MOVIE THERAPY FOR LAW STUDENTS:

Are you Ready for Law School? Prepare for Law School by Watching Movies!

Updated 2020 Edition

By Sonia J. Buck, Esq.

Praise for *Movie Therapy for Law Students*

"Reversal of Fortune has been subject to many analyses over the years. This one is the best I have seen for law students and a legal audience. It really gets to the heart of the legal, tactical, and ethical issues in the case. It would be extremely useful for law students who view the film to read this perceptive and insightful analysis."

-Professor Alan M. Dershowitz, Felix Frankfurter Professor of Law, Harvard University, Author of *Reversal of Fortune: Inside the Claus von Bülow Case* (Random House 1986)

"The analysis of Silkwood brings into focus the complex linkages among labor law, workers' compensation rights, and federal and state statutory protections such as OSHA and whistleblower acts.   It aptly identifies the competing interests of employees and employers relative to job security, worker safety, and environmental protection. Watching Silkwood with the author's insights in mind will deepen the significance of both the movie and the law school experience."

-Jon Oxman, Managing Partner, Linnell, Choate and Webber; Adjunct Faculty, University of New England

"I wish I had this book when going through law school. It's perfect for those times when a student needs to step back from studying legal concepts and yet wishes to learn from a different angle. Attorney Buck's book allows a student to take a couple of hours off and yet apply critical thinking skills, analyze the issues, and critique Hollywood's views on the law. This book will also help all the armchair lawyers who know that there's more to the law than "Judge Judy" and "Law and Order." Reading this book is more than a good read: it will encourage lawyers, law school students, and armchair lawyers alike to look at real cases, which sometimes are even stranger than the movies!"

-Patricia E. Weidler, Esq., lawyer, author, and teacher

"I wish I had this book when I was in law school! Sonia does a great job of educating through her analyses of the movies . . . a great teaching tool!!"

-Susan Quigley, Esq., attorney and recent law school graduate

Contents

ALPHABETICAL LISTING OF MOVIES

12 Angry Men
13th
Absence of Malice
Accused, The
Adam's Rib
Anatomy of a Murder
And Justice for All
Baby Boom
Civil Action, A
Class Action
Deep Water Horizon
Delivery Man
Erin Brockovich
Find Me Guilty
Firm, The
Flash of Genius
Fortune Cookie, The
Fracture
Guilty as Sin
Hurricane, The
I am Sam
Inherit the Wind
Irreconcilable differences
Jagged Edge
Judge, The
Just Mercy
Kramer v. Kramer
Legally Blonde
Liar Liar
Lincoln Lawyer, The
Michael Clayton
Miss Sloan
Mrs. Doubtfire
My Cousin Vinny

Night Falls on Manhattan
North Country
On the Basis of Sex
Paper Chase
Philadelphia
Presumed Innocent
Reversal of Fortune
Reversible Errors
Selma
Silkwood
Suspect
Ted 2
Time to Kill, A
To Kill a Mockingbird
Up In The Air
Verdict, The
Wall Street
Wedding Crashers
What Happens in Vegas
Who Gets the Dog?
You Can't Take My Daughter
Young Mr. Lincoln

MOVIES BY SUBJECT MATTER

Business Law

Wall Street
Up in the Air

Civil Procedure

Class Action
Erin Brockovich
Reversal of Fortune

Contracts

Liar Liar
Paper Chase

Employment & Labor Law

Baby Boom
Deep Water Horizon
Silkwood
The Firm
North Country
Philadelphia
Up in the Air

Family Law

Delivery Man
Kramer v. Kramer
Irreconcilable Differences
I am Sam
Liar Liar
Losing Isaiah
Mrs. Doubtfire
Wedding Crashers
What Happens in Vegas
Who Gets the Dog?
You Can't Take My Daughter

Constitutional Law

13th
Absence of Malice
Find Me Guilty
Fracture
Inherit the Wind
Just Mercy
Legally Blonde
Miss Sloane
On the Basis of Sex
Presumed Innocent
Reversal of Fortune
Reversible Errors
Selma
Ted 2
The Hurricane
Young Mr. Lincoln

Criminal Law/Procedure

12 Angry Men
Adam's Rib
Anatomy of a Murder
Find Me Guilty
Fracture
Legally Blonde
Night Falls on Manhattan
Presumed Innocent
Reversal of Fortune
Reversible Errors
Suspect
The Accused
The Firm
The Hurricane
The Judge
To Kill a Mockingbird
Young Mr. Lincoln

Torts

A Civil Action
Absence of Malice
Class Action
The Verdict
The Fortune Cookie

Evidence

A Time to Kill
Adam's Rib
Anatomy of a Murder
And Justice for All
Jagged Edge
Kramer v. Kramer
Liar Liar
My Cousin Vinny
Presumed Innocent
The Accused
Young Mr. Lincoln

Ethics

A Civil Action
Adam's Rib
And Justice for All
Class Action
Erin Brockovich
Fracture
Guilty as Sin
Jagged Edge
Liar Liar
Michael Clayton
My Cousin Vinny
Suspect
The Firm
The Lincoln Lawyer
The Verdict

Intellectual Property

Flash of Genius

INTRODUCTION

Movie Therapy for Law Students involves putting your legal brains to work on some great movies while enjoying some quality time for yourself during the intense three years that you are a law student. The new 2020 edition includes discussions about more than 55 movies, with 20 movies/chapters that were not included in the original *Movie Therapy for Law Students*. With legal issues being the focal point, you can read this book in conjunction with your movie time and feel no remorse for watching movies when you really should have been reading your torts textbook.

The book may also be a good read during your short break between law school graduation and studying for the bar exam. To give you a head start on the laborious process of studying for final exams and bar exams, I have included certain material that is tested on the multi-state bar exam, some state essay exams, and other law-related tests. I have also included dozens of exam tips throughout the material, which I have marked:

? **Exam Tips.**

In presenting some of the legal questions that these movies raise, I am attempting to elicit thought from you; answers are not necessarily provided in this book, but may be provided in the cited references or the movies themselves. I have provided relevant statutory material, rules, case law, and other resources to guide you in the thought process. The geographic settings spread the country and the temporal settings range from the 1930s to modern day, encompassing over 90 years of legal changes throughout the nation. For ease of discussion and reference, I have tried to use current federal and/or uniform rules and codes, and I encourage you to view the corresponding law in whatever state you plan to sit for the bar exam and/or practice, keeping in mind that the law in your jurisdiction could be changing as you read this. Also, many of these movies are based on actual cases that you may want to read as part of your studies. I have cited sources for additional information about some of the real-life stories. I have placed the movies in chronological order, according to their release. Watch how images and dynamics of gender and race begin to shift. Notice how the faces of the juries, judges, and lawyers become more diverse as the country evolves, both theatrically and socially.

WARNING: It is assumed you have already seen each movie as you read beyond this point. Verdicts and endings of whodunits may be revealed!

YOUNG MR. LINCOLN
(Twentieth Century Fox 1939)

Starring: Henry Fonda; Richard Cromwell; Eddie Quillen

Lessons: Criminal Law/Procedure; Constitutional Law; Evidence

Plot: Starring Henry Fonda as Mr. Lincoln, *Young Mr. Lincoln* highlights America's 16th president and his early career as an attorney. At the heart of the movie is a small-town murder trial at which Mr. Lincoln defends the two accused, brothers Adam and Matt Clay (Richard Cromwell and Eddie Quillen, respectively). The Clay brothers make enemies with local troublemakers, Scrub White and J. Palmer Cass. One night, the Clays wind up in a scrap with White and Cass after an incident at the town fair. White pulls a gun on both Clays, and the three men engage in a struggle and fall to the ground. Cass stands nearby, watching as the three continue to fight. It is dark and we cannot see what is happening, but we hear White's gun fire. Then, we see that White is the only man still lying on the ground. He is dead, but not from a gunshot. Cass runs to him, and it appears as though Cass pulls a knife from his friend's body. Cass accuses the Clays of killing White during the struggle. Apparently, Adam and Matt each think the other is guilty. Each Clay tries to protect his brother by falsely confessing to the crime. So, both Clay brothers are charged with murdering Scrub White. The movie focuses on their joint murder trial, providing entertaining trial scenes and rich attorney/courtroom dynamics that set the groundwork for the many legal movies that follow. The trial ends with that dazzling Hollywood courtroom comedy and drama that would never fly in today's courts but has made for over 80 years of great film.

CRIMINAL LAW/PROCEDURE
Unfair Prejudice

Both brothers are charged with murdering Scrub White. They are tried together for that crime. In Scene 7, they are told they are "equally guilty." Ignoring that it defies logic for the prosecution to prove both brothers are "equally guilty" of the same count of murder when only one could have stabbed Cass, is there any prejudicial effect, either to the defendants or the prosecution, of trying the two brothers together for the crime? Rule 14 of the Federal Rules of Criminal Procedure provides for "relief from prejudicial joinder." Rule 14 states that, "if the joinder of offenses or defendants in an indictment ... or a consolidation for trial appears to prejudice a defendant or the government, the court may order separate trials of counts, sever the defendants' trials, or provide any other relief that justice requires." Relief from joinder under criminal procedure rules is similar to the civil bifurcation principle discussed in *A Civil Action*. How might bifurcation rules - focused on judicial economy and efficiency - affect fairness principles? Can courts strike a workable balance between equity and efficiency?

CONSTITUTIONAL LAW
Fifth Amendment: Self-Incrimination

In Scene 21, Cass takes the witness stand and claims he saw Matt Clay stab White. In the same type of Matlock/Perry Mason fashion that would never pass constitutional muster today, Lincoln manages to elicit a confession from Cass. The Fifth Amendment provides that "no person ... shall be compelled in any criminal case to be a witness against himself." The Fifth Amendment's mandate was not made applicable to the states through the Fourteenth Amendment until the 1969 Supreme Court case of *Benton v. Maryland*, 395 U.S. 784 (1969), however. Today, the Fifth Amendment would have protected Cass, and would have required the judge to take action.

What other actions might the judge in this case have taken to better promote a fair and efficient trial?

EVIDENCE
Witness Testimony

Aside from criminal due process problems, is Lincoln's accusatory cross-examination of Cass improper badgering of a witness under today's rules? What would happen in a modern court under these circumstances? Federal Rule of Evidence 611(a) provides that "the court shall exercise reasonable control over the mode and order of interrogating witnesses and presenting evidence so as to ... protect witnesses from harassment or undue embarrassment." In addition to Rule 611(a)'s mandate, Rule 26(c) of the Federal Rules of Civil Procedure permits a court to take action "to protect a party or person from annoyance, embarrassment, oppression, or undue burden or expense." Based on these guidelines, should the judge have intervened and protected Cass from Lincoln's line of questioning?

In Scene 17, Mother Clay takes the stand and is asked to explain what she saw. She simply testifies: "I ain't saying." Assuming Mrs. Clay knows something (or thinks she does) but "ain't saying" in an effort to protect her sons, how might a modern judge respond? What contemporary laws are invoked in such a situation? Could she be held in contempt of court under modern rules? Indicted for obstruction of justice? What else might the judge have done to be more proactive in securing Mrs. Clay's testimony while still protecting her rights as a witness?

Judicial Notice

Lincoln is able to impeach Cass's ability to see who stabbed White. Cass claims the moon allowed him to see vividly, but Lincoln proves that the moon was not out at the date and hour of the murder. He does this by showing the court a Farmer's Almanac. This clever tactic could be used under today's Federal Rules of Evidence. Moon phases, weather, and visibility on a particular night are the types of facts about which a court will take judicial notice. When a court takes judicial notice of a fact, a party is relieved from having to prove the fact through admissible evidence. Judicially noticeable facts include facts that are "not subject to reasonable dispute" because they are "(1) generally known within the territorial jurisdiction of the trial court or (2) capable of accurate and ready determination by sources whose accuracy cannot reasonably be questioned." FED. R. EVID. 201. Federal Rule of Evidence 201 provides for judicial notice in two situations: when discretionary (Rule 201(a)) and when mandatory (Rule 201(b)). Judicial notice is mandatory "if requested by a party and [the court is] supplied with the necessary information." The Almanac would likely have been held to constitute necessary information for judicial notice. There is nothing in the rule that states the information cannot be hearsay or otherwise inadmissible evidence. If Lincoln had requested judicial notice, the court would have been required to take notice. It appears the court took notice on its own discretion.

? Exam Tips

The areas of constitutional law, criminal procedure, and evidence often overlap. It is the **constitutional** framework that governs the criminal process and delineates criminal procedure rules. **Criminal procedure** rules regulate the way law enforcement officials interact with criminal suspects and investigate crime scenes to gather **evidence** for criminal proceedings. In any course about constitutional law, criminal procedure, or evidence, you should be able to identify and write about these overlapping principles: the constitutional protections that affect criminal investigations and the subsequent admission of evidence at criminal trials. Pay attention to constitutional problems with searches and seizures, failed Miranda warnings, improper custodial interrogations, the deprivation of the right to counsel, coerced confessions, etc. Determine how the facts presented invoke these overlapping legal principles. Outline the issues. Then, frame your answer according to the subject for which you are testing, focusing on the rules, cases, and concepts you learned in the particular class. For a bar exam, organize your essay around each of the three principles, setting forth which constitutional amendments are implicated in the gathering of what evidence, and then analyzing the subsequent admissibility of that evidence at trial.

LEGAL BRIEFS & MOVIE EXTRAS

*Take note of the bases upon which Lincoln dismisses and accepts the jurors during the voir dire process. Also notice the way in which Lincoln enamors the jurors during this initial process – his friendly mannerisms, his tactfully teasing opposing counsel, his entertaining style. He was a great trial attorney and Henry Fonda does a fabulous job bringing out President Lincoln's legal mastermind. Apparently, some things about being a good trial lawyer come naturally and cannot be learned in law school. (Abraham Lincoln never went to law school; he learned the law largely from reading Blackstone's Commentaries.)

*For another legal drama starring Henry Fonda, see *The Wrong Man* (Warner Brothers 1956). In this movie, an older and even more brilliant Henry Fonda sits on the other side of the defense table, as a New York musician wrongly accused of robbing an insurance company when he innocently visited the company to try to borrow money from his wife's policy. *The Wrong Man* is an Alfred Hitchcock film and, as such, it is quite thrilling albeit very disturbing!

*President Lincoln is President Obama's role model. Both men are from Illinois, and both were successful lawyers before becoming President.

"The leading rule for the lawyer, as for the man of every other calling, is diligence. Leave nothing for tomorrow which can be done today."

-Abraham Lincoln
(from *Collected Works of Abraham Lincoln,* vol. 2, p. 81, Rutgers University Press (1953, 1990))

ADAM'S RIB
(MGM 1949)

Starring: Spencer Tracy; Katharine Hepburn; Judy Holliday

Lessons: Ethics; Evidence; Criminal Law

Plot: *Adam's Rib* is one of the best of the many wonderful Spencer Tracy/Katharine Hepburn films. The stars provide an entertaining depiction of the American legal system and gender inequalities in 1950s marriages. The movie opens with the crime scene: Mrs. Attinger, a young blond, brilliantly portrayed by Judy Holliday, walks into a room and catches her husband cheating on her. She becomes hysterical and shoots all six rounds of a gun, one bullet hitting her husband in his shoulder. He lives and she is tried for attempted murder. Katharine Hepburn plays Amanda Bonner, the ambitious attorney who defends Mrs. Attinger. Spencer Tracy plays her husband, Adam Bonner, the Assistant District Attorney assigned to prosecute the case. When Adam learns that his wife will be his opponent, he pleads with her to withdraw from the case. When she refuses, he tells her, "I am going to cut you into 12 little pieces and feed you to the jury so get prepared for it." The scenes switch between daytime (in the courtroom) and evenings (in the home, mostly the bedroom). Gender dynamics are prevalent in both places.

ETHICS
Attorney Relationships

Under current ethical rules, family relationships between opposing counsel give rise to potential conflicts of interest. *See* 2007 American Bar Association Model Rules of Professional Conduct ("ABA Model Rules"). ABA Model Rule 1.7 (Conflict of Interest: Current Client) provides:

1.7(a): Except as provided in paragraph (b) [consent], a lawyer shall not represent a client if the representation involves a concurrent conflict of interest. A concurrent conflict of interest exists if ... there is a significant risk that the representation of one or more clients will be materially limited by the lawyer's responsibilities to another client, former client or a third person or by a personal interest of the lawyer.

(b) Notwithstanding the existence of a concurrent conflict of interest under paragraph (a), a lawyer may represent a client if:

(1) the lawyer reasonably believes that the lawyer will be able to provide competent and diligent representation to each affected client;

(2) the representation is not prohibited by law;

(3) the representation does not involve the assertion of a claim by one client against another client represented by the lawyer in the same litigation or other proceeding before a tribunal; *and*

(4) each affected client gives informed consent, confirmed in writing.

Under Model Rule 1.7, are Mr. and Mrs. Bonnor automatically prohibited from opposing each other in the *Attinger* trial? If not, what do they have to do to ensure compliance? *See* Comment 11 to Rule 1.7:

When lawyers representing different clients in the same matter or in substantially related matters are closely related by blood or marriage, there may be a significant risk that client confidences will be revealed and that the lawyer's family relationship will interfere with both loyalty and independent judgment. As a result, each client is entitled to know of the existence and implications of the relationship [and each client must give his or her informed consent].

See also RESTATEMENT (THIRD), THE LAW GOVERNING LAWYERS §125 ("Unless the affected client consents ... a lawyer may not represent a client if there is a substantial risk that the lawyer's representation of the client would be materially and adversely affected by the lawyer's financial or other personal interests.").

Given the marital roles and gender dynamics between the Bonnors, is simply obtaining informed consent enough to cure the conflict risks in this case? Could a husband and his wife ever be on the opposite sides of an attempted murder trial? Under ABA Model Rule 1.7(b)(1) (above), the attorneys must also have a reasonable belief that they "will be able to provide competent and diligent representation to each affected client." In other words, even with a waiver, if there is a reasonable belief that the attorney could not be completely impartial, or that the familial relationship may affect the client, he or she should not undertake the representation.

Here, it is unlikely that a waiver would alleviate the risk of a client being affected by counsels' marriage. In a marital relationship, particularly when both partners are consumed in a stressful, emotional, felony trial, a wider range of family dynamics might come into play. For the Bonnors, spousal competition and bitterness bred potential for ethical problems in the *Attinger* case. If one of these attorneys felt he or she had to make concessions, even lose, to protect the marriage, there would be a serious conflict of interest and perhaps grounds for a mistrial. More obvious problems involve the "double standards in gender/equality before the law" theme at the heart of the trial. Their focus on this theme causes the attorneys to inject marital strife into their courtroom strategies. The power struggles, outrages, and bickering between the Bonners in open court could improperly influence the jury and seriously impact the attorneys' careers. One of the Bonnors, therefore, probably should have declined representation. At the very least, one of the Bonnors should have withdrawn as soon as this conflict became apparent. I anticipate disagreement among readers as to which Bonnor that should be.

EVIDENCE
Direct/Re-Direct Examination

During what appears to be the prosecution's case, Amanda is cross-examining Warren Attinger. Amanda successfully portrays him to the jury as a bad husband who stays out all night and scolds and hits his wife. On re-direct, Adam starts with a series of yes or no questions: did your wife hit you, scold you, knock you down? And this caused you distress? (All answered "yes"). Should Amanda have objected to some of these questions as leading? *See* FED. R. EVID. 611(c) (Leading Questions) ("Leading questions should not be used during direct examination except as may be necessary to develop the witness's testimony."). *State v. Merced*, 933 A.2d 172, 175 (R.I. 2007) (leading questions that "suggest the desired answer" are generally impermissible on direct examination.). Did the Bonnors ask their clients any other leading or otherwise improper questions during these courtroom scenes? What other objectionable conduct do the Bonnors engage in during this trial?

CRIMINAL LAW
Defenses

During the defense portion of the case, Adam properly objects to Amanda's leading Mrs. Attinger, when Amanda was obviously trying to lead her to say she felt enraged. She is forced to rephrase her question, to which Mrs. Attinger dutifully responds: "I was enraged." Why did Amanda think it was important to prove that Mrs. Attinger was enraged at the time of shooting? Could rage rise to the level of insanity or temporary insanity? Many states offer a defense based on a mental infirmity that is just short of insanity. Under the American Law Institute's Model Penal Code, adopted by most states, "a person is not responsible for criminal conduct if at the time of such conduct as a result of mental disease or defect he lacks substantial capacity either to appreciate the criminality of his conduct or to conform his conduct to the requirements of the law." Model Penal Code, §4.04(1). This concept is similar to that universally known as diminished capacity.

The question becomes: what type of defect or abnormality might have been present in Mrs. Attinger's mental state that could support a lack of capacity or diminished capacity defense? Is rage such a defect? Along those lines, had Mrs. Attinger's bullet killed Mr. Attinger, could her crime be reduced to manslaughter instead of murder under your state law? Consider the requirements under the Model Penal Code for the lesser crime of manslaughter. Manslaughter is defined as:

a homicide which would otherwise be murder ... committed under the influence of extreme mental or emotional disturbance for which there is reasonable explanation or excuse. The reasonableness of such explanation or excuse shall be determined from the viewpoint of a person in the actor's situation under the circumstances as he believes them to be.

Model Penal Code §210.3(1)(b). Is rage an extreme mental or emotional disturbance? Was Mrs. Attinger's rage a reasonable excuse for her actions? Or is there a high enough degree of planning and premeditation for the prosecution to negate Mrs. Attinger's claim that she was under the influence of extreme anger or some other emotional disturbance the entire time she carried out the shooting? Compare Mrs. Attinger's culpable state of mind with that of Lt. Frederick Manion (*Anatomy of A*

Murder), Mrs. Sabich (*Presumed Innocent*), or Carl Lee Haley (*A Time To Kill*).

? Exam Tips

Learning the essential elements of various crimes and their defenses involves a fair amount of memorization, particularly for the multi-state bar exam. An exam study tip that can be helpful for intensive memorizing is the use of a handheld mini-tape recorder. Read into the recorder the portions of your notes that you are struggling to remember, and play it back several times. Not only is there a psychological benefit to hearing your own voice easily recalling vast amounts of information, you can also save study time by listening to your recording while your hands are free to do other tasks, such as baking cookies, lifting weights, or playing with puppies.

Another helpful memorization tactic involves the use of acronyms. For example, for the bar exam, you will need to know what crimes can lead to a charge of felony murder if a death results while a defendant commits certain felonies. Felony murder charges are appropriate when unintentional killings occur during commission or attempted commission of serious or inherently dangerous felony crimes. Felonies presumed to be inherently dangerous for purposes of felony murder charges include **b**urglary, **a**rson, **r**ape, **r**obbery, and **k**idnapping. Use the famous acronym BARRK to assist you in recollecting these crimes. When a death results during the commission of any BARRK, with or without intent to kill, a felony murder charge is appropriate.

LEGAL BRIEFS & MOVIE EXTRAS

*Note that when the attorneys' objections are overruled they mumble: "exceptions." This was the practice under old rules, in order to preserve an overruled objection as grounds for an appeal. The current Federal Rules of Evidence set forth the methods for preserving erroneous evidentiary rulings for appeal by making proper and timely objections and offers of proof. *See* FED. R. EVID. 103(a)(1) and (2).

*Watch how gender dynamics play out in this movie: Amanda's "cause" in the case, equality before the law, is the driving force behind her representation of Mrs. Attinger. Her strive for equality in the courtroom parallels with her strive for equality in the bedroom. She wins her case, but her marriage suffers.

*For another fabulous legal movie invoking themes of gender equality in marriage and before the law, see Richard Gere, Catherine Zeta Jones, and Renee Zellweger in the blockbuster musical *Chicago* (Miramax Films 2002).

"Lawyers should never marry other lawyers. This is called inbreeding. From this comes idiot children ... and other lawyers."

-Says Kip Lurie to his friends and neighbors, Adam and Amanda Bonnor

12 ANGRY MEN
(MGM 1957)

Starring: Henry Fonda; Lee J. Cobb; Ed Bagley; E.G. Marshall; Jack Klugman; Jack Warden; Martin Balsam; John Fieldler; George Voskovec; Robert Webber; Edward Binns; Joseph Sweeney

Lesson: Criminal Law

Plot: *12 Angry Men* begins with a scene outside a courtroom, where a murder trial has just ended and bystanders are congratulating the prosecutor on a job well done. It appears the onlookers assumed the defendant was guilty and that the prosecutor succeeded in proving his guilt to the jury beyond a reasonable doubt. The prosecutor and his fans over-confidently await the jury's verdict. The rest of the movie tracks the jury's deliberations. It is the "hottest day of the year," and the jurors - 12 white males – are stuck in a small room with uncomfortable chairs. Most jurors are eager to get to baseball games and other commitments. They assume their work is essentially finished at this point. Eleven of them are immediately in favor of a guilty verdict. One man, Juror #8 (Henry Fonda), struggles to persuade them not to rush to convict the defendant, a young immigrant boy accused of killing his father. Juror #8 conducts his own investigation after hours. He shares his "evidence" with the jury, negating witness testimony and circumstantial evidence (something the defense attorney failed to do). One by one, Juror #8 has the other jurors questioning their initial assessments. At times, the dialogue is funny; other times, it is quite heated and tense.

CRIMINAL LAW
Juries

The Sixth Amendment to the United States Constitution provides that "in all criminal prosecutions, the accused shall enjoy the right to a speedy and public trial by an impartial jury." Back in the 1950s, however, juries consisted of white males, few of whom were impartial to immigrant youths accused of killing their fathers. Since that time, the United States Supreme Court has consistently held that the Sixth Amendment guarantees to criminal defendants the right to a trial by a jury composed of a fair cross section of the community. *Tennessee v. Lane*, 541 U.S. 509, 523 (2004). *See also, Taylor v. Louisiana*, 419 U.S. 522, 528 (1975) (the selection of a jury "from a representative cross section of the community is an essential component of the Sixth Amendment right to a jury trial."). In *Tennessee v. Lane*, the Supreme Court noted that "the exclusion of 'identifiable segments playing major roles in the community cannot be squared with the constitutional concept of a jury trial.'" *Id.* (quoting *Taylor v. Louisiana*, 419 U.S. 522, 530 (1975)).

To demonstrate a prima facie violation of the fair-cross-section requirement, however, the defendant must establish: "(1) that the group alleged to be excluded is a 'distinctive' group in the community; (2) that the representation of this group in venires from which juries are selected is not fair and reasonable in relation to the number of such persons in the community; and (3) that this under representation is due to systematic exclusion of the group in the jury-selection process." *Duren v. Missouri*, 439 U.S. 357, 364 (1979). The third prong is the largest hurdle for criminal defendants who complain about an "absence from the jury of representatives from an identifiable segment of the community" because courts require proof "that their absence is due to a preconceived plan conceived by those who are responsible for the formulation of the jury lists." *State v. Johnson*, 358 A.2d 370, 375 (R.I. 1976). *See also, Norris v.*

Alabama, 294 U.S. 587 (1935) (prohibiting systematic exclusion of minority groups from jury pools). The problem for immigrant, indigent, criminal defendants, however, is the difficulty in proving on appeal that the jury list resulted from a preconceived plan to exclude a particular group of people.

Conduct of Jurors/Extrinsic Evidence

Was it appropriate for Juror #8 to engage in his own after-hours, "extra-judicial" investigating? What is the legal significance of his actions? The Supreme Court has held that jurors, in conducting their deliberations, have a duty to consider only the evidence presented in open court. *Turner v. Louisiana*, 379 U.S. 466, 472-73 (1965). Evidence not presented at trial, acquired through out of court experiments or otherwise, is deemed "extrinsic." *United States v. Navarro-Garcia*, 926 F.2d 818, 821 (9th Cir. 1991) (internal citations omitted). When extrinsic evidence is presented to a jury that is considering a criminal case, the defendant is entitled to a new trial "if there exist[s] a reasonable possibility that the extrinsic material could have affected the verdict." *Id.*

In *Navarro-Garcia*, a jury convicted defendant Navarro-Garcia on drug offenses stemming from the importation of marijuana. *Id.* at 820. The defendant apparently had claimed she did not know there were drugs in her car trunk. *See id.* She moved for a new trial based on allegations that a juror conducted an experiment to see whether, based on a test of the weight equal to that of the marijuana (344 lbs.) in her own trunk, the defendant should have known about the marijuana. *See id.* at 821. The Ninth Circuit found that the experiment went to a critical issue in case – the defendant's mens rea. *See id.* at 823. The defendant was entitled to an evidentiary hearing as to "whether the jury considered extrinsic evidence and, if so, the nature of that evidence." *Id.* The Court held that if the court found on remand "that there was a reasonable possibility that the extrinsic evidence affected the verdict, defendant would be entitled to a new trial as a matter of law." *Id.*

In *Marino v. Vasquez*, a juror made an unauthorized reference to the dictionary definition of an element of the crime and conducted an unauthorized out of court experiment with a third party, regarding the use of a handgun. 812 F.2d 499, 502 (9th Cir. 1987). The Ninth Circuit found that there was a reasonable possibility that the defendant suffered prejudice as a result of such juror misconduct. *Id.* at 504. The Court held that:

When a jury considers facts that have not been introduced in evidence, a defendant has effectively lost the rights of confrontation, cross-examination, and the assistance of counsel with regard to jury consideration of the extraneous evidence. In one sense the violation may be more serious than where these rights are denied at some other stage of the proceedings because the defendant may have no idea what new evidence has been considered. It is impossible to offer evidence to rebut it, to offer a curative instruction, to discuss its significance in argument to the jury, or to take other tactical steps that might ameliorate its impact.

Id. at 505. The Court therefore granted the defendant's habeas corpus request and ordered a new trial. *Id.* at 503-07.

Following a defendant's conviction in *State v. Hartley*, two jurors came forward with signed affidavits alleging that extraneous information was brought to the attention of the jury after a juror discussed the effects of mace with a policeman, and another juror conducted a test to determine whether the defendant had enough time to leave a party, commit the crime, and return to the party. 656 A.2d 954, 957 (R.I. 1995). The Rhode Island Supreme Court considered the affidavits admissible for purposes of demonstrating that matters not in evidence reached the jury through outside communications. *Id.*

The Court remanded the case because it concluded, based on the affidavits, that "further inquiry into circumstances and conditions under which extraneous information may have been imparted to the jury" was required to ensure that defendant's right to counsel and right to confront witnesses had not been violated. *Id.* at 958. The Court stated: "if [on remand] the trial justice determines that extraneous prejudicial information was improperly brought to the attention of the jury and that such extraneous information would probably influence the decision of an average reasonable juror, then the defendant shall be granted a new trial." *Id.* at 962.

These cases show that, in the real world, juror misconduct can lead to mistrials and other dire consequences. Note, however, that these cases allow convicted defendants new trials due to juror misconduct. The extrinsic evidence affecting the verdict in *12 Angry Men*, in contrast, resulted in an acquittal. What rights does the prosecution have in such a situation?

Presumption of Innocence/Burden of Proof

At the beginning of the movie, the judge instructs the jurors and then sends them off to deliberate. Were the judge's instructions proper under today's due process laws? In *Sandstrom v. Montana,* the United States Supreme Court ruled that the Due Process Clause of the Fourteenth Amendment prohibits jury instructions that have the effect of relieving the state of its burden of proof. 442 U.S. 510 (1979). Criminal juries are instructed that the defendant starts with the presumption of innocence, and that the state has the burden of proving each element of the crime beyond a reasonable doubt. *See id.*

Theoretically, this means it is up to the prosecution to *rebut* the *presumption* of innocence; the defense does not have to *prove* innocence. The reality, however, is that criminal defense lawyers often have to rebut prejudice, preconceptions, and presumptions of guilt, while being careful not to assume a burden they do not have.

? Exam Tips

If an exam fact pattern describes jurors in a criminal trial, their biographical or physical characteristics, conduct, prejudicial tendencies, etc., be thinking about the Sixth Amendment, its body of case law, and its impact on the question presented. Also, to the extent any jurors engage in misconduct or the jury otherwise considers extrinsic evidence in reaching a guilty verdict, discuss the possibilities of a new trial under the Sixth Amendment.

LEGAL BRIEFS & MOVIE EXTRAS

*The twelve angry men are told that, if they find the defendant guilty, he automatically gets the death penalty. Under current criminal procedure, however, a defendant's sentencing may be a separate process. Many state rules and the federal rules of criminal procedure provide for the judge to sentence the defendant after a jury finds him guilty. For an example and explanation, see *Andres v. United States*, 333 U.S. 740 (1948).

*This movie is essentially all dialogue; there is very little action and there are no trial scenes to analyze. It is, however, a short and entertaining classic that invokes legal and philosophical quandaries and should generate productive discussion among law students. Plan a "happy hour" with fellow law students, watching this 90-minute movie and then engaging in some intelligent conversation over coffee, drinks, or snacks. Make it a weekly or monthly event and see how many fabulous legal movies you can watch. Take advantage of being a law student. Enjoy the time that you get to spend simply absorbing knowledge and exchanging thoughts and ideas with the people that share the law school bond and the quest for legal intellect and expertise.

"Nine of us seem to feel the defendant is innocent ... we may even be trying to return a guilty man to the community, but we have a reasonable doubt in our minds and that is a safeguard..."

-Juror #8

"Reasonable doubt?! That's nothing but words!"

 -Juror #3

ANATOMY OF A MURDER
(Columbia Films 1959)

Starring: James Stewart; Ben Gazzara

Lessons: Criminal Law; Evidence

Plot: Lt. Frederick Manion (Ben Gazzara) is an army lieutenant who went to a bar and shot the owner, Barney Quill, after his wife comes home and tells him Quill had beaten and raped her. James Stewart plays Paul Biegler, a defense attorney who cannot even afford to pay his secretary. Biegler takes some time out of his busy fishing schedule to handle an insanity defense for Lt. Manion. Lt. Manion feels strongly that he has the "unwritten law" on his side. Yet, as his lawyer points out, the "unwritten law is a myth." Biegler explains that there are four ways to defend a murder trial: 1. it wasn't murder; it was suicide or an accident; 2. it was somebody else; 3. it was justified because of self-defense, property defense, or defense of a third party; or 4. it was excusable due to some mental defect. There are no facts to support the defenses based on 1-3. Lt. Manion and his attorney therefore need a "real" defense to show that the murder was excusable. They attempt to prove that the crafty lieutenant was operating under an "irresistible impulse" when he loaded his gun, walked to the tavern where he knew he would find Quill, slowly strolled over to the bar, took aim, pulled the trigger, shot Quill dead, and then shot him some more. Well, I take no position. You be the judge!

CRIMINAL LAW
Irresistible Impulse Defense

The defense being put forth is something just short of the insanity defense. Manion's attorney tells him he needs a legal peg so the jury can hang its sympathy on something useful. The defense needs a "legal excuse." They find one: irresistible impulse, a temporary "mental defect," similar to Carl Lee Haley in *A Time to Kill* and Mrs. Attinger in *Adam's Rib*.

In Scene 4, Biegler walks a fine ethical line when he elicits testimony from his client to support some mental defect. Note the dialogue between the attorney and his client:

Client: "I must have been mad."

Attorney: "Bad temper is no excuse."

Can bad temper ever be an "excuse" for committing a crime? What about Mrs. Attinger from *Adam's Rib*? Also, as discussed with respect to the defendant in *A Time To Kill*, extreme anger, though no "excuse," might have lessened the charge to manslaughter instead of murder. Although jurors may be given the option of finding the defendant guilty of the lesser charge of manslaughter, as a practical matter, the defense attorney has to plan his or her case around one theory or the other. Determining whether to shoot for "not guilty by reason of insanity," versus going for a reduction to manslaughter, is sometimes a gamble defense attorneys choose to take. One factor in the decision, not discussed in the movie, is that criminal defendants found not guilty by reason of insanity typically still have to give up years of their lives in an institution.

From the prosecution's standpoint, some cases may be more likely to result in convictions if the prosecutor had pursued manslaughter charges instead of gambling for a murder conviction. Often, the same set of facts that would play into a defense such as irresistible impulse (e.g., a defendant's rage or fear) might also play into a charge of manslaughter. By bringing manslaughter charges, the prosecution could use evidence of fear or rage to its advantage, for instance, focusing on proving the fear or rage was not reasonable. Even though murder juries are typically instructed on the lesser offense of manslaughter, whether to gamble on a murder conviction or settle for a manslaughter charge is an important consideration for prosecutors to make early on, because the entire theory of the case and all of the evidence may take a different course depending upon which charge is brought to trial.

? Exam Tip

When faced with a fact-pattern that suggests both murder and possible defenses to murder, do not overlook the possible lesser crime of manslaughter. The facts relating to a murder defense may be useful to prove manslaughter. In such an essay answer, first discuss the elements of murder, discuss facts supporting a state of mind defense, and then discuss manslaughter, focusing on actions taken under *unreasonable* fear or anger, or an *unreasonable* belief that a deadly type of self-defense was necessary.

EVIDENCE
Rule 404 -- Propensity Bar

Character evidence is introduced at various stages of the *Manion* trial. Was it permissible? Federal Rule of Evidence 404(a) provides that character evidence "is not admissible for the purpose of proving action in conformity therewith on a particular occasion." Similarly, Rule 404(b) provides that "evidence of other crimes, wrongs, or acts is not admissible to prove the character of a person in order to show action in conformity therewith." In other words, parties cannot attempt to show that because someone did something once, they must have done it again. This is called the "propensity bar." There are, of course, exceptions to Rule 404's propensity bar. For instance, under Rule 404(a)(1), a criminal defendant can offer evidence of any "good" character traits he may have. In admitting "good" character evidence during the defense's case-in-chief, however, the defense then opens the door to the prosecution's being able to admit "bad" character evidence in rebuttal.

Also, in certain circumstances, the defense can offer "bad" acts or character evidence of an alleged victim, during the defense's case-in-chief, to show that the victim was the first aggressor in order to support a self-defense claim. Additionally, upon reasonable notice, character evidence and evidence of prior bad acts may be admitted to show "motive, opportunity, intent, preparation, plan, knowledge, identity, absence of mistake or accident." FED. R. EVID. 404(b).

Another exception to the propensity bar is set forth in Rule 404(a)(3), allowing for "evidence of the character of a witness, as provided in Rules 607, 608, and 609." Rules 607, 608, and 609 deal with witness impeachment. Because the defendant himself was a witness in his defense, evidence regarding his credibility is admissible for impeachment purposes. Federal Rule of Evidence 608(b) allows for witness impeachment with specific instances of the witness's conduct, but only on cross-examination. Could evidence of Manion's character be admitted during the prosecution's case for any purpose? (Keep in mind the propensity bar and its exceptions).

Witnesses were impeached on cross-examination by their prior arrests. Is evidence of these prior arrests admissible? Federal Rules of Evidence 609, which makes certain crimes admissible for impeachment purposes, applies only to convicted crimes - not arrests. Rule 609 also imposes time limits and other restrictions. Could prior arrests be admissible under any other rules of evidence? *See* FED. R. OF EVID. 608(b) (specific instances of conduct). Under Rule 608(b), the court has the discretion to admit specific instances of a witness's conduct "if probative of truthfulness or untruthfulness." Do the arrests relate to the witnesses' character for truthfulness? Are the crimes within the permissible time limitation? Attorney Biegler used evidence of a prosecutorial witness's misdemeanor crimes to attack his credibility. Should that evidence have come in?

? Exam Tip

Keep in mind that the propensity bar is just that: a bar against evidence tending to show action in conformity with a character trait on a particular occasion. When a person's character is itself an issue, because a character trait is an element of a claim, charge, or defense, the propensity bar does not apply. For instance, truth is a defense to defamation claims, so evidence as to the character of a slander plaintiff can be admissible to prove that the derogatory statements made about the plaintiff were in fact true.

Also, Rule 404(b) provides a non-exhaustive list of routes around the propensity box. Rule 404(b) allows evidence of specific instances of conduct if the evidence tends to prove knowledge. For instance, if a defendant is charged with a specialized computer hacking crime, evidence of any prior specific acts of computer hacking might be offered to prove that the defendant had the capacity, not the propensity, to commit the crime. Evidence to show proof of identity is another example of a Rule 404(b) exception. Consider the case of a signature serial killer. A prosecutor might offer evidence to show that it would be extremely unlikely that two different criminals are involved in a particular serial crime. The prosecution would have to prove that the prior crime and the current crime are sufficiently similar, however. Evidence of prior conduct might also be admitted to show proof of motive.

Hearsay: State of Mind Exception

Lt. Manion's defense is that he murdered Quill because he believed Quill raped his wife. He claims "irresistible impulse" as a murder defense. Manion testifies that his wife told him Quill had raped her. Is Manion's testimony as to what his wife told him hearsay? If so, how might the statement nevertheless be admitted?

Hearsay is defined in Federal Rule of Evidence 801(c) as "a statement, other than one made by the declarant while testifying at the trial or hearing, offered in evidence to prove the truth of the matter asserted." In other words, hearsay is:

-an out of court
-statement
-made to prove that the fact it states is true

Mrs. Manion's accusation of rape against Quill is an out of court statement that she made to her husband. But is it being offered for its truth? The statement is relevant to explain how Lt. Manion was *feeling* when he shot Quill. Federal Rule of Evidence 803(3), generally known as the state of mind exception to the hearsay bar, excludes from the hearsay bar "a statement of the declarant's then existing state of mind, emotion, sensation, or physical condition (such as intent, plan, motive, design, mental feeling, pain and bodily health)." It does not necessarily matter whether Mrs. Quill's accusation of rape is true. What is at issue is that Lt. Manion heard the statement and reasonably believed it to be true, creating in his mind an irresistible impulse to kill the man he thinks raped his wife. Therefore, Mrs. Manion's statement comes in under the Rule 803(3) state of mind exception. We never know if Quill actually raped and beat Mrs. Manion, but it is enough that Manion thought he did.

? Exam Tip

On evidence essay exams, be able to spot the hearsay problem presented in fact patterns where knowledge or intent are at issue. First discuss the hearsay rule, explain why the facts show hearsay on its face, and then raise the Rule 803(3) state of mind exception. Focus on ways in which the facts presented make the statement relevant for purposes other than truth, such as the speaker's or the listener's state of mind, knowledge, belief, or mental or physical condition, feeling, etc.

LEGAL BRIEFS & MOVIE EXTRAS

*This movie highlights several evidentiary questions that go to critical issues in the defense. Often, certain evidentiary questions are decided upon well before trial and have a significant impact on the defense attorney's strategic planning process. Judges act as gatekeepers of evidence, determining in advance of the trial what evidence the jury will hear. Federal Rule of Evidence 104(a) (Preliminary Questions) provides that "preliminary questions concerning the qualification of a person to be a witness, the existence of a privilege, the admissibility of evidence shall be determined by the court" [i.e., the judge, not the jury]. Then, defense attorneys and prosecutors plan their jury trial in accordance with initial evidentiary rulings.

*Biegler's "irresistible impulse" defense does in fact come from an actual case, *People v. Durfee*, 62 Mich. 487 (1886), as (almost) accurately portrayed in the movie, when Biegler is conducting legal research the old fashioned way: using actual books as opposed to Westlaw or Lexis. Can you imagine?!?!

*There are many good trial scenes to evaluate in this movie, from Scene 12 onward. There are some improprieties, but the attorneys' objections are right on, and the "easily awakened" judge provides fantastic comic relief.

*How many ethical violations can you spot in this movie? By the prosecutor? By Biegler? Was there anything ethically wrong with Biegler and Manion's fee arrangement? (That is, anything aside from the fact that Biegler was never paid!)

"12 people go off into a room ... 12 different minds, 12 different hearts, from 12 different walks of life; 12 sets of eyes, ears, shapes, and sizes. And these 12 people are asked to judge another human being as different from them as they are from each other. And in their judgment, they must become of one mind - unanimous. It's one of the miracles of man's disorganized soul that they can do it, and in most instances, do it right well. God bless juries."

- James Stewart (as defense attorney Paul Biegler)

INHERIT THE WIND
(MGM 1960)

Starring: Spencer Tracy; Fredric March; Dick York

Lesson: Constitutional Law

Plot: Based on an actual case, *Scopes v. State,* 278 S.W. 57 (Tenn. 1925), otherwise known as the Monkey Trial, this film dramatizes the controversy over the teaching of evolution in American public schools, as opposed to the then more-accepted divine creation (Christianity) theories. Bertram Cates (Dick York, star of 1970s sitcom *Bewitched*), a science teacher in 1960s Hillsboro, Tennessee, is arrested for teaching Charles Darwin's theory of evolution, in violation of state law. Many of the townspeople consider Cates an atheist and feel he should be hanged for his scientific teachings. Henry Drummond (Spencer Tracy) handles Bertram Cates's defense; highly-respected "Honorary Colonel" Matthew Harrison Brady (Fredric March) prosecutes Cates. The lengthy yet entertaining courtroom scenes are rich with objections to analyze and legal tactics to observe. Other parts of the movie, however, drag. To avoid sheer boredom while waiting for trial, I recommend watching this movie while engaging in some secondary task (such as knitting, sewing, exercising, cooking, cleaning, emailing, texting, Facebooking, on-line shopping, etc.).

CONSTITUTIONAL LAW
First Amendment

Bertram Cates was charged with violating the Butler Act. The Butler Act declared it:

> unlawful for any teacher in any of the Universities, Normals, and all other public schools of the State which are supported in whole or in part by the public school funds

of the State, to teach any theory that denies the Story of the Divine Creation of man as taught in the Bible, and to teach instead that man has descended from a lower order of animals.

Tennessee's Butler Act does not pass First Amendment muster under today's law. The Establishment Clause under the First Amendment provides that "Congress shall make no law respecting an establishment of religion, or prohibiting the free exercise thereof." The First Amendment was extended to the states through the Fourteenth Amendment. *Gitlow v. New York,* 268 U.S. 652, 666 (1925). Many years after the Butler Act and the Monkey Trial, in 1968, the United States Supreme Court struck down as unconstitutional a similar Arkansas statute, mandating Christian teachings. *Epperson v. Arkansas*, 393 U.S. 97, 109 (1968). The Supreme Court held that the First Amendment prohibits a state from requiring "that teaching and learning [be] tailored to the principles or prohibitions of any religious sect or dogma." *Id.* at 106 (citing the Establishment Clause). The Court, therefore, ruled that the Arkansas statute was "contrary to the mandate of the First, and in violation of the Fourteenth, Amendment to the Constitution." *Id.* at 109. The *Epperson* Case created much national controversy. In response to its holding, some states enacted legislation mandating *equal* treatment in the public schools for both evolution science and Christian principles based on creation.

For example, Louisiana passed the Creationism Act in 1981, which forbade "the teaching of the theory of evolution in public schools unless accompanied by instruction in 'creation science.'" The Act declared that "[n]o school is required to teach evolution or creation science…If either is taught, however, the other must also be taught." *Edwards v. Aguillard*, 482 U.S. 578, 578 (1987). A group of interested parents, teachers, and religious leaders challenged the constitutionality of the law. *Id.* The Supreme Court ruled that the Creationism Act (and similar "equalization laws"), like the Butler Act, served a religious purpose and violated the First Amendment's separation of church and state. *Id.* at 593.

For more information about this line of First Amendment cases, see Steven K. Green, *Religious Liberty as a Positive and Negative Right*, 70 ALB. L. REV. 101 (2007).

Sixth Amendment

Under the Sixth Amendment, "in all criminal prosecutions, the accused shall enjoy the right to a speedy and public trial, by an impartial jury." Cates's neighbors consider his actions so blasphemous that they would just as soon see the friendly teacher hanged "by the sour apple tree." In Scene 6, we see the voir dire process play out, and we immediately see that Cates will not be afforded a fair trial by an impartial jury of his peers. The jury panel consisted only of white, Christian, townsmen, at least one of whom appears to worship "Colonel" Brady, the prosecutor. Had Cates's attorney not used a peremptory challenge, the judge apparently would have allowed Brady's fan to remain on the jury despite obvious prejudice. Under today's laws, what, if anything, should the judge have done differently? Should the court have excluded the witness on its own accord, without the need for Cates to use one of his limited peremptory challenges? *See State v. Lindell,* 629 N.W.2d 223, 235 (Wis. 2001) (encouraging judges to strike prospective jurors for cause when they "reasonably suspect" that the potential juror is biased). If all of the potential jurors on the panel were of this same mindset, would that have been grounds for a mistrial? *See United States v. Martinez-Salazar,* 528 U.S. 304, 316-17 (2000).

Not surprisingly, the jury finds Cates guilty, but the townspeople were disappointed with the sentence: no hanging. Cates was simply ordered to pay a $100 fine. On a teacher's salary in 1960, the fine was no small burden.

? Exam Tips

A constitutional law essay exam might pose a newly enacted statute or other state action and you will have to decide whether the government's act is constitutional or unconstitutional. When taking the position that a new statute violates the First Amendment's free speech protection, for example, the first thing you want to do is make a facial attack on the statute. For instance, perhaps the statute is overbroad, in that it reaches both protected as well as unprotected speech in its prohibition. Obviously, be skeptical of words like "all," "any," or "every." Similarly, the statute presented might be defeated if it is too vague. A vague law is one that leaves a person guessing as to what precisely it prohibits (e.g., "annoying or offensive statements are illegal.").

A key to a good score on such an essay is not whether you correctly identify the action as constitutional or not. Federal judges would disagree on that issue. Your grade depends on your constitutional analysis. Often, the constitutional question raised on your exam is analogous to a case in your textbook, in which the government takes essentially the same action, but your professor has creatively disguised the scenario by putting it in a slightly different context. If you can properly spot the issue, and its analogy to a case you studied in class, you can then utilize the familiar constitutional reasoning of our Supreme Court justices. If your professor seems to have a "favorite" case or two, re-read those cases just prior to your Con Law exam.

Another important preparatory tip for constitutional law courses and exams – and for law school itself – is to read the United States Constitution in full. It is short so read it twice. For quick and easy reference, obtain a pocket-sized constitution, or download an app. You can likely score one for free from one of the Westlaw or Lexis representatives at your school. Get as much free stuff as you can from these people.

LEGAL BRIEFS & MOVIE EXTRAS

*Bertram Cates openly admitted to committing the crime with which he was charged: violating Tennessee's Butler Act. Having confessed, his best chance was that the Butler Act would be found unconstitutional. Today, federal law provides a mechanism to challenge a statute's constitutionality prior to any adverse ruling in a proceeding to enforce the questionable statute:

In any action, suit, or proceeding in a court of the United States to which a State or any agency, officer, or employee thereof is not a party, wherein the constitutionality of any statute of that State affecting the public interest is drawn in question, the court shall certify such fact to the attorney general of the State, and shall permit the State to intervene for presentation of evidence, if evidence is otherwise admissible in the case, and for argument on the question of constitutionality. The State shall, subject to the applicable provisions of law, have all the rights of a party and be subject to all liabilities of a party as to court costs to the extent necessary for a proper presentation of the facts and law relating to the question of constitutionality.

28 U.S.C. §2403(b). Thus, modern attorneys can attempt to change the law before their clients' criminal trials.

*Constitutional challenges may also be brought after a conviction for a violation of a constitutionally questionable criminal statute, such as the Butler Act. *See* 28 U.S.C.A. §1257 (providing for the United States Supreme Court's review of a final judgment or decree from the "highest court of a State in which a decision could be had.").

*There is also a 1988 made-for-television remake of *Inherit the Wind*, starring Kirk Douglas. Suffice it to say that the original is better, particularly for a legal audience.

"He that troubleth his own house shall inherit the wind."

— *Proverbs 11:29*

TO KILL A MOCKINGBIRD
(Brentwood Productions 1962)

Starring: Gregory Peck; Mary Badham; Brock Peters

Lesson: Criminal Law/Procedure

Plot: This story takes place during the Great Depression in fictional Maycomb, Alabama. At the heart of the movie is the story of attorney Atticus Finch (Gregory Peck). Atticus Finch is a well-respected small-town southern lawyer who accepts hickory nuts for legal fees. Atticus Finch is a widower with two children. His youngest, Jean Louise "Scout" Finch (Mary Badham) narrates much of the story. Scout is a six-year-old tomboy who seems ahead of her time, using a vast vocabulary and referring to her father by his first name. Also at the heart of the movie is the story of Tom Robinson (Brock Peters), a black man accused of beating and raping a local white woman, Mayella Ewell. At the request of the town judge, Atticus defends Tom Robinson. Atticus is scorned by some of the Maycomb townspeople, who would prefer to skip the trial and get right to Robinson's lynching. But Atticus considers it his duty to represent Robinson. We hear the story of the trial through Scout, who is certain her father is virtuously defending an innocent man being falsely accused of rape by a white-trash tramp and her bigoted father, Bob Ewell. According to Scout, her father succeeds in proving the Ewells' lies and Tom's innocence, even though a guilty verdict by the all-white, racist Maycomb jury was inevitable. (The Sixth Amendment's guarantee of an impartial jury may not have been available to Tom Robinson; the Sixth Amendment was not made applicable to the states through the Fourteenth Amendment until 1966. *See, e.g., Parker v. Gladden,* 385 U.S. 363 (1966).

The movie has many interesting courtroom scenes, including persuasive closing arguments and compelling witness interrogations. Although not completely realistic, these scenes nevertheless offer educational value. Pay attention to Atticus Finch's courtroom style, noting what tactics seem effective, what is unattractive, etc.

CRIMINAL LAW (this also relates to Evidence)
Rape Cases

Like *The Accused*, the trial at the heart of *To Kill a Mockingbird* is a rape case. Like the defense attorneys in *The Accused*, Atticus Finch painted the rape victim, Mayella, as a sexual aggressor who consented to the sexual encounter at issue. This is standard operating procedure in rape defenses: invoke the consent defense. As discussed in the evidence section of *The Accused*, modern rape shield laws provide some protection for alleged rape victims. Federal Rule of Evidence 412(a) (Sex Offense Cases) declares inadmissible: (1) evidence offered to prove that any alleged victim engaged in other sexual behavior; and (2) evidence offered to prove any alleged victim's sexual predisposition. Rule 412(b), however, carves out exceptions to the rape shield rule. A victim's sexual history may come into evidence when: (1) it is offered to "prove that a person other than the accused was the source of the semen, injury, or other physical evidence;" (2) it is offered to prove consent by "specific instances of sexual behavior by the alleged victim with respect to the person accused;" and (3) exclusion "would violate the constitutional rights of the defendant."

Rule 412 minimizes an attorney's ability to attack these women on cross-examinations, badgering them about their sexual propensity, the way that Atticus tortured Mayella Ewell. The difference between the two rape stories, however, is the audience perception of whether or not the victims are telling the truth. In *The Accused,* Jodie Foster's character is regarded as telling the truth about the gang rape, whereas Mayella is commonly thought to be lying. From a defense attorney's standpoint, does this distinction matter? Does the propriety of Atticus Finch's cross-examination of Mayella depend upon Tom Robinson's guilt or innocence? For a thought-provoking article exploring these and other interesting issues about Tom Robinson's trial and Atticus Finch's role, see Steven Lubet, *Reconstructing Atticus Finch,* 97 MICH. L. REV. 1339-1362 (1999). Professor Lubet queries: Does the virtue of Atticus Finch "depend at all on Tom's innocence, or is it just as noble to use one's skills in aid of the guilty?" *Id.* at 1339.

CRIMINAL LAW/PROCEDURE
Motion for Judgment of Acquittal/Directed Verdicts

When the prosecution rested, Atticus immediately proceeded with his case and called Tom to the stand. Was this the appropriate next step for Atticus to take? Federal Rule of Criminal Procedure 29 (Motion for a Judgment of Acquittal) provides that:

After the government closes its evidence or after the close of all the evidence, the court on the defendant's motion must enter a judgment of acquittal of any offense for which the evidence is insufficient to sustain a conviction. The court may on its own consider whether the evidence is insufficient to sustain a conviction. If the court denies a motion for a judgment of acquittal at the close of the government's evidence, the defendant may offer evidence without having reserved the right to do so.

In other words, when a prosecutor has not met his burden of proving every element of a crime, a motion for a judgment of acquittal (also called a motion for directed verdict) should be made at the close of the prosecution's case so that the defense only has to present a case if the motion is properly denied. In some instances, the failure to make such a motion at this window of opportunity may result in the failure to preserve certain issues for an appeal. *Leary v. United States*, 395 U.S. 6, 32 (1969). In this case, Atticus successfully negates the medical evidence offered to show that Tom beat Mayella (and, in fact, convincingly establishes that it was more likely Mayella's blackened right eye came from her father's left hand). He paints the prosecution's star witnesses, the victim and her drunken father, as low-life liars who, out of embarrassment, are attempting to hide Mayella's sexual aggression and Tom's rejection of her advances. Without credible testimony from the Ewells, the prosecution had very little - not enough for a conviction. The problem, of course, was that Tom had a racist jury and a guilty verdict was assumed. Nevertheless, did Atticus miss an opportunity in going forward with his case without making a Rule 29 motion?

Despite a complete lack of evidence of guilt and, in fact, significant evidence of innocence, the jury convicts Tom Robinson. Had Robinson not been shot trying to escape from prison, how would you handle his appeal? Based on current law, what are your best appellate arguments?

LEGAL BRIEFS & MOVIE EXTRAS

*During Atticus's cross-examinations, Bob and Mayella Ewell are impeached to shreds. Although this is a great scene, proving Atticus's fine advocacy abilities, how many evidentiary and/or ethical violations can you spot?

*This movie is, of course, based on Harper Lee's Pulitzer Prize winning novel *To Kill a Mockingbird*. The novel is also narrated by Scout Finch, the young daughter of Atticus. The story is loosely based on Harper Lee's own family and neighbors. In fact, Harper Lee's father was the inspiration for Atticus Finch, and Scout was likely modeled after Harper Lee herself. Certain other characters are based on Harper Lee's childhood neighbors.

To Kill a Mockingbird was Robert Duvall's movie debut. He plays the Finches' mentally challenged neighbor, Boo Radley. Boo Radley both terrifies and mystifies the Finch children. He adds a certain comic relief to the film.

"Be not too hard on lawyers, for when we are at our best we can give you an Atticus Finch."

-Steven Lubet, Professor of Law, Northwestern University of Law (from *Reconstructing Atticus Finch,* 97 MICH. L. REV. 1339-1362 (1999))

THE FORTUNE COOKIE
(MGM 1966)

Starring: Jack Lemmon; Walter Matthau; Ron Rich; Judi West

Lesson: Torts

Plot: An unethical personal injury attorney, Willie Gingrich (Walter Matthau), convinces his brother-in-law, Harry Hinkle (Jack Lemmon), to commence a $1,000,000 lawsuit after Harry was knocked down at a football game. Harry worked as a television cameraman for CBS. While Harry was working on the sidelines filming a Cleveland Browns v. Minnesota Vikings game, the Browns' running back, Luther "Boom Boom" Jackson, crashed into him. He was rushed to the hospital. He was not seriously injured, however, but "Whiplash Willie" concocts a scheme. He convinces Harry to pretend to be paralyzed. Harry went along with Willie's scam because he hoped the prospect of a large cash settlement would win him back his wife (Judi West), a materialistic woman who longed for fame and fortune and had recently left Harry for another man. Willie and Harry sue the Cleveland Browns, CBS, and the football stadium owners for $1,000,000. With Willie's help and the use of an old x-ray, Harry manages to trick a team of doctors and a private investigation team into thinking he was paralyzed. But then Harry's conscience begins to threaten Willie's plan, particularly as he befriends a guilt-ridden "Boom Boom" Jackson. *The Fortune Cookie* is a hysterically funny movie that raises a number of tort law issues. Obviously, it raises ethical and criminal law issues as well.

TORTS
Premises Liability

The theory upon which Willie attempts to sue the Cleveland Browns' municipal stadium owner is based on premises liability.

Premises liability is a form of negligence. As such, a plaintiff suing for injuries sustained on the property of another must prove the four elements of negligence: (1) duty, (2) breach of that duty, (3) causation, and (4) harm to the plaintiff. Here, the questions become: did the stadium owners have a duty to keep the sidelines completely clear of equipment and, if so, did a breach of that duty result in damages to Harry?

Employer Vicarious Liability: Respondeat Superior

As Willie points out in Scene 4, the Hinkle case is based on negligence. The question becomes, who is responsible for the negligence? When injury results from a person negligently performing his job duties, many plaintiffs seek redress from a deeper pocket than the employee tortfeasor; plaintiffs find a way to reach the employer's deep pockets – or the employer's liability insurance policy. Most states have held employers vicariously liable for their employees' negligence under the doctrine of respondeat superior. Literally translated, the Latin phrase respondeat superior means "let the master stand." This concept of letting the master stand means that plaintiffs can look to deep-pocket employers when they are injured by an employee who may not have the financial ability to cover all of the damages sustained. In order to prevail against the employer, the plaintiff must show that the employee caused the accident while acting within the scope of the employment relationship. The question of whether or not a negligent employee was within the scope of his employment when he caused injury is heavily litigated and fact-specific. An employee's act is considered to be within the scope of his employment only if:

(a) the act is of the kind he is employed to perform;

(b) the act occurs substantially within the authorized time and space limits;

(c)   the act is actuated, at least in part, by a purpose to serve the master; and

(d)   if force is intentionally used by the servant against another, the use of force is not unexpectable by the master.

RESTATEMENT (SECOND) OF AGENCY §228(1). The Restatement further provides that "[c]onduct of a servant is not within the scope of employment if it is different in kind from that authorized, far beyond the authorized time or space limits, or too little actuated by a purpose to serve the master." RESTATEMENT (SECOND) OF AGENCY §228(2). *See also* RESTATEMENT (SECOND) OF AGENCY §229(2), which offers ten factors to be considered in deciding whether an employee's conduct occurred within the scope of the employment.

As you should note, Luther "Boom Boom" Jackson was clearly acting within the scope of his employment when he crashed into Harry. So, fearing that Boom Boom's own pockets were not deep enough, Willie and Harry sued Boom Boom's employer (the Cleveland Browns), Harry's employer (CBS), as well as the property owners of the football stadium.

Employer Direct Liability: Negligent Supervision

Even where the employee is outside of the scope of his employment when he negligently causes harm, many states recognize the tort of negligent supervision as an independent, direct cause of action against an employer (in contrast to the vicarious liability imposed under a respondeat superior theory). These states generally do so through the adoption of Restatement (Second) of Torts §317, Duty of Master to Control Conduct of Servant. *See, e.g., Davis v. USX Corp.*, 819 F.2d 1270, 1273-74 (4th Cir. 1987) (relying on §317 and holding that "[u]nder a theory of negligent supervision, an employer may be held liable for a failure to exercise reasonable care to control an employee from intentionally harming third parties while acting outside the scope of his employment."). *See also, Platson v. NSM, America, Inc.,* 748 N.E.2d 1278 (Ill. App. Ct. 2001). Section 317 provides:

A master is under a duty to exercise reasonable care so to control his servant while acting outside the scope of his employment as to prevent him from intentionally harming others or from so conducting himself as to create an unreasonable risk of bodily harm to them, if

(a) the servant

(i) is upon the premises in possession of the master or upon which the servant is privileged to enter only as his servant, or

(ii) is using a chattel of the master, *and*

(b) the master

(i) knows or has reason to know that he has the ability to control his servant, and

(ii) knows or should know of the necessity and opportunity for exercising such control.

RESTATEMENT (SECOND) OF TORTS §317 (1965).

Additionally, some states recognize the tort of negligent supervision via their adoption of the Restatement (Second) of Agency §213, Principal Negligence or Recklessness. Section §213 provides that "[a] person conducting an activity through servants or other agents is subject to liability for harm resulting from his conduct if he is negligent or reckless … in the supervision of the activity."

RESTATEMENT (SECOND) OF AGENCY §213 (1958).

Under these common law principles, negligent supervision allows for a broader basis to impose employer liability than the respondeat superior doctrine alone. Many states, however, have not yet recognized the tort of negligent supervision. Research whether or not your state has adopted either the Restatement (Second) of Torts §317 or the Restatement (Second) of Agency §213 and the factors considered in imposing employer liability.

? Exam Tips

When a torts exam fact pattern presents an employee causing injury to another while performing his job duties, you are in the realm of respondeat superior. As you think about the facts presented, consider whether the tortfeasor was within the scope of his employment (whether the employee was expressly or impliedly authorized to perform the task, whether the incident occurred within the employee's authorized time or space limits, and whether the employee's activities were performed for an employer-related purpose). When the facts do not support employer liability, for instance, because the employee was outside of the scope of his employment, consider whether negligent hiring or negligent supervision torts may apply to the given facts.

Tort Defenses
Assumption of Risk

An affirmative defense often invoked in tort law is the assumption of risk doctrine. If a defendant can show that the plaintiff voluntarily and knowingly assumed the risks inherent to a particularly dangerous activity, the assumption of risk doctrine may act as a complete bar to any recovery against the negligent tortfeasors. *See* RESTATEMENT (SECOND) OF TORTS §496A (1965). The assumption of risk defense is often raised in cases involving injuries sustained during sporting events. If a person attending a baseball or football game is hit by a flying ball, a bat, or even a player, the players, team owners, stadium owners, or other possible defendants may avoid liability completely. The theory behind this broad defense is that anybody attending a ball game knows or should know about the normal risks associated with being in close proximity to the sport. The law therefore holds a would-be plaintiff responsible for any harm suffered as a result of choosing to take those risks by going to the game. The defendants in Willy and Harry's case may have been able to avoid liability based on the assumption of risk doctrine, assuming the doctrine had been adopted in the jurisdiction at that time. Harry would still have been able to obtain workers' compensation, however, had he truly been hurt.

Comparative Negligence

Even where the assumption of risk doctrine does not act as a complete bar to recovery, another defensive legal tool used in personal injury claims based on negligence is the concept of comparative negligence. Although not a complete bar to recovery, comparative negligence can reduce the liability or the amount of damages the defendant has to pay a plaintiff if the defendant can show that the plaintiff's own negligence was a contributing factor in his or her own injuries. Courts often try to determine the fault ratio and award damages accordingly. To illustrate, suppose a court finds that a plaintiff was 10% responsible for her own injuries. The defendant might then be liable for 90% of the damages suffered. Some courts deny recovery under comparative negligence principles if it is determined that the plaintiff was at least 50% responsible for her own injuries. It depends on whether the applicable state law is based on a contributory negligence theory (which, like the assumption of risk doctrine, bars recovery if the plaintiff is even 1% at fault) or a comparative negligence state (which reduces or prohibits the plaintiff's recovery based on that plaintiff's percentage of fault). Some states use a pure comparative method, while others use a modified comparative negligence standard. Research which method is used in your state.

What, if any, comparative negligence did Harry engage in prior to colliding with the football player?

? Exam Tip

For state bar exam purposes, make sure you know how your state deals with the issues of assumption of risk and comparative negligence of a plaintiff. Know when these defenses are a complete bar to recovery and when they simply reduce the amount of damages. Know the formula your state courts use to account for a plaintiff's own negligence in awarding damages.

LEGAL BRIEFS & MOVIE EXTRAS

*When Harry Hinkle is in his hospital bed faking paralysis, he is watching the movie *Young Mr. Lincoln.*

*For more information about the tort concepts discussed above, two famous tort treatises are particularly helpful: D. Dobbs, *The Law of Torts* (2000) and W. Keeton, D. Dobbs, R. Keeton, D. Owen, *Prosser and Keeton on The Law of Torts*, 655-56 (5th ed. 1984).

*In Scene 4, the defendant insurance company's attorney states that the Hinckle case is one of "simple workmen's compensation." The workers' compensation issue was brushed off as Willie cited, by memory, a handful of cases involving negligence. (I do not think the cases "Whiplash Willie" cited were actual cases in New York or Ohio.) Every state and the federal government has a workers' compensation statute that provides no-fault medical and lost wage benefits to workers who are injured, killed, or become ill during the course of their employment. Negligence and fault are, for the most part, immaterial under these laws. In exchange for the no-fault medical and lost wage benefits under workers' compensation laws, however, employees are generally barred from suing the employers for injuries sustained at work, except under limited circumstances (e.g., failure to pay claims or employer discrimination based on a workers' compensation claim). Thus, had the CBS cameraman actually been injured on the job, under modern laws, he would have been entitled to workers' compensation through the station's insurance carrier. Exceptions to this system are discussed in *Deep Water Horizon.*

"Too bad it didn't happen further down the street...in front of the May Company. From them, you can collect! Couldn't you have dragged yourself another twenty feet?"

-Says Attorney Willie Gingrich to a potential personal injury (slip and fall) client

PAPER CHASE
(Twentieth Century Fox 1973)

Starring: Timothy Bottoms; Lindsay Wagner; John Houseman

Lesson: Contracts

Plot: James Hart (Timothy Bottoms) is a struggling first-year Harvard law student, desperately trying to impress his strict and intimidating contracts professor, Charles Kingsfield (John Houseman). He is overwhelmed with the law school workload and the pressure of competition, reaching his own high goals, and meeting Kingsfield's expectations. Hart proves to be one of the brightest students in his class. He appears to be winning Kingsfield's approval, until he meets Susan (Lindsay Wagner), and falls in love with her before discovering that she is the good Professor's daughter.

The Paper Chase is a back-to-the-classroom look at the law, sans the intriguing plots, dazzling courtroom moments, crooked cops, and murderous spouses that fashion some of the other movies discussed in this book. Still, it is something of a rite of passage for law students to see this movie, especially those from Harvard Law. For more information about the plot and history of *The Paper Chase*, see the many reviews at www.amazon.com, several of which are written by law students.

CONTRACTS

In Scene 2, on the first day of class, Professor Kingsfield uses the Socratic Method to elicit discussion about a case he calls the "Hairy Hand" case. Kingsfield is referring to the infamous 1929 New Hampshire Supreme Court decision in Hawkins v. McGee, 146 A. 641 (N.H. 1929) (although the case nickname came from a subsequent suit, *McGee v. United States Fidelity & Guaranty Co.*, 53 F.2d 953 (1st Cir. 1931), in which McGee sued his malpractice carrier for refusing to cover the damages he was ordered to pay in the original *Hawkins* lawsuit.). In the *Hawkins* case, the plaintiff, young Hawkins, suffered electrical burns that scarred his hand. *Id.* at 642. Dr. McGee approached Hawkins and made strong promises about his ability to remove the hand scars with skin grafting, using the boy's chest skin. *Id.* Dr. McGee promised to "make the hand a hundred percent perfect hand." *Id.* at 642-433. Dr. McGee, however, was apparently unfamiliar with the new technique and botched the procedure. *See id.* at 643. Hawkins sued for breach of contract and negligence, but the negligence portion was dismissed. *Id.* at 641. The Court had no trouble finding Dr. McGee liable for breach of contract; the issue in the case focused on the remedies to which Hawkins was entitled. *See id.* at 644. Hawkins wanted remedies for his pain and suffering. *Id.* Remedies for physical pain and suffering, however, sound in tort. In *Hawkins*, the basis for liability was contract, due to the doctor's guarantee of "perfection." *Id.* The Court therefore determined that remedies were limited to Hawkins' expectation damages, i.e., the difference between the value of what Hawkins would have received had the contract been properly carried out and the actual value he obtained from the doctor's work (and reasonably anticipated incidental losses incurred as a result of the breach). *Id.*

This case raises a distinction between damages in tort law and contract law that resembles the modern "economic loss rule." In order to preserve the bright line between contract and tort law, the economic loss rule prohibits the recovery of purely economic losses in tort where the relationship between the parties is governed by a contract. *See Jones & Laughlin Steel Corp. v. Johns-Manville Sales Corp.,* 626 F.2d 280, 287 n. 13 (3d Cir. 1980) (citing cases holding that economic losses from breaches of contract are not recoverable under tort theories). As courts have explained, "[t]he economic loss rule, adopted by the majority of states ... marks the fundamental boundary between the law of contracts, which is designed to enforce expectations created by agreement, and the law of torts, which is designed to protect citizens and their property by imposing a duty of reasonable care on others." *Fireman's Ins. Co. v. Childs*, 52 F. Supp. 2d 139, 142 (D. Me. 1999). *See also* W. Keeton, D. Dobbs, R. Keeton, D. Owen, *Prosser and Keeton on The Law of Torts*, 655-56 (5th ed. 1984) (stating that the economic loss doctrine upholds "obligations based on the manifested intention of the parties to a bargaining transaction" as opposed to duties of reasonable care under tort theories).

Note that it is unlikely a contracts course would begin with a remedies case. Professor Kingsfield used FULLER ON CONTRACTS, which does begin with the *McGee* case and a discussion of remedies. A modern contracts class typically starts with the basic requirements of a contract: offer, acceptance, mutual assent, consideration, capacity, legality, and a lack of other defenses (*see, e.g.,* STEVEN J. BURTON, BURTON'S PRINCIPLES OF CONTRACT LAW (3rd Edition) (West 2006). Kingsfield does not talk about the nature of an offer, acceptance, and consideration and other elements of a binding contract until Scene 10, when he discusses the Carbolic Smokeball Company case (I am unable to confirm, through a search on Westlaw, whether the Smokeball case was an actual case; if a reader can find it on-line or in a case book, please let me know). According to Professor Kingsfield, the Carbolic Smokeball Company placed an advertisement in the November 1891 *Gazette* offering a $100 reward if anyone caught a cold or influenza while using the smokeball product, which was supposed to combat viruses. The plaintiff, Mrs. Cardale, developed influenza while on the product. The company refused to pay the reward, so she sued. The Court apparently found in her favor, and Hart properly explains the basis for a finding of adequate consideration in this hypothetical. The consideration Mrs. Cardale provided was her agreement to use the product.

? Exam Tips

Contracts law is essentially incorporated into two bodies of authority: the Restatement of Contracts and the Uniform Commercial Code ("UCC"). The Restatement is a secondary source, which means it is not necessarily binding on courts; it is a summary of the common law doctrines of contracts. Most state courts, however, regard the Restatement as authoritative. The UCC (Article II) has been adopted and codified into the statutes of every state, almost in its entirety (with only minor exceptions). The UCC governs contracts for the sale of goods valued at over $500. So, if you are dealing with goods, you analyze the problem under the UCC. For most other contracts, such as service contracts, you analyze the facts under the Restatement. Basically, the UCC and the Restatement overlap. It is crucial, however, to understand where the UCC differs from the common law Restatement, and to fully understand which one applies to a particular situation. Also, watch out for "mixed deals," involving both goods and services. If an agreement involves both a sale of goods as well as services, determine whether the goods or the services constitute the most important part of the agreement. Then, follow an "all or nothing" rule and analyze the facts only under the Restatement or only under the UCC - not both, unless of course you are specifically asked to do so.

When writing an essay exam answer, be sure to use all of the facts provided in the given hypothetical. This is particularly true with respect to contracts law essays. In an essay question about contract formation, for example, the facts provided should correspond to each of the necessary elements for contract formation: offer, acceptance, consideration, capacity, etc. Any remaining facts likely relate to defenses or damages. Also, never assume any facts not specifically provided.

The first step in acing a contracts essay for a state bar exam is recognizing that you are in the realm of contracts. If you read a fact pattern in which liability is being debated because of some promise or statement made by one of the parties, you know you can move from recognition of a contract to isolating the major issues the question raises. Consider these basic contract issues to determine the proper focus of your answer:

1. Did the parties have the capacity to form an agreement?

2. Did the parties form an agreement by exchanging a valid offer for a valid and timely acceptance?

3. If so, has each party exchanged consideration?

4. If there is no consideration, or if some other contractual defect exists, do any equitable grounds provide relief? For example, has there been detrimental reliance or partial performance?

5. Do the terms of the deal or the subsequent actions of the contract parties confer any rights or impose any duties upon third parties?

6. Have contractual obligations become due?

7. If the contract obligations are due, has performance been excused for any reason?

8. If performance has not been excused, has it been properly and fully tendered?

9. If performance has not been properly and fully tendered, identify the breach at hand.

10. If there is a breach, what remedies are appropriate?

You may see variations of this list, but the point is: if you can remember a list of basic contract questions, you can spot all of the issues on an exam, quickly outline them, and draft an ace essay.

LEGAL BRIEFS & MOVIE EXTRAS

The Paper Chase is based on John Jay Osborn, Jr.'s novel. The novel and the movie inspired a television series of the same name. John Houseman again played Professor Kingsfield.

One L, published in 1977, is best-selling author Scott Turow's entertaining memoir of his first year as a Harvard Law student. Although you may be worlds away from a Harvard law student in the 1970s, any law student of any age or gender at any law school in the world will be able to relate to this book. Attorney Turow's prose is so profound and insightful, you are sure to find yourself saying: "that's me!"

"You come in here with a head full of mush, and you leave thinking like a lawyer."

-Says Professor Kingsfield to his first-year law students on their first day of law school.

KRAMER V. KRAMER
(Columbia Films 1979)

Starring: Dustin Hoffman; Meryl Streep

Lessons: Family Law; Civil Procedure; Evidence

Plot: Dustin Hoffman plays Mr. Kramer, a big shot New York City advertising executive. Meryl Streep fabulously plays Mrs. Kramer, a troubled homemaker with a Smith education who tries to run away from her own emotional turmoil. She leaves her husband – and her 5-year-old child – to travel to California in search of ... something. On her journey, she regains "self-esteem," and decides to return to New York to seek sole custody of her son. This is an intense and very well acted movie. It won best picture and its brilliant stars won best actor and actress. *Kramer v. Kramer* also illustrates the emotional aspects of practicing family law.

FAMILY LAW

The "best interests of the child" standard is today's guide in child custody determinations. The best interests of the child principle affords the trial court judge significant discretion. Ideally, judges work with the divorcing parents to develop a custody plan that both of the parents, the children, and the court system can embrace. The best interests of the child standard is imperfect. For one reason, depending on the age and preference of a child, he or she may take the stand in a custody battle and be put in the difficult position of having to tell which parent is the better parent. Further, when parents fight for sole custody, as the Kramers did, each parent attempts to show that the other is unfit to be a parent. As this movie shows, the best interests of the child standard results in the bashing of both parents in open court. On the other hand, properly handled, the best interests of the child standard provides a workable means of court-facilitated childcare plans tailored to the specific needs of each child. In some cases, a *guardian ad litem* may be appointed by the court to protect the rights and advocate for the best interests of the children as their parents' divorce goes through the court system. A neutral, outsider serving as guardian can make the process less stressful and more constructive (or less destructive).

Would joint custody be feasible for the care of this child? What factors should properly be taken into consideration in determining what is best for Billy? Mrs. Kramer's attorney focuses on Mr. Kramer's imperfect work history, trying to show that he is irresponsible because he misses deadlines and that his general negligence would not serve the best interests of his son. He uses the boy's playground accident as dirt to diminish Mr. Kramer's parenting skills. Mrs. Kramer's attorney attempts to connect the incident to Mr. Kramer's being a neglectful workaholic, even though the Kramers had previously discussed the incident and Mrs. Kramer was supportive and understanding. So he has a few work problems and is present when Billy gets hurt on the playground; she admits to promiscuity, child abandonment, and mental health issues. She gets custody. He gets visitation rights. Luckily, she has another breakdown and decides to let Billy stay with his Dad.

If this case were decided today, would it have come out differently? Should it? Why or why not?

? Exam Tips

Many state bar examiners include an essay question on family law issues, including divorce, child custody, and property distribution. Generally speaking, there are a few terms that should be included in any essay answer involving family law. The first involves child custody. When analyzing a child custody problem, focus on the buzzwords "best interests of the child standard" and what facts from the hypothetical would be used to assess the case under this standard. Another key term to use in essays about divorce cases is "shared parental rights and responsibilities," which seems to have replaced the terms "joint custody" and "child support." Also important in writing about divorce cases, from a property rights standpoint, is an analysis of the "equitable divisions of assets" – the buzzwords for determining how to fairly split whatever wealth the couple acquires throughout the marriage. When appropriate, discuss grounds, if any, for spousal support (a term that seems to have replaced "alimony"). Think in terms of what is equitable, in light of the length of the marriage, the respective marital roles, contribution, income, debt, etc.

CIVIL PROCEDURE
Appeals

When Ted Kramer and his attorney discuss an appeal, they talk about putting Billy on the witness stand. Aside from whether or not it is in Billy's best interest to take the stand, under what circumstances could that happen on appeal? Appellate courts generally do not hear new evidence, so the only way Billy could testify is if the appellate court remanded the case to the lower court and ordered a new trial. New trials in custody cases are uncommon. It is more common for a court to simply hear attorney arguments on motions to modify the original order. *See, e.g., Lovin v. Lovin,* 561 N.W.2d 612, 616 (N.D. 1997) (holding that a motion for a new trial based on newly discovered evidence is inappropriate in custody cases because the court has continuing jurisdiction to modify custody orders when new evidence is adduced).

Search the appellate courts of your state for divorce cases and note the grounds upon which these appeals are filed. What factors tend to result in reversals when it comes to child custody disputes?

EVIDENCE
Direct Examination

The later scenes in this film, from Scene 20 forward, take place mostly in the courtroom. Some portions of the witness questioning during these lengthy trial scenes follow the civil rules of evidence and procedure, but other parts follow the rules of Hollywood. During the direct examinations of Mr. and Mrs. Kramer, the attorney actors have very little to do, while the stars shine as their clients. Meryl Streep and Dustin Hoffman provide moving narratives that would not be proper witness testimony in an actual courtroom but won them both Oscars. Outside of Hollywood, such narrative testimony and voluntary statements are objectionable. *See* 98 C.J.C. *Witnesses* §403 (Testimony in narrative form; voluntary statements). There are limited circumstances in which a trial judge has the discretion to allow a witness to testify in the narrative form. Narrative testimony might be allowed in order to expedite a trial, for example, or to refresh a witness's recollection about prior testimony. *See Goings v. United States*, 377 F.2d 753, 762 (8th Cir. 1967). But the Kramers' narratives go far beyond those limited situations and are objectionable.

Such narrative testimony is particularly objectionable where, as here, the testimony begins to take on an argumentative tone. *See Bilby v. Owen,* 181 P. 724, 727 (Okla. 1919) (holding that witnesses must simply state the facts and "leave the jury to draw their conclusion from such facts"). Witnesses "are not permitted to usurp the province of the [court] and give testimony in the nature of conclusions, opinions, or argument." *Id.* Here, the Kramers usurp. When Ted Kramer takes the stand, for example, he provides an emotional soliloquy about gender biases and inequalities in parenting. Clearly such narrative testimony, Oscar-winning as it was, crosses into objectionable territory.

What other objections do you note regarding the Kramers' direct examinations? Did they provide testimony objectionable as hearsay? For instance, might hearsay objections have been successful as to Mrs. Kramer's testimony about various things Ted said to her? Or were the statements properly admitted as party opponent admissions?

Cross-Examination

Upon cross-examination of Mrs. Kramer, Ted's lawyer is able to elicit testimony about her love life. Was this properly admitted? What degree of relevance does the testimony have to determining what is in the best interests of the child? Mrs. Kramer's attorney objects on vagueness grounds. What other objections might have been made? Federal Rule of Evidence 403 allows for the exclusion of even relevant evidence "if its probative value is substantially outweighed by the danger of unfair prejudice, confusion of issues, or misleading the jury" or if it is cumulative and will cause undue delay or waste of time. Could you make 403 arguments to exclude this evidence?

The non-party witness, Ms. Phelps, after being cross-examined by Joanna's lawyer, turns to Joanna and exclaims, "Ted is not the same man … if you could see them together Joanna maybe you wouldn't be here now." As discussed above, ordinarily, a court will not permit a witness to volunteer statements or provide narratives not specifically asked in the proper question and answer manner, particularly where the witness blurts out her own opinion without being asked the question. Forgetting for a moment that an objection would have ruined the dramatic effect of the scene, should Joanna's attorney have objected to this outburst? Should it have been stricken from the record? What specific grounds for objection might have been made? Is the outburst argumentative? Non-responsive? Speculative? Might the outburst have a prejudicial impact on the outcome?

Whether or not improper in form, was Ms. Phelps's outburst relevant to the issue of Billy's best interests? If so, could her statements pass a Rule 403 balancing test, weighing the probative value against the prejudicial effect?

? Exam Tips

Whether relevant evidence might be excluded as prejudicial under Rule 403 is a heavily litigated issue – and a heavily tested subject. Watch for fact patterns containing shocking or disturbing testimony or other evidence, particularly if the evidence has only marginal relevance or a low probative value when balanced against its prejudicial impact. Other clues that you may need to discuss a Rule 403 balancing test include offensive visual or audio aids, grotesque photographs, and other graphic material. When it comes to the question of evidence admissibility in a family law case, perhaps you can make arguments that the child's best interest weighs in favor of or against the admission of the evidence in question. For example, evidence quite prejudicial to a parent may nevertheless be admitted if it is highly probative of a child's risk of danger if left in that parent's care. If, however, the evidence at issue is only remotely related to the best interests of the child analysis, Rule 403 may justify its exclusion.

LEGAL BRIEFS & MOVIE EXTRAS

*Joanna is the party petitioning for custody, so her lawyer begins the hearing. Notice he does not begin with an opening statement. Aside from whether opening statements are allowed in this New York Family Court in the 1970s, are there any strategic reasons why Joanna's attorney might have wanted to put Joanna on the stand immediately, foregoing an opening statement? Would the presence of a jury matter? Note that some states do not allow jury trials in divorce cases. If you are not already familiar from life experience or otherwise, now is a good time to learn your state's nuances on divorce law and procedure.

*For a more recent film involving parental rights and the "best interests of the child" analysis, see *I Am Sam* (New Line Cinema 2001). There are many movie references in I AM SAM, including a very obvious reference to *Kramer v. Kramer*.

"What law is it that says a woman is a better parent?"

- Mr. Kramer rhetorically questions the court.

AND JUSTICE FOR ALL
(Columbia Pictures 1979)

Starring: Al Pacino; John Forsythe; Jack Warden

Lessons: Evidence; Ethics

Plot: Al Pacino plays attorney Arthur Kirkland, a passionate criminal defense attorney who truly cares about his clients and tends to walk a straight ethical line. When Judge Henry T. Fleming (John Forsythe) is accused of rape, the judge believes Kirkland's sparkling reputation will create a semblance of innocence. The judge wants to hire Kirkland, and he will not take no for an answer. Ironically, Judge Fleming and his brethren use an alleged ethical violation, from Kirkland's past, to blackmail him into taking the judge's rape defense. Kirkland's representation of Judge Fleming unleashes an ethical dilemma that proves disastrous to Kirkland's career.

EVIDENCE

In Scene 28, Kirkland, in an opening statement, tells the jury that his client passed a lie detector test. His reference to the lie detector test was inappropriate. As the judge points out, Kirkland was "out of order." Generally, the results of a lie detector test are inadmissible when offered by either party, "either as substantive evidence or as relating to the credibility of a party or witness." *State v. Legrand*, 864 So.2d 89, 98 (La. 2003) (quoting *State v. Humphrey*, 445 So.2d 1155, 1158 (La. 1984)). Even where the lie detector test results are exculpatory, courts have historically excluded the results because such tests lack reliability. *State v. Robertson*, 712 So.2d 8, 34 (La. 1998); *People v. Forte*, 18 N.E.2d 31, 32 (N.Y. 1938); *See also People v. Leone*, 255 N.E.2d 696, 697 (N.Y. 1969) (holding that the reliability of lie detector tests "has not yet been sufficiently established to give them an evidentiary standing in the administration of the criminal law."). Kirkland therefore should not have made this reference in his opening statement, because it is impermissible to discuss evidence in opening statements that will not be admitted in the trial (or to refer, during closing arguments, to facts that were not introduced and admitted into evidence). *See United States v. D'Amico,* 496 F.3d 95, 104 (1st Cir. 2007). Obviously, however, his opening statement had much bigger problems.

ETHICS

The only reason Kirkland agrees to defend the Judge is because other members of the bench threaten to turn him in for breaching client confidentiality years prior. Kirkland's client had described his visions of murders he would commit. After a series of killings conducted in the manner his client described, Kirkland told the police about the visions and his client's confidential revelations. Was he prohibited from reporting the visions, after the crimes occurred, under the ethical rules of client confidentiality?

Under ABA Model Rule 1.6(b) (Confidentiality of Information), "a lawyer may reveal information relating to the representation of a client to the extent the lawyer reasonably believes necessary … to prevent the client from committing a crime." Also applicable is ABA Model Rule 4.1(b) (Truthfulness in Statements to Others), providing that, "in the course of representing a client a lawyer shall not knowingly … fail to disclose a material fact when disclosure is necessary to avoid assisting a criminal or fraudulent act by a client, unless disclosure is prohibited by Rule 1.6." Arguably, however, the Rule 1.6 exception carved out of Rule 4.1(b) effectively swallows Rule 4.1(b). In fact, a lawyer needs to be careful not to read the Rule 1.6 exception too broadly. The lawyer may breach confidentiality *only* if he has a reasonable belief that the breach will prevent a *future* crime. As this scene points out, a lawyer better be sure that he is disclosing a crime that is happening in the future, not past crimes. When the client confidence involves a serial type crime, where does the attorney draw the line between reporting past crimes that his client committed and preventing similar crimes in the future?

Also, in order to be sure to fall within the exception, the attorney needs to be quite certain that a crime *is* imminent, and that he is not simply speculating about what *might* happen.

As to Kirkland, would the Rule 1.6 exception, for preventing harm to people, save him from a violation of confidentiality rules? Or did Kirkland turn in his client for a crime already committed? How would you argue for Kirkland that no ethical violation occurred with respect to his prior revelations?

Regardless of whether he breached his prior client's confidentiality, Kirkland's days as a trial attorney are finished in the final scene. Kirkland's new client, the judge, confessed his guilt to Kirkland. Kirkland ultimately gives up his law license and reveals the judge's secret right in front of the jury. That clearly is a violation of Rule 1.6 confidentiality! What other attorney ethical violations are apparent in this movie?

The judges that blackmail Kirkland into taking Fleming's case are obviously guilty of ethical and other legal violations. Their actions violate, at the very least, the first two Canons of the ABA Model Code of Judicial Conduct (2002) (Upholding Integrity and Avoiding Impropriety or the Appearance of Impropriety). The judges' conduct may also be criminal. Further, to the extent the judges truly believed Kirkland's prior actions violated client confidentiality rules, the judges would have been obligated to report such conduct at that time, pursuant to ABA Model Rule 8.3 (Reporting Professional Misconduct) ("A lawyer who knows that another lawyer has committed a violation of the Rules of Professional Conduct that raises a substantial question as to that lawyer's honesty, trustworthiness or fitness as a lawyer in other respects, shall inform the appropriate professional authority."). This is known as the "rat rule." Comment 1 to Rule 8.3 suggests that judges are subject to this "squealing" rule too: "self-regulation of the legal profession requires that members of the profession initiate disciplinary investigation when they know of a violation of the Rules of Professional Conduct." In addition, Comment 1 states that "lawyers have a similar obligation with respect to judicial misconduct," such that Kirkland should have reported the judges' blackmail to the Board of Overseers of the Bar. As a practical matter, however, taking that route may have had just as disastrous of an impact on Kirkland's career.

? Exam Tips

Ethics exams can be tricky because doing what seems like the "right thing" may just run afoul of duties that an attorney has to his or her clients. Be sure you fully understand the interplay and overlap between the various ethical rules. Be familiar with the exceptions to client confidentiality rules that allow an attorney to reveal secrets to prevent harm. Be cognizant of nuances in the language of the rules, noting differences, like which rules use the word "shall" and which use the word "may." Also, make sure you can properly distinguish between a client's future plans to commit a crime and criminal actions that have already occurred. The difference could be subtle, particularly when dealing with a client who is suspected of being a repeat offender or "serial" criminal.

LEGAL BRIEFS & MOVIE EXTRAS

*Al Pacino won an Academy Award for his performance as Arthur Kirkland.

*Jack Warden appears in *And Justice for All* as the senior Judge Rayford, who engages in some outrageous and risky behavior and seems to have a death wish. Warden also appears in 12 *Angry Men, The Verdict*, and *Guilty as Sin*. He appears in the greatest scene from *And Justice for All*, Scene 28, where Judge Rayford tells Kirkland he is out of order, to which Kirkland famously responds:

"I'm out of order? You're out of order! The whole trial is out of order! They're out of order!"

-Says Arthur Kirkland, during what I assume was his last courtroom appearance as an attorney.

ABSENCE OF MALICE
(Columbia Pictures 1981)

Starring: Sally Field; Paul Newman; Bob Balaban

Lesson: Torts/Constitutional Law

Plot: Mike Gallagher (Paul Newman) is a Miami liquor distributor and the son of a bootlegger. He is also believed to be involved with the Mafia. The United States Department of Justice investigates Gallagher for murder after an obsessive prosecutor suspects him of being responsible for the disappearance of Joey Diaz, a local leader in the labor movement and a headache to certain mobsters. Baited by the prosecutor, a Miami newspaper reporter, Megan Carter (Sally Field), writes a sensational yet unflattering story about Mr. Gallagher. Megan soon becomes overly involved in the investigation, as she develops an intense relationship with Mr. Gallagher. Her values and beliefs start to change as she and Gallagher become romantically involved. (I was surprised that the chemistry between Paul Newman and Sally Field was somewhat believable). This movie is not a courtroom drama, but it raises interesting legal issues surrounding the media and ethical questions about what really constitutes "truth." *Absence of Malice* also features Bob Balaban, as Prosecutor Elliott Rosen, who resorts to desperate means and unscrupulous conduct in his efforts to destroy Mike Gallagher and end the Mafia. Through Rosen, the movie highlights attorney ethical violations and prosecutorial tactics to avoid.

TORTS/CONSTITUTIONAL LAW
Defamation and the First Amendment

In Scene 4, Megan meets with the paper's attorney, seeking approval to run a story connecting Mr. Gallagher to Mr. Diaz and suggesting that Gallagher is a murder suspect. The attorney questions the truth of the allegation, but he is not overly concerned about whether the intriguing and newsworthy rumor is true. Truth is a defense; but even if they are uncertain of the truth, the paper can avoid liability for the tort of defamation by showing the absence of malice – a media privilege that stems from the First Amendment and the U.S. Supreme Court's case law regarding free press.

In *New York Times v. Sullivan*, the Supreme Court had to balance the First Amendment's protection of freedom of the press against a party's right to sue for libel. 376 U.S. 254 (1964). It did so by carving out a limited privilege that protects Megan and her employer against liability for defamation when they publish inaccurate material about public figures concerning public issues. The Supreme Court held that "the constitutional guarantees require, we think, a federal rule that prohibits a public official from recovering damages for defamatory falsehood relating to his official conduct unless he proves that the statement was made with actual malice." *Id.* at 279-80. The *New York Times v. Sullivan's* actual malice standard requires an increased level of culpability, above and beyond the mere negligence standard used in analyzing cases where the plaintiff is not a public figure. Actual malice is either: 1. actual knowledge that the published statement is false, or 2. a reckless disregard of the statement's truth or falsity. *Id.* at 280. In other words, to prove actual malice, the plaintiff must show that the writer or publisher had subjective, serious doubts about the truth of the statement, but published it anyway. Actual malice therefore becomes hard to prove, giving the media wide latitude in printing even speculative stories. The privilege might also be allowed as to non-media defendants, where the defamatory statement concerns a public issue and the plaintiff is a public official. *Avins v. White*, 627 F.2d 637 (1980). In addition, the Supreme Court has held that a mere failure to adequately verify sources does not, in itself, constitute actual malice. *Harte-Hanks Communications v. Connaughton*, 491 U.S. 657 (1989).

The issue in Scene 4 is whether Gallagher is a public figure. In determining whether this limited privilege applies, the cases often focus on two major issues: "who is a public figure?" and "what is a public issue?" There are two types of public figures: general public officials, who are considered public officials for all purposes, and limited public figures, who obtain public official status by becoming involved in certain current public issues or controversies that are important to society. For the media privilege to apply with respect to a limited public figure, the defamatory statement must be related to the issue that renders the plaintiff a public official.

Megan and her employer's attorney discuss the distinction between a public official and a limited public figure. Megan asks what it takes for him to be a public figure and the attorney replied that if he knew, he would be a judge. *New York Times v. Sullivan* does offer some guidance to reporters in Megan's situation, however. The attorney advised Megan to contact Mr. Gallagher, even though he would likely refuse to talk to her. Either way, if the story contains inaccuracies, they at least tried to give him a chance to correct them. This way, he says, the paper has no direct knowledge that the story is false; the paper, therefore, will be able to show an absence of malice and avoid liability for defamation. But as the movie points out, even though there is, legally, an absence of malice defense, Megan walks a fine ethical and moral line with her story. She looks to the attorney for legal "rules" to guide her in deciding what to print. Sometimes one's own conscience might serve as a better guide. This movie shows that lawyers (like Jan Schlichtmann, in *A Civil Action,* for example) are not the only professionals who embark on personal career quests at the expense of others.

While Jan clearly crosses ethical lines, Megan wants to know exactly where the line is so she can stay just shy of it. Was that enough? Or does Megan's and her newspaper's conduct show that there can be a high price to pay even just walking too close to the line?

? Exam Tips

Torts exams always test the more common tort concepts, such as negligence and intentional torts like assault and battery. If your torts professor spends a long time discussing *New York Times v. Sullivan,* be prepared for exam questions about defamation torts: libel (written defamation) and slander (spoken defamation). Be able to distinguish these torts and identify their necessary elements. Also be able to spot the defamation defenses provided under *New York Times v. Sullivan* and its line of cases.

Additionally, when it comes to a torts essay exam, know whether or not your torts professor will expect you to cite certain key cases by name. If so, *New York Times v. Sullivan,* may be one, as would *Palsgraf v. Long Island R.R. Co.,* 162 N.E. 99 (N.Y. 1928).

LEGAL BRIEFS & MOVIE EXTRAS

*In Scene 28, the Assistant Attorney General was questioning Gallagher and others about the Diaz investigation. Does the AAG's "inquiry" pass constitutional muster? What constitutional amendments are implicated? Consider the AAG's question: "Mr. Gallagher do you want a lawyer?" Gallagher said "No." The AAG replied: "Good, there's no room in here anyhow." Does this questioning invoke the Sixth Amendment's right to counsel? If so, does the AAG's conduct fall short of protecting Gallagher's constitutional rights? Are the Fourth or Fifth Amendments implicated in this scene?

*Another movie involving the law and starring the very talented Sally Field is *Norma Rae* (Twentieth Century Fox 1979). Norma Rae is a small-town southern mill worker who organizes her fellow factory workers to fight for better working conditions and wages – a great story about the labor movement.

"As a matter of law, the truth of your story is irrelevant. We have no knowledge the story is false. Therefore, we're absent malice."

-Says the Miami newspaper's attorney, to staff reporter, Meg Carter

THE VERDICT
(Twentieth Century Fox 1982)

Starring: Paul Newman; Jack Warden

Lessons: Torts; Ethics

Plot: Here, Paul Newman plays Frank Galvin, a Boston lawyer with a drinking problem, who hits rock bottom personally and professionally. A friend, Mickey Morrissey (Jack Warden), tries to help by referring to Frank an "open and shut" medical malpractice case, assuming Frank would get himself a third of a quick, quiet, and large settlement. Galvin takes on the case, which involves a young woman, Deborah Ann Kay, who slipped into a coma giving birth at a hospital run by the Boston Archdiocese. Her baby did not survive and her husband abandoned her. Galvin represents the woman's sister and brother-in-law, Mr. and Mrs. Doneghy. The "open and shut" referral turns into complex litigation against powerful defendants, including the Boston Archdiocese, St. Catherine's Hospital, and two "gallant" physicians of the hospital. Galvin must prove the defendants were negligent and that Mrs. Kay was given the wrong anesthesia. With a twisted sense of justice, Galvin wants to expose the hospital's wrongdoings in court. In the process, he violates several ethical rules and gives up a substantial settlement offer that might have felt more like justice to his client.

TORTS
Medical Malpractice

The plaintiffs' case is one of medical malpractice – a subcategory of tort law. Although strict liability torts (e.g., defective products, drugs, medical supplies, or equipment) and intentional torts (e.g., assault and battery) may come into play in the healthcare arena, most medical malpractice claims are premised on the concept of negligence. Plaintiffs therefore need to show that the defendants had a duty to provide a certain standard of care, and that their failure to meet that standard resulted in injury. Here, Galvin must show that, had the defendants exercised a reasonable standard of care, they would have administered the proper anesthesia. Instead, the defendants breached their duty and caused Mrs. Kay's coma.

As medical malpractice litigation and medical liability insurance claims began to rise across the country, many states began to institute pretrial medical malpractice screening panels. Pretrial screening panels seek to encourage parties to settle meritorious claims and to eliminate "nuisance" suits. Massachusetts law provides for a pre-screening tribunal made up of a judge, a doctor, and an attorney. Mass. Gen. Law Title II, Chapter 231: Section 60B. The tribunal evaluates the medical evidence and decides whether the case raises a legitimate question of liability. *Id.* Other states with medical malpractice screening panels include Montana (Mont. Code Ann. §27-6-704(2) (2005)), Nebraska (Neb. Rev. Stat. §44-2843 (2005)), Maine (24 M.R.S.A. §§2851-2859 (2005)), and New Hampshire (NH RSA 519-B). According to the American Medical Association, as of August 2007, at least 16 states were using medical malpractice screening panels of some form to evaluate claims before they reach a court. Some states tried the screening panels for a short time, but later altered or repealed them entirely. Catherine T. Struve, *Improving the Medical Malpractice Litigation Process,* HEALTH AFFAIRS, vol. 23, no. 4 (2004) fn. 8. Research the prerequisites and the process for bringing medical malpractice claims under your state's statutes and civil procedure rules.

? Exam Tips

On a torts essay exam involving negligence, use the four essential elements of negligence as the outline for your answer, regardless of the setting. Whether the facts present medical malpractice, legal malpractice, premises liability, a car accident, or any other mishap causing personal injury or property damage, always address duty, breach, causation, and damages, in that order. Group the facts into these four categories before sketching out an answer. Typically, the facts will also warrant a discussion of defenses. Common tort defenses include comparative negligence, assumption of the risk, misuse or abuse of a product, self-defense, defense of a third party, defense of property, recapture of chattels, privilege, or public or private necessity.

ETHICS
Attorney Misconduct

This movie highlights a number of ethical violations that can occur when attorneys fall victim to substance abuse and become desperate. ABA Model Rules 1.1 and 1.3, requiring competence and diligence, are implicated from Galvin's lack of preparation and procrastination, not to mention his perpetual hangover. Another obvious violation Galvin commits occurs in Scene 2, when he hands his business card to a widow at a funeral, telling her "it's a crime what happened" to her husband and offering his help as an attorney. ABA Model Rule 7.3(a) (Direct Contact with Prospective Clients) provides that "a lawyer shall not by in-person ... contact solicit professional employment from a prospective client when a significant motive for the lawyer's doing so is the lawyer's pecuniary gain." *See* Comment 1 to Rule 7.3 (explaining that "there is a potential for abuse inherent in direct in-person ... contact by a lawyer with a prospective client" because the prospective client "may already feel overwhelmed by the circumstances giving rise to the need for legal services ... the situation is fraught with the possibility of undue influence, intimidation, and overreaching."). Galvin's conduct at the funeral is exactly the type of attorney business solicitation that Rule 7.3 proscribes.

Additionally, like Attorney Jan Schlichtmann from *A Civil Action,* Galvin fails to present a $210,000 settlement offer to his client, in violation of Rule 1.4, regarding communications with clients. Comment 2 to Rule 1.4 requires that "a lawyer who receives from opposing counsel an offer of settlement in a civil controversy ... must promptly inform the client of its substance." Instead of letting Mr. and Mrs. Doneghy know of their chance for justice in the amount of $210,000 less Galvin's cut, Galvin decides he wants to take the defendants to court. Then, in Scene 17, Galvin crosses the line preparing for trial with his expert witness, Dr. Lionel Thompson, an obstetrician. The manner in which he essentially dictates his witness's testimony is a violation of ABA Model Rule 3.4(b) (Fairness to Opposing Party and Counsel) ("A lawyer shall not ... falsify evidence, [or] counsel or assist a witness to testify falsely.").

All of these actions may also be violations of ABA Model Rule 3.4(c) (Fairness to Opposing Party and Counsel) ("A lawyer shall not ... knowingly disobey an obligation under the rules of the tribunal."), ABA Model Rule 3.5 (Impartiality and Decorum of the Tribunal) ("A lawyer shall not ... engage in conduct intended to disrupt a tribunal."), and ABA Model Rule 8.4 (Misconduct) (providing that a violation of a Rule constitutes professional misconduct). The "rat rule," ABA Model Rule 8.3 (Reporting Professional Misconduct), may also be implicated, to the extent lawyers in the film failed to report other lawyers' misconduct. Rule 8.3 provides that "a lawyer who knows that another lawyer has committed a violation of the Rules of Professional Conduct that raises a substantial question as to that lawyer's honesty, trustworthiness or fitness as a lawyer in other respects, shall inform the appropriate professional authority."

The hospital is no ethical model either. In Scene 29, Mrs. Kay's admitting nurse, Kaitlin Costello, reveals on the witness stand that one of the defendant doctors asked her to alter Mrs. Kay's hospital admittance form. The doctor wanted to hide the fact that the hospital knew Mrs. Kay had recently eaten, creating a greater anesthesia risk. Obviously, the doctor is guilty of obstruction of justice for altering Mrs. Kay's hospital admission form. The doctor, and possibly his co-defendants, are also subject to court sanctions and "negative inferences" if found to have concealed evidence. *See Olszewski v. Spencer*, 466 F.3d 47, 52 n.4 (1st Cir. 2006) (holding that, if jurors believe a party has destroyed or concealed evidence, they may infer that the destroyed or concealed evidence contained something unfavorable to the party); *Zubulake v. UBS Warburg LLC,* 2004 WL 1620866 at *6, n.62 (S.D.N.Y. July 20, *2004*) (imposing sanctions and holding that an "adverse inference instruction may … be warranted, in some circumstances, for the untimely production [or non-production] of evidence.").

As to Attorney Concannon, he too obstructed justice and certainly violated ethical rules if he advised his clients to conceal or assisted them in concealing the witness, Nurse Costello, and the copy of the original admission form showing that Mrs. Kay had recently eaten. *See* Rule 3.4 (a) (Fairness to Opposing Party and Counsel) ("A lawyer shall not … unlawfully obstruct another party's access to evidence or unlawfully alter, destroy or conceal a document or other material having potentially evidentiary value.").

Was it improper for the judge to exclude Nurse Costello's copy of Mrs. Kay's "real" admission record? Should the judge have excluded the defense's altered copy? *See, e.g., Sacramona v. Bridgestone/Firestone, Inc.,* 106 F.3d 444 (1st Cir. 1997) (the court has inherent power to exclude evidence that has been improperly altered or damaged by a party where necessary to prevent the non-offending side from suffering unfair prejudice.).

Organization as Client

This movie highlights the conflicts of interest that can arise from an attorney's representation of organizations and the people who comprise them. In Scenes 17 and 25, Galvin arguably violates ABA Model Rule 4.2 (Communication with Persons Represented by Counsel) ("A lawyer shall not communicate about the subject of the representation with a person the lawyer knows to be represented by another lawyer in the matter, unless the lawyer has the consent of the other lawyer or is authorized to do so by law or a court order."). He approaches a hospital employee, Maureen Rooney, a nurse who was present while his client was a patient, and asks her questions about his client and the case. How would one determine whether or not the nurse, as an agent of the hospital, is a represented party for purposes of Rule 4.2? Comment 7 to Rule 4.2 provides that:

> [i]n the case of a represented organization, this Rule prohibits communications with a constituent of the organization who supervises, directs or regularly consults with the organization's lawyer concerning the matter or has authority to obligate the organization with respect to the matter or whose act or omission in connection with the matter may be imputed to the organization for purposes of civil or criminal liability.

In other words, the test is typically whether the employee exercises control or decision-making ability over the subject matter of the litigation. Here, the nurse decided to administer an anesthesia that turned out to be the wrong one – this is the very subject matter of the litigation. Her actions may be imputed to the hospital. Galvin walks a fine line even talking to this nurse, much less tricking her into providing material information about tracking down Kaitlin Costello, the admitting nurse on duty when Mrs. Kay went into the hospital. Does Galvin's contacting Ms. Costello also violate Rule 4.2? Does it make a difference that she was no longer a hospital employee? Does it matter that she was not in the operating room? What other factors might be considered in determining whether Galvin's actions violate Rule 4.2? *See Frank v. L.L. Bean Inc.,* 377 F.Supp.2d 233, 237 (D. Me. 2005) (holding that "former employees, as well as many current [non-decision-making] employees, are not within the scope of an attorney's representation of an employer" and may therefore be contacted by opposing counsel.).

Either way, his trickery violates other ethical rules. *See, e.g.,* ABA Model Rule 4.1(a) (Truthfulness in Statements to Others) ("In the course of representing a client a lawyer shall not knowingly ... make a false statement of material fact or law to a third person.").

LEGAL BRIEFS & MOVIE EXTRAS

*What legal interests do Galvin's clients, Mr. and Mrs. Doneghy, have in the lawsuit against the defendants? Mrs. Kay, after all, is still alive, as is her husband (though he has abandoned his wife). Are they simply next of kin, representing Mrs. Kay's interests? Or could a sister and brother-in-law stake a loss of consortium claim? What about wrongful death, as to Mrs. Kay's baby? Most states have statutes permitting a wrongful death lawsuit to be brought by the relatives of a person who died as a result of negligence. Additionally, many states have survivor statutes that allow the relatives to step into the shoes of the deceased person to bring claims belonging to the deceased. Wrongful death statutes and survivor statutes vary greatly from state to state. Some state survivor statutes exclude siblings, aunts, and uncles from their scope.

*Note the attorney/client communications about the anticipated outcome of the case. Galvin tells his clients they have a very good case and he doubts the case will ever go to trial. Worse, the defense assures the Archdiocese they will win. Clients should never be given false hope about uncertainties, and no guarantees should ever be made about the results of a jury trial.

*Is there anything interesting about the amount of the settlement offer, $210,000? Is it curious that this number is easily divisible by three? Did the defense extort the desperate Galvin's one-third contingent fee arrangement? Is this defense tactic ethical?

*Paul Newman passed away on September 26, 2008. In subsequent celebrations of his life and achievements, *The Verdict* was proclaimed as one of his top five performances, along with *Cool Hand Luke, Butch Cassidy And the Sundance Kid, Cat On A Hot Tin Roof,* and *Nobody's Fool.*

"There are two Newman's laws. The first one is: 'it is useless to put on your brakes when you're upside down.' The second is: 'just when things look darkest, they go black.'"

-Paul Newman

SILKWOOD
(Twentieth Century Fox 1983)

Starring: Meryl Streep; Kurt Russell; Cher

Lessons: Labor and Employment Laws

Plot: Karen Silkwood (Meryl Streep) is a working-class southerner, who, like many people living in her small Oklahoma town, depended upon the local nuclear power plant for her income. Silkwood suffers a workplace injury after being exposed to radiation at the plant. She conducts her own investigation of the accident, after discovering that somebody had tampered with the official investigation for cover-up purposes. Kurt Russell plays Drew, Silkwood's live-in boyfriend, also a plant employee. Cher won a well-deserved Best Supporting Actress Golden Globe for her role as Karen's co-worker and housemate "Dolly."

Labor conditions at an Oklahoma nuclear power plant in the 1980s were about as bad as it gets. At Silkwood's plant, many employees live with the fear of cancer. Whenever employees are accidentally exposed to radiation (i.e., "cooked"), they are subjected to a painful naked scrub down and heightened cancer scare. Silkwood is one of them. She becomes a voice of concern and a union activist. Some of her fellow employees, including her boyfriend, do not appreciate her efforts. Many fear losing their jobs if things like hazardous waste leaks and company cover-ups were revealed. There are federal and state statutes that aim to protect not only Silkwood's labor-related activities, but also employees who refuse to participate in or report illegality, including safety and health violations at the workplace.

State workers' compensation laws also provide remedies for injuries sustained on the job. These statutes contain anti-retaliation provisions that protect employees from facing adverse employment action for exercising their rights under these statutes or for testifying in enforcement proceedings.

EMPLOYMENT LAW
National Labor Relations Act of 1935

The employees at this power plant have a union. Union activities are protected under the National Labor Relations Act, 29 U.S.C. §§151-169, ("NLRA"), administered by the National Labor Relations Board ("NLRB"). The NLRA protects the rights of employees who wish to organize into labor unions for purposes of bargaining collectively with their employers through chosen representatives. Section 7 and Section 8 of the Act come into play most often. Section 7 of the Act outlines the rights of employees:

> Employees shall have the right to self-organization, to form, join, or assist labor organizations, to bargain collectively through representatives of their own choosing, and to engage in other concerted activities for the purpose of collective bargaining or other mutual aid or protection, and shall also have the right to refrain from any or all such activities except to the extent that such right may be affected by an agreement requiring membership in a labor organization as a condition of employment as authorized in section 8(a)(3) [section 158(a)(3) of this title].

29 U.S.C. §158. Section 8 of the Act defines and prohibits unfair labor practices, making it illegal for an employer "to interfere with, restrain, or coerce employees in the exercise of the rights guaranteed in section 7." 29 U.S.C. §158. One of the most important rights under the Act is the right for employees to engage in "concerted activity." Concerted activity is not expressly defined in the Act; one must look to relevant case law for a functional definition of the term. Discussing unionization,

striking, and picketing are some of the most obvious types of concerted activities. What concerted activities do plant employees engage in at the plant? *See, e.g., NLRB v. City Disposal Systems*, 465 U.S. 822, 828 (1984) (in which the Supreme Court held that when an employee complains about safety or job conditions "which are embodied in a contract, he is acting not only in his own interest, but is attempting to enforce such contract provisions in the interest of all the employees covered under that contract. Such activity we have found to be concerted, and protected under the Act."). Does the plant interfere with concerted activities or any other rights protected under the Act? Keep in mind that the NLRB also contains provisions to protect employers from business interference during strikes or other concerted activities. Further, employers are allowed to voice their opinions, but they must be very careful when doing so. An employer may express any views, arguments, or opinions about unionization, so long as the expressions do not contain threats of reprisal or promise of benefit for supporting or not supporting unionization. 29 U.S.C. §158.

In Scene 10, plant employees are told at a union meeting that there is a decertification election pending, in which the NLRB will hold an election so employees can vote on whether the union will remain at the plant. The union leader explains that decertification means "deep shit" for the plant employees. Lost faith among employees about union benefits threatens the union's very existence, which is exactly what the plant managers want. The leader tells the group that union activists need to act in concert to encourage union representation. The union needs to stand up to management and protect against unfair or harmful working conditions, among other things. Silkwood is immediately on board.

In Scene 11, she is on the telephone with a fellow union activist. She says: "management is putting up memos saying no union business on our breaks ... they just think they can get away with anything." Is prohibiting union business during employee breaks an employer interference with concerted activity? Are any other Section 7 rights violated in the plant's attempts to dissuade union activity?

The NLRA also contains an anti-discrimination provision, prohibiting an employer's "discrimination in regard to hire or tenure of employment or any term or condition of employment to encourage or discourage membership in any labor organization." 29 U.S.C. §158(3). At what point does §158(3) come into play in this movie? Shortly after vocalizing problems with radiation exposure and scrub downs, Silkwood gets transferred to a job she finds less favorable, in which she works with only one other employee. Was Silkwood's transfer an attempt by the employer to thwart organization efforts? How would you prove it?

Occupational Health and Safety Act of 1970

In Scene 9, Dolly and Karen are discussing "acceptable levels" of plutonium. The federal statute governing hazardous materials is the Occupational Safety and Health Act, administered by the Occupational Safety and Health Administration (the federal administrative agency known as "OSHA"). President Richard M. Nixon signed the Act (also known as OSHA) into law in 1970, but it underwent significant amendment in 1998. OSHA is codified at 29 U.S.C. §661 et seq. Generally, the Act requires that places of employment be free "from recognized hazards that are causing or are likely to cause death or serious physical harm to [the] employees." 29 U.S.C. §661(a). Like the National Labor Relations Act, OSHA contains anti-discrimination provisions. 29 U.S.C. §660(c)(1) (an employee may not be discharged or otherwise discriminated against because the employee "filed any complaint or instituted or caused to be instituted any proceeding under or related to this Act or has testified or is about to testify in any such proceeding or because of the exercise of any … right afforded by this Act."). To the extent Dolly and Karen reported OSHA violations, they would be protected from discrimination under modern laws.

Whistleblower Protection

The plant is a company that wants its secrets kept and does not like the sound of whistles. It is more worried about government contracts than employee health and welfare. From the corporate standpoint, whistleblowers are worse than union activists to the plant's bottom line. Today, whistleblowers are protected under state whistleblower laws and federal laws with provisions prohibiting employer retaliation for reporting violations of the laws, refusing to engage in any action made unlawful by the laws, or participating in proceedings under the laws. OSHA and the NLRA are two such federal laws that include protections against discrimination and retaliation. Other federal statutes with whistleblower protections include: the Americans with Disabilities Act (42 U.S.C. §12203), the Age Discrimination in Employment Act (29 U.S.C. §623), the Federal Coal Mine Safety and Health Act (30 U.S.C. §§801 et seq.), the Fair Labor Standards Act (29 U.S.C. §215(a)(3)), the Family Medical Leave Act (29 U.S.C. §2615), the Employee Retirement Income Security Act (29 U.S.C. §1140), the Sarbanes-Oakley Act (18 U.S.C. §1514A), Title VII (the 1964 Civil Rights Act) (42 U.S.C.A. §2000e-3), the False Claims Act (31 U.S.C. §3730), and the Labor Management Reporting and Disclosure Act (29 U.S.C. §401). As a practical matter, however, people need their jobs more than they need the task of proving a discrimination or retaliation lawsuit.

Watch for retaliation and implications of whistleblower protection laws at the plant. Consider, for example, Silkwood's transfer, immediately after voicing anger about the company's treatment of her co-worker, Thelma, after Thelma is "cooked" and "scrubbed." Is Silkwood's transfer connected to her voicing concerns about safety, or reporting health risks and illegalities? Is the transfer an "adverse employment action?" For a recent Supreme Court interpretation of what constitutes an adverse employment action, see *Burlington Northern v. White*, 548 U.S. 53 (2006). Regarding what constitutes protected activity, see *Crawford v. Metro. Gov't of Nashville*, 129 S.Ct. 846 (2009) (holding that an employee's answering questions during an employer's internal investigation about sexual harassment is protected against retaliation).

Workers' Compensation Laws

The injuries and illnesses that the nuclear power plant employees suffered are also compensable under state and federal workers' compensation laws. Most workers' compensation laws allow victims of work-related injuries to receive prompt, reasonable compensation for injury or illness sustained during the course of their employment. Such laws offer wage replacement for partially or wholly incapacitated workers, medical benefits, vocational assistance, and benefits for survivors of workers who suffer fatal injuries. In exchange for these no-fault medical and lost wage benefits under workers' compensation laws, however, employees and surviving heirs are barred from civil suits against the employers for injuries sustained at work, except in certain limited circumstances. State workers' compensation laws also provide remedies for discrimination against employees who report or assert claims of injury, including reinstatement with back pay when discrimination leads to termination of employment.

? Exam Tip

You may have heard that it is not necessary to memorize the names and details of all of the cases in most law classes, as long as you master their black letter law holdings. If you take a specialized course such as labor or employment law, however, your professor may expect you to be able to identify and explain certain important or landmark cases. Ask all of your professors where they stand on this issue and plan accordingly.

LEGAL BRIEFS & MOVIE EXTRAS

*Another "fact-based" movie about labor conditions and the labor movement is *Norma Rae* (Twentieth Century Fox 1979), starring Sally Field in an unforgettable performance as the title character. Norma Rae is a small-town southern mill worker, who organizes her fellow factory workers to fight for better working conditions and wages.

*For yet another great legal thriller starring Meryl Streep, also the star of *Kramer v. Kramer*, you may want to watch *Before And After* (Buena Vista Films 1996), co-starring Liam Neeson. Key scenes deal with forensic investigations, destruction of evidence, perjury, and other crimes and criminal law themes.

JAGGED EDGE
(Columbia/TriStar Pictures 1985)

Starring: Jeff Bridges; Glenn Close; Peter Coyote

Lessons: Ethics; Evidence

Plot: Glenn Close plays Teddy Barnes, a former prosecutor turned corporate lawyer. Peter Coyote plays District Attorney Tom Krasny, Teddy's former boss turned opposing counsel. Teddy quit the DA's office after helping power-hungry Krasny prosecute Henry Styles, an innocent man wrongly convicted of a "newsworthy" crime. Teddy was guilt-ridden after Styles hanged himself in prison. After the *Styles* case, Teddy renounced criminal law. But four years later, the partners in her large corporate law firm want her to defend Jack Forrester (Jeff Bridges), a wealthy publisher client accused of murdering his wife and her maid. Attorney Barnes gets a little too close to Jack. He temporarily convinces her he is innocent, and Teddy again realizes she is a poor judge of character. Both a legal thriller and a murder mystery, this movie turns quite scary, so grab some popcorn and a close friend.

ETHICS
Attorney Misconduct

The prosecutor, Thomas Krasny (Peter Coyote), is guilty of several ethical violations. Hungry for a career-boosting conviction in the Henry Styles case, Krasny withheld exonerating evidence. (Scene 25). In the Forrester case, Krasny again withheld evidence - a police report. (Scene 24). The report implicated a suspect other than Forrester, so the report was exculpatory evidence. Krasny therefore should have provided it to the defense. *Brady v. Maryland,* 373 U.S. 83, 87-88 (1963) (holding that a prosecutor's withholding exculpating evidence from the defense "does not comport with standards of justice.");

ABA Model Rule 3.8(d) (Special Responsibilities of a Prosecutor) (stating that "the prosecutor in a criminal case shall … make timely disclosure to the defense of all evidence or information known to the prosecutor that tends to negate the guilt of the accused or mitigates the offense.").

Teddy commits ethical violations as well. Most notably, Attorney Barnes has a sexual relationship with her client. ABA Model Rule 1.8(j) (regarding conflicts of interest) provides that a "lawyer shall not have sexual relations with a client unless a consensual sexual relationship existed between them when the client-lawyer relationship commenced." *See also* ABA Comm. on Ethics and Professional Responsibility, Formal Op. 92-364 (1992). Teddy commits another serious ethical violation in Scene 18. She visits the home of Judge Carrigan, the judge presiding of over Forrester's trial. She laments to the judge about her ethical dilemma, having realized her client may be a murderer. How many ethical rules does Teddy violate in this scene? First, this constitutes ex parte communications with the court. Second, she is alerting the presiding judge of the defendant's guilt! ABA Model Rule 3.5(a) (Impartiality and Decorum of the Tribunal) prohibits a lawyer from seeking "to influence a judge, juror, prospective juror or other official by means prohibited by law … [or] communicate ex parte with such a person during the proceeding unless authorized to do so by law or court order." *See also,* American Bar Association Model Code of Professional Responsibility 7-108(B) (1998).

Judicial Misconduct

The ABA Model Code of Judicial Conduct also contains a prohibition against ex parte communications with judges. *See* Rule 2.9(A) ("A judge shall not initiate, permit, or consider ex parte communications, or consider other communications made to the judge outside the presence of the parties or their lawyers, concerning a pending or impending matter."). What should

Judge Carrigan have told Teddy when she came to his house? What else should he have done in light of her inappropriate visit? Did the judge misbehave in any other ways? Was it proper for the judge to threaten the lawyers, stating: "I'll tell you now, I see this trial degenerating and I'll hit you like a freight train coming down the High Sierra!"

? Exam Tips

If an essay question presents facts about lawyers doing bad things, think not only ethical violations, think also malpractice torts and criminal violations. If an attorney's misconduct results in a criminal defendant's conviction, the Sixth Amendment's right to effective counsel is also invoked. In law school, your discussion of the legal implications of attorney misconduct fact patterns will of course depend upon what course you are taking and the specific issues discussed in class. For state bar exams, however, you should be able to spot all of the issues raised in a particular fact pattern.

EVIDENCE
Hearsay

Jagged Edge has plenty of witness examinations, so watch for hearsay (Scene 14-16; 19-23). In Scene 14, witness Virginia Howe testifies that the victim, the late Paige Forrester, had told her she would be dumping her husband, the defendant. Is this hearsay? It is an out of court statement, but is it being offered to prove the truth of what it asserts (that the defendant's wife had planned to divorce him)? If the victim's statement to Ms. Howe is hearsay, under what exception might the statement come into evidence? *See* FED. R. OF EVID. 803(3) (setting forth an exception to the hearsay exclusion with respect to a statement of the declarant's then existing state of mind, emotion, sensation, or physical condition). Rule 803(3) is generally known as the state of mind exception to the hearsay bar.

Evidence that divorce was on the horizon - and that Mrs. Forrester's money would be divorcing Jack as well - is relevant to show his motive. Whether true or not, the statement is evidence of what was going on in Jack Forrester's mind before his wife was killed.

If Ms. Howe's testimony about Paige Forrester's plans for divorce could be admitted under a hearsay exception, could you make any Rule 403 arguments to exclude the statement? If you were the judge, how would you rule on the issue? Is the statement highly probative of motive, or is it more prejudicial than anything else?

LEGAL BRIEFS & MOVIE EXTRAS

*What if Forrester had survived? Could he have been brought to justice? See the Fifth Amendment to the United States Constitution (the "Double Jeopardy" Clause). The Double Jeopardy Clause provides that no person shall, for the same offense, "be twice put in jeopardy of life or limb." Because Jack Forrester was already put in jeopardy for the offense of murdering his wife, the same state could not re-prosecute him for that same offense. Forrester might have been brought up on other charges had he survived, however, including, without limitation, aggravated assault/assault with intent to kill, obstruction of justice, etc.

*When it comes to the attorney/client relationship, how close is too close? Like *Guilty as Sin*, this movie presents another hard lesson about an attorney becoming blindsided by her relationship with her client - at the cost of her career, and even lives.

"How can you defend me if you think I'm guilty?"

-Jack Forrester to his attorney, Teddy Barnes

"It happens all the time; it's the way our legal system works."

-Teddy, in response

BABY BOOM
(United Artists 1987)

Starring: Diane Keaton; Sam Wanamaker

Lesson: Employment Law

Plot: Diane Keaton plays J. C. ("Tiger Lady") Wiatt, an unmarried, childless women ruled by her career as a high-powered executive at a Manhattan advertising agency, Sloane Curtis. That all changes when a long-lost cousin dies and J.C. is designated caregiver to the cousin's young baby, Elizabeth. After her conscience would not let her give Elizabeth up for adoption, she does what a typical 1980's career woman would do: takes it all on. She hires a nanny to watch Elizabeth while it is business as usual at her Manhattan high rise office. Her hopes of "having it all" are dashed when her job performance starts to falter. When her boss, Fritz Curtis, pulls her from an account that J.C. herself landed, he tells her she will handle low profile accounts from now on, as he feels they would be better suited for her now that she is raising a child. J.C. is not one to step down; so she quits her job and moves to the country. Fortunately, she starts a gourmet baby food business that "boomed" and she was all set. She even ditches her boring city boyfriend and finds love in the Vermont veterinarian who treated her for exhaustion.

Discrimination – particularly in the form of gender stereotyping – is rampant at Sloane Curtis. It plays out in a funny, witty way in the movie and the audience is left with a feel-good ending.

Gender Discrimination – Domestic Responsibilities

An up-and-coming area of discrimination, often couched in terms of gender discrimination, relates to bias against domestic responsibilities. As the Supreme Court has recognized, gender-based stereotypes about traditional family values and female domestic responsibilities tend to "create a self-fulfilling cycle of discrimination." *Nevada Dept. of Human Resources v. Hibbs*, 538 U.S., 721, 736 (2003). *See also, Phillips v. Martin Marietta Corp.,* 400 U.S. 542, 544 (1971) (finding evidence showing that the employer defendant had a policy of not hiring women with young children, but had no such policy with respect to men with young children). There may also be state law protections more specific to familial responsibilities.

In other words, new moms might claim they are treated differently from new dads in terms of conditions and privileges of employment. For these women, a discrimination case could fall within the purview of Title VII or similar state laws protecting against gender discrimination in all of its forms. Consider J.C.'s boss early in the movie, before Elizabeth, when he tells her she is being considered for partnership. Even though he never "thinks of J.C. as a women," Fritze warns her of the sacrifices she will have to make as a partner at Sloane Curtis. Of course he does not come right out and tell her she will not be allowed a family. But he does state that he is lucky because, as a man he has not had to make those sacrifices; as a man, he can "have it all" (to which J.C. responds, "I don't want it all"). Clearly, such comments can be construed as gender bias, which can lead to risks of discrimination claims. But, that was the 1980's. Most management professionals, even if they still hold these archaic believes, do not vocalize them to their subordinates. That being said, keep in mind most plaintiff's lawyers typically issue "litigation hold" letters to ensure electronic communications are preserved for discovery and trial. This could include texts and social media communications among management members, even outside of the workplace, and even when people think they are "off the record."

In short, the law is addressing some of the more subtle types of discrimination and stereotyping in the workplace, and employers should be mindful of these trends as they conduct interviews and make employment decisions. The bottom line is that employers are best advised to treat all employees the same, to enforce all company policies evenly, and not to allow stereotypes to affect employment decisions.

Family Medical Leave Act

The Family Medical Leave Act would also protect J.C. in this situation – but not if she were to have become a partner. The FMLA only protects employees. See 29 U.S.C. §2611. As an eligible employee, J.C. would be entitled to up to a total of 12 workweeks of unpaid, job-protected leave in any 12-month period for … the placement with the employee of a child for adoption or foster care, and to bond with that child. 29 U.S.C. § 2612(a)(1)(B). Of course, her boss probably would have retaliated against her by assigning all the good clients to the men. That too would be illegal. It is unlawful under the FMLA to "interfere" with, "restrain" or "deny" "the exercise of or attempt to exercise, rights provided" by the Act, or to discriminate against employees for exercising rights under the Act. *See* 29 U.S.C. § 2615(a); 29 C.F.R. §825.220(c).

LEGAL BRIEFS & MOVIE EXTRAS

*What if an employer seems to value the flexibility of non-parents, and treats all parents, regardless of gender, as though they are not 100% committed to the job due to family responsibilities? Would this type of discrimination be actionable? Changing times may broaden the scope of court treatment of gender-stereotyping about raising children.

*For a funny movie about gender discrimination in the workplace, try the classic *Nine to Five* (Dolly Parton; Lily Tomlin; Jane Fonda). There, three women, after a series of follies surrounding their boss, take matters into their own hands in trying to create equality in the office.

*The fictitious advertising agency in *Baby Boom*, Sloan Curtis, is also the advertising agency where Mel Gibson and Helen Hunt's characters worked in the movie *What Women Want*, although they worked in the fictitious Chicago office as opposed to the fictitious Manhattan office. Coincidence? The writer of *Baby Boom*, Nancy Meyers, directed *What Women Want*.

SUSPECT
(Columbia/TriStar Pictures 1987)

Starring: Cher; Liam Neeson; Dennis Quaid

Lessons: Ethics; Criminal Law; Evidence

Plot: Cher stars as Washington, D.C., public defender, Kathleen Riley. Riley is assigned to represent Carl Wayne Anderson (Liam Neeson) – a deaf-mute Vietnam War veteran who is wrongfully charged with murder. Carl was in the vicinity where a young Supreme Court secretary was found murdered. Unfortunately, he had been trying to break into cars at the time and looked quite guilty. Attorney Riley, however, becomes determined to prove his innocence. Crossing legal and ethical lines in her quest, she accepts the help of one of the jurors in Anderson's case, Eddie Sanger (Dennis Quaid). Sanger is a Washington lobbyist, versed in forensic evidence and legal research, and something of a busybody. He and Riley embark on their own private investigation, breaking laws and risking lives in the process. The movie keeps you on the edge of your seat as Riley and Sanger uncover scandal and corruption in trying to find the secretary's real killer. *Suspect* also provides substantive courtroom scenes and insight into the criminal process. The witness examinations, however, are unrealistic, in terms of what a court would allow. Can you spot the problems?

ETHICS

Obviously, Riley and Sanger's joint endeavor violates ABA Model Rule 3.5 (Impartiality and Decorum of the Tribunal) (prohibiting a lawyer from seeking "to influence a judge, juror, prospective juror or other official by means prohibited by law ... [or] communicate ex parte with such a person during the proceeding unless authorized to do so by law or court order."). In Scene 13, Eddie gives Riley an anonymous telephone call, alerting her to the fact that her client is left-handed. Riley is then able to show the jury that the forensic evidence revealed that the deadly knife wound was most likely inflicted by a right-handed person.

In Scene 14, Eddie approaches Riley and tells her she should thank him for his tip. Riley is angry. She tells him she cannot speak to him and that what she should do is go to the judge and have Eddie thrown off of the jury. That is exactly what she should have done, under ABA Model Rule 3.3(b) (Candor to the Tribunal) ("A lawyer who represents a client in an adjudicative proceeding and who knows that a person intends to engage, is engaging or has engaged in criminal or fraudulent conduct related to the proceeding shall take reasonable remedial measures, including, if necessary, disclosure to the tribunal."). In violation of Rule 3.3(b), Riley takes no remedial measures. Riley can be sanctioned – even disbarred – for her behavior; her relationship with Eddie Sanger has even greater implications, however.

Another ethical violation occurs in Scene 11. Riley appears in the judge's chambers. Riley's opponent, the prosecutor, is not present. Granted, Hollywood probably wanted Cher to own the scene, but Riley and the judge are engaging in ex parte communications concerning an important issue in the case: whether or not Riley may be granted a continuance in order to locate a witness for the defense. Such ex parte communications are prohibited under rules governing the conduct of and communications between lawyers and judges. Specifically, ABA Model Rule 3.5(a) (Impartiality and Decorum of the Tribunal) prohibits a lawyer from seeking "to influence a judge, juror, prospective juror or other official by means prohibited by law … [or] communicate ex parte with such a person during the proceeding unless authorized to do so by law or court order." *See also,* American Bar Association Model Code of Professional Responsibility 7-108(B) (1998). Additionally, the ABA Model

Code of Judicial Conduct contains a prohibition against ex parte communications with judges, at Rule 2.9(A) ("A judge shall not initiate, permit, or consider ex parte communications, or consider other communications made to the judge outside the presence of the parties or their lawyers, concerning a pending or impending matter."). Of course, the prosecutor would likely not complain about the judge's in-chambers ex parte discussion with Riley, given that the judge's decision is a striking blow to the defense.

CRIMINAL LAW
Motions to Continue

Riley's basis for her motion for a continuance in Scene 11 was her stated need to locate a key witness, a man named Michael, who might have been able to offer exculpating information. The judge denied the request, stating that, if we had to wait for every supposed witness, the justice system would "grind to a halt." Not only does the judge deny continuance, he also admonishes Riley about not mentioning Michael in open court. Could such a ruling be a "reversible error," grounds for an appeal of a guilty verdict? *See State v. Hill,* 449 S.E.2d 573, 576 (N.C.1994) ("When a motion for a continuance raises a constitutional issue and is denied, the denial is grounds for a new trial only when a defendant shows that the denial was erroneous and also that his case was prejudiced as a result of the error."); *Hughey v. State,* 512 So.2d 4, 11 (Miss.1987) ("Generally, this Court has found prejudice when there was a loss of evidence, the death of a witness, or the investigation became stale.").

Does the absence of a witness who may have exculpatory information raise a constitutional issue? Could Michael's absence prejudice the case? If so, how could such prejudice be proven, after-the-fact, through an appeal of a guilty verdict? What, if anything, has your state's highest court said about these issues?

Jury Tampering/Juror Misconduct

Jury tampering is a federal crime for which both Sanger and Riley are guilty due to their improper influence on the other jurors. Title 18 of the United States Code prohibits and heavily punishes this type of jury tampering. Title 18 U.S.C. §1503 provides that "[w]hoever corruptly, or by threats or force, or by any threatening letter or communication endeavors to influence, intimidate, or impede any grand or petit juror" in certain felonies, including murder, is subject to punishment "of imprisonment for not more than 20 years, a fine under this title, or both," 18 U.S.C. §1503(a)-(b). Additionally, 18 U.S.C. §201 prohibits juror bribery and subjects violators to up to 15 years in prison and heavy fines.

Juror misconduct is also grounds for a mistrial under certain circumstances. *See Turner v. Louisiana*, 379 U.S. 466 (1965); *Marino v. Vasquez*, 812 F.2d 499 (9th Cir. 1987); *United States v. Navarro-Garcia*, 926 F.2d 818, 821 (9th Cir. 1991); *State v. Hartley*, 656 A.2d 954 (R.I. 1995) and the discussion of these cases in *12 Angry Men*.

EVIDENCE
Opening Statements/Closing Arguments

In Scene 12, the prosecutor, Charlie Stella (Joe Mantegna) provides impermissible commentary in his opening statement. He brags to the jury about having prosecuted over forty murder cases, and tells them: "this is the most horrible one." Here, Stella was out of line. A prosecutor is prohibited from injecting personal opinions into opening statements and closing arguments. *U.S. v. Young*, 470 U.S. 1, 8-9 (1985). *See also, Arrieta-Agressot v. United States,* 3 F.3d 525, 527 (1st Cir. 1993). As a general rule, it is improper for attorneys to talk about themselves and their own personal experiences during presentations to juries.

Was there anything else about Stella's or Riley's opening presentations or closing arguments that was improper or highly prejudicial?

LEGAL BRIEFS & MOVIE EXTRAS

*In this movie, it seems every attorney breaks rules: Riley, the prosecutor, even the judge. Quite interesting is Scene 26, during which Riley listens to the judge's confession concerning *United States v. Cook*. There, the judge conspired to "fix the case." He accepted a bribe: in exchange for appointment of a federal court seat, he dismissed the charges of a rich and influential defendant. The atmosphere of corruption in this scene is sinister.

*For another interesting story about some serious jury tampering, see the film *The Juror* (Columbia Pictures 1996), and/or read John Grisham's novel *The Juror*.

"Your cross has been weak and your behavior in this courtroom has been unprofessional."

"I desperately need a continuance!"

"It would be imprudent of me to grant you a continuance because your case is weak."

-Exchange between Kathleen Riley and the Judge

WALL STREET
(Twentieth Century Fox 1987)

Starring: Michael Douglas; Charlie Sheen; Martin Sheen

Lessons: Business Law; Criminal Law

Plot: An eager and greedy new day trader, Bud Fox (Charlie Sheen), gets ahead in the Wall Street game by taking extraordinary measures to obtain insider information about publicly traded companies, and then making and sharing investment decisions based on the confidential information. As Martha Stewart and others can attest, such conduct is illegal. Nevertheless, Bud obtains insider information from his father, Carl Fox (Charlie Sheen's real-life father, Martin Sheen). Carl Fox is an airline mechanic for corporate giant Bluestar Airline. In talking to his father, Bud learns of a Federal Aviation Administration ruling clearing Bluestar of an alleged safety violation after a crash. The FAA's ruling had not yet been publicly disclosed – not even to the victims of the crash. Bud shares this insider information with an even greedier, seasoned, wealthy investor, Gordon Gekko (Michael Douglas). Influenced by Gekko, Bud sparks an insider-trading scheme that makes him rich but ultimately gets him into a world of trouble.

BUSINESS LAW/CRIMINAL LAW
Insider Trading

Insider trading is taking action within the market based on material, non-public knowledge. Such activity disrupts the natural course and integrity of the marketplace and normal market forces. Insider trading is unlawful under Rule 10b-5 of the Securities and Exchange Commission's regulations, although the Rule does not use the term insider trading. *See* 17 C.F.R. §240.10b-5. The Rule prohibits the "Employment of Manipulative and Deceptive Practices," stating that:

It shall be unlawful for any person, directly or indirectly, by the use of any means or instrumentality of interstate commerce, or of the mails or of any facility of any national securities exchange:

(a) To employ any device, scheme, or artifice to defraud,

(b) To make any untrue statement of a material fact or to omit to state a material fact necessary in order to make the statements made, in the light of the circumstances under which they were made, not misleading, or

(c) To engage in any act, practice, or course of business which operates or would operate as a fraud or deceit upon any person, in connection with the purchase or sale of any security.

Taken together, the restrictive language of the above three paragraphs, regarding dishonesty with respect to material facts, effectively prohibit insider trading. The question often becomes: What is a material fact, for purposes of Rule 10b-5? The answers are in case law. The Supreme Court defines a material fact as one in which there is "a substantial likelihood that a reasonable shareholder would consider it important in deciding how to vote." *TSC Industries, Inc. v. Northway, Inc.*, 426 U.S. 438, 449 (1976).

Consider, for example, the Securities and Exchange Commission's 1968 case against Texas Gulf and Sulphur. The case created some bright line rules and therefore appears in most business law textbooks. In *SEC v. Texas Gulf and Sulphur*, the SEC sued individuals and the corporation itself for Rule 10b-5 violations based on insider trading. 401 F.2d 833, 839 (1968). Texas Gulf and Sulphur made a significant discovery of valuable mineral deposits and sought to quickly and quietly acquire the surrounding land. *Id.* Certain corporate employees concealed the information, pending the company's land purchase. *Id.* at 848. Meanwhile, they purchased large amounts of their company stock. *Id.* at 853. Some had never before purchased any shares. *Id.* Further, a misleading press release was issued to suppress the effect of rumors regarding the company's precious find. *Id.*

The Second Circuit held that, where corporate employees come into possession of material information affecting their corporation's securities, they may have no duty to disclose the information, if there is a valid business reason for nondisclosure. *Id.* They may not, however, benefit from transactions made based on the non-disclosed information. *Id.* The defendants "should have kept out of the market until disclosure was accomplished." *Id.* at 848. In other words, the employees cannot try to "beat the press."

As to Texas Gulf and Sulphur itself, the court ruled that a corporation that issues public statements relating to material information concerning a matter which could affect the company's securities in the marketplace must fully and fairly state the facts upon which investors could reasonably rely. *Id.* at 860. The corporation departed from that standard, and was therefore subject to liability under Rule 10b-5. *Id.*

The *Texas Gulf and Sulphur* Court provided guidance for determining if a certain piece of information is material. The Court looked at what the insiders actually did, and when. They all inexplicably bought significant shares of stock in a short time period, while sitting on material information. Obviously, the insiders knew something, kept the information out of the marketplace, yet traded on the information. If the insiders considered the information important for their own trading purposes, a reasonable shareholder would as well; the information must therefore be material.

? Exam Tips

In a business law course, be able to recognize the "insider trading" fact pattern. If anything resembling a rumor or a secret appears on your exam, think insider trading. Ask yourself whether the information is material and non-public and discuss Rule 10b-5 and the cases you learned in class. You may be called upon to raise defenses to such a charge. You should be alerted to that calling when a fact pattern presents a valid business reason that could require information to be kept confidential. If so, query whether a straight-faced argument can be made that no action was taken based on the confidential information for the benefit of insiders, aside from actions taken in the ordinary course of business (which ... coincidentally ... resulted in large profits to executives).

LEGAL BRIEFS & MOVIE EXTRAS

*One could hardly forget domestic goddess Martha Stewart's missteps into the realm of insider trading. Martha was not an insider, but she had access to inside information, and she used that information to make lucrative trade decisions. Bud Fox was an insider who accessed and utilized inside information for his benefit. Both are violations of Rule 10b-5.

*Michael Douglas won several awards for his depiction of Gordon Gekko. This was one of his many very fitting roles.

"Greed, for lack of a better word, is a good thing."

-Gordon Gekko

THE ACCUSED
(Paramount Pictures 1988)

Starring: Jodi Foster; Kelly McGillis

Lessons: Criminal Law; Evidence

Plot: Three men gang rape Sarah Tobias (Jodie Foster) at a bar. Because the defense attorneys' strategy was to paint Sarah, the victim, as a woman of "questionable character," all three defendants were given fairly easy deals under a plea bargain. Enraged at the light sentences her attackers received under the plea bargain, Sarah's second chance at justice rested entirely with Assistant District Attorney, Kathryn Murphy (Kelly McGillis). The prosecution faced bad facts for a rape trial: the victim had taken drugs and was acting provocatively in a bar just prior to the incident. The victim also had something of a reputation for promiscuity. So instead of bringing the three men to trial on rape charges, Murphy allows them to plead guilty to a misdemeanor reckless endangerment charge. Sarah Tobias criticizes Murphy for allowing the rapists to receive less than a year in jail. Sarah Tobias demanded justice and Murphy went on a crusade to get it for her. Creatively, however impractically, she decides to charge the onlookers who watched and encouraged the rapists with the crime of solicitation, even after her boss threatens to fire her for wasting time and resources on such a cause. There are some disturbing scenes in this movie.

CRIMINAL LAW

In perfect Hollywood heroine style, Murphy winds up getting the onlookers a harsher jail sentence than the actual rapists. Why? In perfect Hollywood convenience, the prosecutorial problems that arose because of Tobias's history and actions at the bar suddenly disappear when it is time for the movie to give way to a suitable ending. Murphy charged the onlookers with solicitation. Was solicitation her best bet for convictions as against the onlookers? What, if any, other charges might have been considered?

In order for the crime of solicitation to have occurred, there must be more than an agreement or an intention to commit the crime. Although the crime need not be completed, there must at least be an overt act toward the crime, such as inducement, enticement, urging, commanding, or requesting. *Allen v. State*, 605 A.2d 960, 976 (1992). An overt act can be any sort of inducement or enticement, or other invitation or request of another to commit a crime. *See id*; *see also*, 21 AM. JUR. 2D *Criminal Law* §181 (2005) ("the gist of the offense [of solicitation] is incitement; the policy behind the prohibition of solicitation is to protect people from exposure to inducements to commit or join in the commission of a crime."). A key element to a solicitation crime, however, is that the underlying requested act actually be a crime. If Tobias consented to the sexual activity, there was no crime to encourage or solicit. So why didn't the defense again use Tobias's promiscuity to show that there was no rape, given the consent, and therefore no solicitation of any crime? Hollywood.

Would Murphy have been wise to bring conspiracy charges as well? Had Murphy brought conspiracy charges, like solicitation, she would not have needed to prove that the underlying rape was completed to convict the onlookers. *Garrett v. United States*, 471 U.S. 773, 778 (1985) (holding that conspiracy is a "distinct offense from the completed object of the conspiracy.").

Would she have also been relieved of proving that the defendants committed an overt act toward rape? What else would Murphy have had to prove under a conspiracy theory? What do your state's statutes and cases say about the distinctions between solicitation and conspiracy crimes? Assuming Murphy could prove the underlying rape, what other charges might she have brought against the onlookers?

EVIDENCE
Rape Shield Laws

During her preliminary investigation, Murphy asked Sarah Tobias, the rape victim, several questions about her own criminal conduct and character, including her sexual propensity. Murphy explains to Sarah that she will be a witness, and that the defense will be allowed to ask certain questions about her character in order to impeach her. But are Murphy's questions about Sarah's sexual past relevant to the issue of rape?

The defense suggests that Sarah "put on a show" and "consented enthusiastically," such that there was no rape. Would questions about the victim's sexual history be permissible to support these allegations to show consent? Under your state's current law, would any of the evidence of Tobias's sexual history be excluded from trial? In the late 1970s/early 1980s, almost all jurisdictions across the country began to pass "rape shield" laws, which prevent the defense from admitting the sexual history of the alleged victim into evidence, except under limited circumstances. Federal Rule of Evidence 412(a) declares inadmissible: (1) evidence offered to prove that any alleged victim engaged in other sexual behavior; and (2) evidence offered to prove any alleged victim's sexual predisposition.

Rule 412(b), however, carves out exceptions to the rape shield rule. A victim's sexual history may come into evidence when: (1) it is offered to "prove that a person other than the accused was the source of the semen, injury, or other physical evidence;" (2) it is offered to prove consent by "specific instances of sexual behavior by the alleged victim with respect to the person accused;" and (3) exclusion "would violate the constitutional rights of the defendant." For a great article on the history of rape shield laws, and an argument that the exceptions swallow the rape shield rule, see "Understanding Rape Shield Laws," by Michelle J. Anderson (available at:

https://vawnet.org/material/understanding-rape-shield-laws)
(last visited November 2, 2020). Research the rape shield laws in your state. Does it need an update?

Exculpatory Evidence

With such bad facts against her client, Murphy already had a tough prosecution in Tobias's case. To make matters worse, Tobias had been fighting with her boyfriend before she headed to the bar. She was overheard saying that she might take one of the accused rapists home and have sex with him in front of her boyfriend, to get even with him and make him jealous. Already an underdog, why did Murphy admit such a damaging fact to the defense? Was that just bad lawyering? Or did Murphy have a choice?

Sarah Tobias's statement could be considered exculpatory evidence. Consent is always a defense to rape, and Tobias's apparent willingness to sleep with the guy could be considered evidence of consent. *See* Rule 412(b)(2), above. When a prosecutor has exculpatory evidence, he is to produce that evidence to the defense. *Brady v. Maryland,* 373 U.S. 83, 87-88 (1963). So, Murphy, unlike some of the other prosecutors that appear in this book, did the right thing.

? Exam Tip

The various rape shield laws and their rich history is an interesting issue that varies among the states. Many state bar examiners enjoy testing distinct features of their states' rules of evidence. If your state has a unique rape shield law or other evidentiary rule, it may very well be the subject of an essay question.

LEGAL BRIEFS & MOVIE EXTRAS

The Accused was based on an actual crime that occurred at a bar in New Bedford, Massachusetts. For information about the New Bedford Gang Rape, see

http://law.jrank.org/pages/3382/New-Bedford-Rape-Trial-1984.html (last visited October 28, 2020).

*Jodie Foster won the 1988 Best Actress Oscar for her outstanding performance as Sarah Tobias.

PRESUMED INNOCENT
(Warner Brothers 1990)

Starring: Harrison Ford; Brian Dennehy; Raul Julia

Lessons: Criminal Procedure/Constitutional Law; Evidence

Plot: Rusty Sabich (Harrison Ford) is a prosecutor who himself becomes a criminal defendant accused of killing a colleague with whom he was having an extramarital affair. The movie focuses around the arrest and trial of Sabich, giving us flashback glimpses into the events leading up to the murder, Sabich's prosecution, the trial, and the aftermath. Based on a Scott Turow novel, this movie is both a suspenseful murder mystery and a thrilling legal drama. It is packed with excellent courtroom scenes (Scenes 21 – 30).

CRIMINAL LAW/PROCEDURE
(CONSTITUTIONAL LAW)

Through Rusty's attorney, Sandy Stern, played by Raul Julia (who is an attorney in real life), the movie realistically highlights some of the difficult choices defense counsel and their clients must make. One of the most important decisions that must be made in a criminal trial is whether the defendant will take the stand, or whether he will exercise his Fifth Amendment right not to "be a witness against himself." U.S. Const. amend. V. Evaluating whether or not a client will make a good a witness for himself is a legal, tactical decision. The lawyer needs to analyze and explain to her client the pros and cons of taking the stand. The ultimate decision, however, belongs to the client. *See* ABA Model Rule 1.2(a) (Scope of Representation and Allocation of Authority between Client and Lawyer) ("In a criminal case, the lawyer shall abide by a client's decision, after consultation with the lawyer, as to a plea to be entered, whether to waive jury trial and whether the client will testify."). Rusty takes his attorney's advice and reluctantly, and awkwardly, exercises his Fifth Amendment right.

EVIDENCE
Hearsay Rules

Would you have put Rusty on the stand? In deciding whether or not Rusty should take the stand, Rusty's attorney, Sandy Stern, states, "clearly we will not allow you to testify." The two lawyers argue briefly over the decision, with Sandy warning: "you don't want to [give the prosecutor] pretrial statements, do you"? (Scene 19). Are Rusty's pretrial statements hearsay, inadmissible under Federal Rule of Evidence 802? How does whether or not Rusty takes the stand affect this hearsay question?

If the prosecution introduced Rusty's prior out of court statements to try to prove that what he said was true, the defense could argue that it is inadmissible hearsay (i.e., that the statement falls within the definition of hearsay and that none of the exceptions to hearsay apply). If Rusty testifies, however, the prosecution could use the statements during cross-examination. Under Federal Rule of Evidence 613(a), Prior Statements by Witnesses, any witness that testifies in a trial can be impeached by his prior statements, including a criminal defendant. This means a jury can hear about pretrial statements that might otherwise be inadmissible hearsay.

One pretrial statement Rusty makes is when he first learns that he is a suspect, in Scene 16. In response to prosecuting attorney Nico Della Guardia's stating, "you killed her; you're the guy," Rusty states "yeah, you're right. You're always right." In Scene 21, we learn that the prosecution's plan was to admit the statement in its case-in-chief – through Attorney Della Guardia himself! ABA Model Rule 3.7(a) (Lawyer as Witness) provides that "a lawyer shall not act as advocate at a trial in which the lawyer is likely to be a necessary witness." The only reason Attorney Della Guardia needed to be a witness was to introduce Rusty's response to his accusation of murder. After opining that Rusty was being facetious, the judge gives Della Guardia a choice: if he insisted on testifying about Rusty's statement, he would be removed as prosecutor. Based on the judge's input, the prosecution decides not to call Attorney Della Guardia as a witness to Rusty's statement and he remains the prosecuting attorney.

Go through the analysis of how the statement could come in during the prosecution's case-in-chief. To do that, first determine if the statement is hearsay. The prosecution would be offering Rusty's out of court statement for the truth of what it asserts: that Rusty admitted Della Guardia was right in accusing him of murder. This appears to be textbook hearsay on its face. However, Rule 801(d)(2), dealing with admissions by party opponents, provides that a statement is not hearsay if the "statement is offered against that party ... and is the party's own statement." In other words, an admission by a party opponent is excepted from the definition of hearsay. So, if Rusty's affirmation of the prosecutor's accusation can be construed as an admission, it is excluded from the hearsay definition. As the judge humorously points out, however, the prosecution would have been hard pressed to make a straight-faced argument that Rusty's statement was anything more than "polite" anger and sarcasm.

From the defense's standpoint, how would you establish the foundation at trial to show that Rusty's statement was merely angry sarcasm and therefore inadmissible hearsay? Even if the statement were not barred by hearsay rules, what, if any, other grounds for exclusion are available? Could you make any constitutional arguments for exclusion?

Note other pretrial statements Rusty makes throughout the movie. Are any of Rusty's pretrial statements admissible because they are excluded from the definition of hearsay by Federal Rule of Evidence 801(d) or because one of the Rule 803 or 804 hearsay exceptions applies? Does Rule of Evidence 403 come into play with respect to any of these pretrial statements? Does the Constitution?

? Exam Tips

Note that the above example does not even explore the many exceptions to the hearsay exclusion, set forth in Federal Rules of Evidence 803 and 804. The issue of hearsay and its exceptions is a complex area and one heavily tested on bar exams and other legal tests. When analyzing hearsay problems, do not jump into the exceptions before going through a definitional analysis and explaining why the statement is or is not hearsay. In doing so, do not overlook Rule 801(d)(1) and 801(d)(2) exceptions to the definition.

Also, be able to distinguish between the 803 exceptions, under which it makes no difference whether or not the declarant of the hearsay is available for trial, and 804 exceptions, which are five limited exceptions that apply only when it can be shown that the declarant of the statement is not available to testify. The five hearsay exceptions that exist when the witness is unavailable are:

1. former inconsistent testimony;

2. a belief of impending death;

3. statements against the interest of the declarant;

4. statements of personal or family history; and

5. forfeiture by wrongdoing (which creates a hearsay exception permitting the introduction of "a statement offered against a party that has engaged or acquiesced in wrongdoing" that caused the declarant of the statement to become unavailable).

There is also a "residual" hearsay exception under Federal Rule of Evidence 807, which is not available in many states. Federal Rule 807 provides a hearsay exception for "a statement not specifically covered by Rule 803 or 804 but having equivalent circumstantial guarantees of trustworthiness." The residual rule also requires that the evidence be relevant (of course), and have more probative valuable than any other evidence the party "can procure through reasonable efforts." In order to utilize Rule 807, an attorney must be able to lay some preliminary foundation at trial. In other words, before attempting to have the witness testify about the hearsay statement, the trial attorney needs to introduce evidence to show the context of the hearsay, its "circumstantial guarantees of trustworthiness," and the lack of any better evidence. Also, before attempting to admit hearsay evidence under Rule 807, an attorney must give advance notice to her opponent. Know whether a residual exception to the hearsay bar exists in your state because state bar examiners love to test distinctions between their state's rules and the federal rules.

Marital Privileges

In a trial against Mrs. Sabich, would Mr. Sabich be *required* to testify against her? Could he be *prevented* from testifying against her? Note that Rule 501 of the Federal Rules of Evidence provides simply that privileges "shall be determined in accordance with State law." Most state rules of evidence provide for two types of privileges that may apply to married couples: the marital communications privilege and the spousal privilege. The marital communications privilege protects confidential communications made during marriage in both civil and criminal cases. Both spouses are entitled to assert the marital communications privilege; therefore, each spouse may prevent the other from disclosing certain confidential marital communications, but this privilege does not prevent the spouses from testifying altogether. On the other hand, the spousal privilege can prevent one spouse from having to testify against the other spouse in a criminal case. The spousal privilege protects all communications between spouses, regardless of confidentiality, and regardless of whether the communications were made prior to or during the marriage. Upon divorce, the whole privilege is lost. At common law and in a minority of states, the holder of the spousal privilege is the defendant in the criminal case, so a criminal defendant could prevent his spouse from ever taking the stand at his trial. Now, however, in the majority of jurisdictions, the witness spouse is the holder, and can decide whether or not to take the stand at the spouse's criminal trial. Once on the stand, however, the marital communications privilege may prevent disclosure of confidential communications made during the marriage.

Under this majority rule, Mr. Sabich can elect not to take the stand in his wife's criminal trial. He cannot be required to take the stand. Mrs. Sabich, however, could not prevent him from doing so; the witness - not the defendant - holds the spousal privilege. Certain of his testimony may nevertheless be objectionable because both spouses are still entitled to a marital communications privilege. In sum, in most states, he could not testify as to her confession but he could take the stand if he wanted to.

? Exam Tip

In distinguishing the marital communication privilege from the spousal privilege, it is helpful to recall that the marital communications privilege is broader in that it applies in both civil and criminal cases, but narrower in that it only protects confidential communications and does not prevent a spouse from taking the stand altogether.

LEGAL BRIEFS & MOVIE EXTRAS

*Now that we know who the real killer is, assume Mrs. Sabich retains you to defend her. What possible defenses could be raised under your state's laws? Are there any defenses based on Mrs. Sabich's state of mind when she killed her husband's mistress? For discussions about diminished mental capacity defenses, see the chapters regarding *Adam's Rib, Anatomy of a Murder*, and *A Time to Kill.*

*Note in Scene 30 that, when the prosecution rests, the defense motions for dismissal on the grounds that the prosecution did not have enough evidence to convict Rusty. A motion for a decision in the defense's favor at this stage of the trial is actually called a motion for direct verdict or a motion for a judgment of acquittal. In Rusty's case, his attorney's motion was a good decision. Criminal defense attorneys quite often move for a directed verdict before putting on their client's case. Not only is there a chance of victory on the spot, as in this case, but a motion for judgment in your client's favor at every window of opportunity is often necessary to preserve certain issues for appeal.

*In Scott Turow's novel *Presumed Innocent*, upon which the movie was based, the prologue presents some of a prosecutorial opening statement, which Rusty says he "always starts with." It is a good sample of a generic prosecutorial opening from which you may get some helpful ideas for your trial practice course.

*Rusty Sabich appears as a character in Scott Turow's later novel, *Limitations* (2006). Like *Presumed Innocent, Limitations* is set in the fictional Kindle County, Illinois.

REVERSAL OF FORTUNE
(Warner Brothers 1990)

Starring: Jeremy Irons; Glenn Close; Ron Silver

Lessons: Criminal Law; Civil Procedure

Plot: This movie is based on one of several actual cases in which Claus von Bülow (Jeremy Irons) was a named party. The case at hand involves a successful criminal appeal. Attorney Alan M. Dershowitz (Ron Silver) manages to reverse von Bülow's conviction of two counts of attempted murder. Claus von Bülow's wife "Sunny" (Glenn Close) slipped into a permanent coma, apparently due to an extremely high blood insulin level. Claus von Bülow was accused of injecting his wife with insulin in an attempt to kill her for her millions. Claus, who had a million-dollar net worth himself, says he does not know what happened to Sunny. But he is able to offer many alternative theories that would explain the coma and exonerate him.

Sunny's two children, from her first marriage, hired their own personal private investigator to help the Rhode Island prosecutors prove their case. With the evidence stacked up against him, von Bülow was convicted by a Rhode Island jury and was sentenced to 30 years in prison. He hired Alan Dershowitz to file an appeal. All the while, Claus remained out of prison on his $1,000,000 bail. *Reversal of Fortune* tells of von Bülow's successful appeal from the perspective of his attorney, Alan Dershowitz (also a Harvard Law Professor). Glenn Close beautifully narrates small portions of the movie, telling the story from Sunny's comatose point of view.

In addition to its interesting story, fantastic cinematography, and fine acting, this movie has much to offer law students. This is one of the many legal films that motivated and inspired me as a law student. Several scenes show Professor Dershowitz working with his students on probably their first real-life case – much like the students in *Legally Blonde*, except that this was a real-life, real-life case. These scenes include Scenes 8, 10, 17, 18, 21, and 26. The students are smart, engaged, and impressionable. In Scene 8, Professor Dershowitz gives a heartfelt speech about the meaning of justice and his students were all moved by his words. One student goes from finding von Bülow "obviously guilty" in Scene 8 to "obviously framed by Sunny's children" in Scene 21.

CRIMINAL LAW
Criminal Appeals

Scene 29 shows the oral arguments before the Rhode Island Supreme Court. We do not get to see much of the actual arguments, but we do get to see Alan Dershowitz's brilliance. As the appellate judge points out, new evidence is almost never allowed on appeal. Dershowitz's plan, however, is to show that the circumstantial theory of the case and the chain of the circumstantial evidence should not have been enough to convict von Bülow. As the very same court held in *In re Derek*, cases based on circumstantial theory as opposed to fact only hold up if no alternate theories make sense. 448 A.2d 765, 768 (R.I. 1982). Evidence "based on conjecture and speculation does not support a criminal conviction." *Id.* The Court did state that if an "inference is the only reasonable one to be drawn from the underlying facts, then a secondary inference may be drawn from the primary inference." *Id.* The State of Rhode Island relied almost exclusively on this "chain of inference" logic: insulin in the black bag in von Bülow's bedroom, insulin on the needle, and insulin in Sunny's blood creates an inference of Claus's guilt. Mere inference, however, "must be rejected as being without probative force where the facts from which it is drawn are susceptible of another reasonable inference." *Id.* The holding in *Derek* set the stage for Dershowitz's success.

As Dershowitz tells the court: "the only way to show a better theory is to present it." Dershowitz needs to offer new evidence to show alternate theories for the coma. He is allowed to do so. Evidence from medical experts suggested that the comas could have been caused by any number of factors: eggnog-induced hypoglycemia, attempted suicide, or some diet fad or concoction Sunny had created. Dershowitz is then able to "bait" the prosecutor by getting him to talk about the evidence too. The prosecutor starts defending the circumstantial evidence and theory, without undermining the key point: legitimate alternative theories exist. Dershowitz broke the prosecution's circumstantial chain. If one link breaks, the whole chain has to be thrown out. Without the circumstantial case, the prosecution had very little. The prosecution having been baited into discussing its (weak) case before the Rhode Island Supreme Court, the judges may have come to believe that Claus von Bülow was innocent. By utilizing the court's decision in the *Derek* case, Dershowitz provided the judges with a hook upon which to hang that belief. Also, this strategy of breaking the chain of inference helped pave the way for von Bülow's victory at the second trial.

CRIMINAL PROCEDURE/CONSTITUTIONAL LAW
Fruit of the Poisonous Tree Doctrine
– Fourth Amendment

The Fourth Amendment to the United States Constitution reads, in part: "The right of the people to be secure in their persons, houses, papers, and effects, against unreasonable searches and seizures, shall not be violated." U.S. Const. amend. IV. To protect against improper police and prosecutorial conduct, such as unlawful searches and arrests, the Supreme Court has carved out the so-called "exclusionary rule" to keep any ill-gotten evidence out of trial. *Brown v. Illinois,* 422 U.S. 590, 599 (1975). The rationale is that, if the evidence cannot be used, the police will be less likely to resort to improper means to obtain such evidence. *See id.* A subset of the exclusionary rule is known as the "fruit of the poisonous tree doctrine." If the illegal search is "poisoned" by impropriety, any evidence obtained through the poisonous process is excluded from evidence at a criminal trial as "fruit of the poisonous tree."

In Scene 21, Dershowitz and his staff attorney discuss evidentiary issues. Dershowitz makes reference to the fruit of the poisonous tree doctrine (without expressly saying so). Can you spot the reference? What evidence was the poisonous tree and what tainted fruit resulted? What other constitutional problems do you note with respect to the criminal investigation? Why was Dershowitz not inclined to rely on technicalities or prosecutorial defects for purposes of von Bülow's appeal?

Double Jeopardy – Fifth Amendment

Under the Double Jeopardy Clause, a criminal defendant may not "be twice put in jeopardy of life or limb." *See* the Fifth Amendment, made applicable to the States through the Fourteenth Amendment in *Benton v. Maryland,* 395 U.S. 784, 794 (1969). The Double Jeopardy Clause of the Fifth Amendment "protects against a second prosecution for the same offense after acquittal ... [a]nd it protects against multiple punishments for the same offense." *North Carolina v. Pearce,* 395 U.S. 711, 717 (1969).

Suppose Sunny had died shortly after von Bülow's acquittal at the second trial. Assume that the autopsy report confirmed positively that she was injected with insulin, and that the injection could not have been self-inflicted. Ignoring the question of whether this scenario would be medically feasible, query whether Claus von Bülow could have then been tried for murder, without running afoul of Double Jeopardy protections. *See Blockburger v. United States,* 284 U.S. 299 (1932) (defining "same offense"). Also note that Sunny fell into her coma in Rhode Island, but died in New York. What, if any, charges could the State of New York bring against Claus von Bülow? *See Heath v. Alabama,* 474 U.S. 82, 87 (1985) (regarding the dual sovereignty doctrine); *See also People v. Helmsley,* 170 A.2d 209 (N.Y. 1991) (discussing double jeopardy protections under New York statutes). For more information about the Double Jeopardy Clause, see the discussion in FRACTURE.

CIVIL PROCEDURE

The Claus von Bülow case resulted in several different court battles and appeals, some around the same time frame as the publication of Alan Dershowitz's book *Reversal of Fortune.* After Claus von Bülow's successful criminal appeal, Martha von Bülow's children sued him on their mother's behalf. Although von Bülow could not be proven beyond a reasonable doubt to have committed the acts for purposes of a criminal conviction, proving civil liability only requires a preponderance of evidence, or a more likely than not chance that Claus von Bülow injected Sunny with insulin. With an easier burden than the prosecutor had, the plaintiff in the civil suit, Martha von Bülow (by her next-of-kin, her two children from her first marriage), used the same facts to sue civilly. The civil causes of action included assault, negligence, fraud, and racketeering charges.

The plaintiff sought to discover certain documents and information about conversations between Claus and his attorneys regarding the criminal case. *In re Claus von Bülow,* 828 F.2d 94, 96 (2d Cir. 1987). When Claus raised the attorney/client privilege in an attempt to avoid turning over the evidence, the plaintiff claimed Claus had waived the privilege by acquiescing to Dershowitz's publishing the book. *Id.* The trial judge agreed and granted plaintiff's motion to compel discovery. *Id.*

Claus von Bülow then filed a writ of mandamus with the Second Circuit. A writ of mandamus is a request for an exception to the finality rule, which holds that a case cannot be appealed until a final judgment upon its merits is rendered. This is no small request of a Circuit Court. Writs of mandamus are to be exercised in extraordinary situations only. *Id.* at 97. Generally, discovery orders are not subject to review by writ of mandamus. *Id.* The Second Circuit recognized, however, that in cases where a privilege is at issue, "taking an appeal afterwards is often an exercise in futility" and found that "courts have often entertained petitions for a writ of mandamus challenging discovery orders on grounds of attorney/client privileges." *Id.* at 99. The Second Circuit determined that von Bülow found himself in this very vulnerable situation:

> an order that information be produced that brushes aside a litigant's claim of a privilege not to ... leaves only an appeal after judgment as a remedy. Such a remedy is inadequate at best. Compliance with an order destroys the right sought to be protected. ... Often, to deny review is to deny the privilege. Although petition may ultimately succeed on appeal, his confidential communications will already have been exposed during the trial.

Id. at 98 (internal quotations omitted). The Court therefore granted the writ and vacated the trial court's ruling. *Id.* at 104. The Second Circuit outlined the scope of von Bülow's waiver, finding that the waiver only applied to confidential communications actually disclosed in the book. *Id.* at 103. The waiver did not extend to undisclosed portions or related communications involving the same subject matter. *Id.*

In addition to being a subject for civil procedure courses, this Second Circuit *von Bülow* opinion appears in Professional Responsibility and Ethics textbooks for its discussion about attorney/client communications and its guidance regarding client waiver of the attorney/client privilege.

Despite the small victory in the Second Circuit, facing these civil charges, Claus von Bülow ultimately gave up his claim to Sunny's $14,000,000, divorced her, and moved to London.

? Exam Tips

If you take a civil procedure exam in which you are provided with a copy of your state's procedural rules, do not expect to have time to search through them to find the answers. You need to know right where to look. When studying, focus on ways to quickly find the right information, as opposed to memorizing the information or relying on your ability to look up the rules during the exam.

Also, on a civil procedure essay exam with fact patterns full of torts, contracts, and other legal issues, do not become too sidetracked by the facts about the underlying civil action. In other words, discuss the case from a procedural standpoint, without overly analyzing the substantive areas of law that put the matter into court. As obvious as it sounds, you need to think procedurally and avoid wasting time writing about things like liability and remedies unless they directly relate to the procedural issue at hand. You may feel safe, if time permits after nailing the procedure, to show off some and discuss your knowledge of the underlying lawsuit. Just make sure your time is not better spent reviewing your civil procedure discussion. Time management is a critical component of complicated essay exams like civil procedure. On a civil procedure or other law school exam, always utilize all of the time provided. If you finish early, go back over the exam, check for apparent errors (without second-guessing yourself!) and make sure your exam is perfectly legible. Then, turn it in and forget about it. I am reminded of a law school exam tip I, regretfully, did not follow:

after the exam, do not discuss your answers with fellow classmates. Your answers will not be exactly the same and that will cause you anxiety that you do not need. If you go to lunch with classmates after an exam, talk sports or current events!

LEGAL BRIEFS & MOVIE EXTRAS

*This movie is based on the novel by Alan M. Dershowitz entitled: *Reversal of Fortune: Inside the Claus von Bülow case* (Random House 1986). Professor Alan Dershowitz appears in cameo as a judge on the appellate court in Scene 29

*Martha "Sunny" von Bülow fell into her coma December 21, 1980. She was never expected to recover. She passed away on December 6, 2008 at a New York nursing home. Claus von Bülow still lives in London.

*Most legal movies involve trials. Like *The Hurricane* and *Reversible Errors*, however, *Reversal Of Fortune* takes us through the appellate process. All three movies result in successful appeals, of course, or their stories would hardly make for Hollywood. In reality, only a small fraction of all criminal cases are reversed on appeal.

"Never let defendants explain...puts most of them in an awkward position...lying."

-Alan M. Dershowitz

CLASS ACTION
(Twentieth Century Fox 1991)

Starring: Gene Hackman; Elizabeth Mastrantonio

Lessons: Torts; Ethics; Civil Procedure

Plot: Two attorneys, Jedediah Tucker Ward (Gene Hackman) and his daughter Maggie Ward (Elizabeth Mastrantonio) find themselves on opposite sides of a large personal injury/products liability case. Jed Ward is a powerful plaintiff's lawyer who has made both a name and a fortune for himself in the personal injury realm. Jed Ward represents Mr. Kellen, a man injured in the car accident that killed his wife. Maggie takes on the defense for one of her firm's largest corporate clients, Argo Motors. As can soon be seen, the lawyers are adversaries in ways that go much deeper than the tort case at hand.

The lawsuit seems to be loosely based on the infamous Ford Pinto litigation, a major products liability case in the 1970s. *See Grimshaw v. Ford Motor Co.,* 119 Cal. App. 3d 757 (4th Dist. 1981). The Pinto case involved Ford's liability for an unsafe product, its economy style Pinto. *Id.* The Pintos were improperly designed, in that their gas tanks were positioned just behind the rear bumper. *Id.* at 774. When the small car was struck from behind, the gas tank could catch fire, and the car and its occupants could become engulfed in flames. *Id.* at 773. One woman was killed in a collision that caused her Pinto to explode, and her passenger, 13-year-old Richard Grimshaw, suffered severe burns and permanent impairment. *Id.* at 771. The jury awarded close to $3,000,000 in compensatory damages and $125,000,000 in punitive damages. *Id.* The judge reduced the punitive damages award to $3,500,000, however. *Id.* at 772. The case was appealed to the California Court of Appeals, which upheld the compensatory damages, as well as the judge's reduction of the punitive damages. *Id.* at 836.

As this movie and the Pinto case show, products liability cases can be lucrative for the attorneys. This movie is a must see for any personal injury attorney hopeful. There are only a few trial scenes, toward the end of the movie, at Scenes 23-25. But CLASS ACTION also explores pretrial practice and provides a look into the discovery process; this is a lesson in what not to do, for the most part.

TORTS
Products Liability

Like the Pinto litigation, the lawsuit in this movie involves a defective consumer product – a car. Products liability is a type of strict liability tort. To recover under a products liability theory, plaintiff must demonstrate:

1. That the product was in a defective condition that made the product unreasonably dangerous to the user or his property;

2. That the product was left in the defendant's control, whether or not the default actually caused the defect;

3. That the product did not undergo any significant changes before it gets in the hands of the user;

4. The seller of the product is in the business of selling the product; and

5. The product causes damages to anyone foreseeably endangered from the defective product.

RESTATEMENT (SECOND) OF TORTS, §402A.

There are at least two categories of defective products: manufacturing defects and design defects. To prove a manufacturing defect, the product must be different and more dangerous than non-defective manufactured products of the same type. The plaintiff may prevail if the product "departs from its intended design" so far as to render the product dangerous beyond the expectation of the ordinary consumer. *Id.* In other words, to prove a design defect, the product must be *unreasonably* dangerous. Because many products pose some danger to consumers, the plaintiff prevails only if he can show that there was an available, economically feasible, safer modification of or alternative to the product, such that the risk of harm posed by the product could have been avoided. RESTATEMENT (THIRD) OF TORTS §2. A product might also be "defective" if there are inadequate instructions or warnings. *Id.*

What facts from *Class Action* help to prove each element of products liability from a strict liability standpoint? (See Scene 18). What are the defenses to strict liability? If, under principles of "simple actuarial analysis," strict liability failed, could the plaintiff recover under a negligence theory? What are the defenses to negligence?

? Exam Tips

When faced with a torts essay, do not forget to include a discussion of damages. Often, some of the facts presented go directly to damages as opposed to liability. Use all of the facts you are given. Also, remember to discuss defenses. For instance, in products liability cases, there may be facts presented that invoke the defenses of assumption of risk or unreasonable misuse of the product. Also, where elements for strict liability in products cases are missing, analyze the scenario under a negligence standard as well.

ETHICS
Conflicts of Interest

As was true in *Adam's Rib,* family relationships between opposing counsel give rise to potential conflicts of interest and require a waiver, as well as an objective and subjective belief by the attorneys that the relationship will not interfere with the ability to provide proper representation. Does this father/daughter relationship pass that test? In other words, can this conflict of interest or potential conflict of interest be cured by client waiver? Recall that, under ABA Model Rule 1.7(b)(1) (Conflict of Interest: Current Client), in addition to obtaining a client's informed consent in such a situation, the attorneys must also have a reasonable belief that they "will be able to provide competent and diligent representation to each affected client" notwithstanding the familial relationship. Can the Wards reasonably claim such a belief under the circumstances? At what, if any, point in the movie might that change? Is Maggie a heroine – a model of ethics – when she turned over the evidence her firm and its client were trying to hide? Or was that decision influenced by her relationship with opposing counsel? Either way, Maggie clearly crosses ethical lines in helping her father beat Argo Motors.

CIVIL PROCEDURE
Discovery

Also an ethical violation, discovery rules are gravely violated in this movie. For example, in Scene 17, Maggie and her firm attempt to hide a critical piece of evidence among boxes upon boxes of paperwork (not knowing it had already been unethically removed). They claim they are within the "letter of the law" in doing so. But take a closer look. Under Federal Rule of Civil Procedure 34(b) (dealing with the production of documents), a party must produce documents in the same manner "as they are kept in the usual course of business or shall organize and label them to correspond with the categories in the request." Whether they were hiding something or not, the defense's "paper blizzard" was improper. When it comes to document productions, "do unto others as you would have done to you."

Further, Rule 26 of the Federal Rules of Civil Procedure requires initial disclosures and imposes ongoing duties among parties to cooperate with respect to discovery. Under Federal Rule of Civil Procedure 26(a)(5)(E)(2), a party has a duty to amend a prior response to a discovery request "if the party learns that the response is in some material respect incomplete or incorrect and if the additional or corrective information has not otherwise been made known to the other parties during the discovery process." The most obvious violation of Rule 26 is, of course, the way the defendants deal with the report of Argo's research scientist, Dr. Alexander Pavel, concluding that the cars were unsafe and recommending they not be sold. Certainly, hiding and destroying evidence and lying about its existence breaches Rule 26 - and constitutes criminal and ethical violations! See Scenes 17 and 24. What are the implications for such violations? What recourse do parties have for their opponent's violation of discovery rules? See Rule 37, Federal Rule of Civil Procedure (Failure to Make Disclosures or to Co-operate in Discovery; Sanctions). What types of sanctions are appropriate?

If a court finds that a party has destroyed or concealed evidence, a negative inference may be appropriate, allowing the court to infer that the destroyed or concealed evidence contained something unfavorable to that party. *Zubulake v. UBS Warburg LLC,* 2004 WL 1620866 at *6, n.62 (S.D.N.Y. July 20, *2004*) (imposing sanctions and holding that an "adverse inference instruction may … be warranted, in some circumstances, for the untimely production [or non-production] of evidence.").

For more information on these discovery issues, evidence withholding, and sanctions, see the ethics discussion regarding *The Verdict*.

LEGAL BRIEFS & MOVIE EXTRAS

*Does Maggie have a cause of action against her law firm for the way it handled her complaints about evidence withholding and ethical violations? Does Maggie have a whistleblower retaliation claim against her firm? What do your state's laws have to say about the handling of employee complaints within an organization, and about whistleblowing and retaliation?

*In Scene 3, Jed discusses his new contingency case, Mr. Kellen's lawsuit against Argo Motors. In Scene 4, however, Maggie and her co-workers discuss the same case against Argo Motors, filed a few years prior, as a class action. Based on the facts of the movie, and looking at Rule 23 of the Federal Rules of Civil Procedure, can we tell if the Wards' battle was an actual class action lawsuit?

*Class Action star Gene Hackman also plays senior partner Avery Tolar in *The Firm* (based on John Grisham's novel *The Firm*). Gene Hackman certainly has a lawyerly look about him.

MY COUSIN VINNY
(Twentieth Century Fox 1992)

Starring: Joe Pesci; Marisa Tomei; Ralph Macchio

Lessons: Ethics; Evidence

Plot: Two youths from New York, Bill Gambini and Stan Rothenstein, hit the highway, bound for college. They run into trouble in small town Alabama when they are accused, in a case of misunderstanding and mistaken identity, of shooting a grocery clerk and robbing the store. Luckily, one of the boys (Ralph Macchio) has a lawyer in the family: Cousin Vinny (Joe Pesci). Vinny Gambini and his fiancée, Mona Lisa Vito (Marisa Tomei), travel from Brooklyn, New York, to Beechum County, Alabama, so Vinny can defend the boys, who are facing the death penalty. Vinny had never handled a murder trial before. He was a personal injury settlement attorney who had never been to trial and who had only recently passed the bar exam after six attempts. He is hilarious.

Marisa Tomei brilliantly portrayed Mona Lisa Vito, an out-of-work hairdresser who also happened to know a thing or two about cars. She won a well-deserved Best Supporting Actress Golden Globe for that role. Her famous scene is when the prosecution challenges her qualifications as an expert witness (Scene 21).

ETHICS
Competence of Attorney

Vinny went from being a New York City personal injury lawyer who settled all of his cases to a criminal defense lawyer in Alabama county court. Is there anything wrong with Vinny's taking on a capital murder case when he has never even had to go to court? ABA Model Rule 1.1 (Competence) provides that "[a] lawyer shall provide competent representation to a client. Competent representation requires the legal knowledge, skill, thoroughness, and preparation reasonably necessary for the representation." Comment 2 to Rule 1.1 explains that a lawyer "need not necessarily have special training or prior experience to handle legal problems of the type with which the lawyer is unfamiliar." After all, every one of us has a "first trial" or a "first case," the memory of which we will take to our graves. Further, Comment 3 to Rule 1.1 explains that "in an emergency a lawyer may give advice or assistance in a matter in which the lawyer does not have the skill ordinarily required where ... association with another lawyer would be impracticable." Does the youths' situation qualify as an emergency? It's Vinny or the stuttering public defender! Comment 4 to Rule 1.1 provides that "a lawyer may accept representation where the requisite level of competence can be achieved by reasonable preparation." Did Vinny reasonably prepare and achieve the requisite level of competence?

Unauthorized Practice of Law

ABA Model Rule 5.5 (Unauthorized Practice of Law; Multi-jurisdictional Practice of Law) prohibits a person from practicing law without a license or from practicing in a jurisdiction other than one in which an attorney is licensed. Rule 5.5(c), however, provides that a "lawyer admitted in another United States jurisdiction, and not disbarred or suspended from practice in any jurisdiction, may provide legal services on a temporary basis." A lawyer not licensed in a particular jurisdiction may practice in that jurisdiction where the legal services:

(1) are undertaken in association with a lawyer who is admitted to practice in this jurisdiction and who actively participates in the matter;

(2) are in or reasonably related to a pending or potential proceeding before a tribunal in this or another jurisdiction, if the lawyer, or a person the lawyer is assisting, is authorized by law or order to appear in such proceeding or reasonably expects to be so authorized;

(3) are in or reasonably related to a pending or potential arbitration, mediation, or other alternative dispute resolution proceeding in this or another jurisdiction, if the services arise out of or are reasonably related to the lawyer's practice in a jurisdiction in which the lawyer is admitted to practice and are not services for which the forum requires pro hac vice admission; or

(4) are not within paragraphs (c)(2) or (c)(3) and arise out of or are reasonably related to the lawyer's practice in a jurisdiction in which the lawyer is admitted to practice.

Is Vinny authorized to practice in the jurisdiction under any of the above provisions? What, if any, additional steps would have needed to be taken for Vinny to properly appear before this court?

EVIDENCE
Hearsay Exception: Admission

During the preliminary proceedings (Scene 10), the good sheriff testified that, during the initial interrogation (Scene 2) the defendant stated: "I shot the clerk!" Obviously, there are Fifth Amendment problems with the so-called confession, given that he blurted out the statement in his confusion when he suddenly realized he was being charged with murder as opposed to shoplifting tuna. Aside from the constitutional problems with the statement being admitted as a confession, what other evidentiary issues does the statement present? Is the statement hearsay? Might it be excepted from the hearsay definition as an admission? *See* FED. R. EVID. 801(d)(2). Does it fall under any Rule 803 hearsay exceptions? *See* FED. R. EVID. 803(1) (present sense impression); 803(2) (excited utterance); and 803(3) (then existing mental, emotional, or physical condition).

Even if the statement were not hearsay, or an exception applied, how might you argue for the defense that the statement should be excluded from evidence at trial? The admission of any statement taken so completely out of context might be excluded under Federal Rules Evidence 403. Without seeing the defendant's confusion, or hearing the questioning tone of his voice, jurors would be confused about the true meaning of the defendant's four words.

Cross-Examination

As with any criminal defense, Vinny does not have to prove anything; he just has to provide the jury with reasonable doubt. Using his analogy, he has to pull apart the bricks that make up the prosecution's illusionary case. So, his cross-examinations are all about discrediting the witnesses (i.e., impeaching) in different ways. There are many ways to do this, as the "quintessential Gambini" successfully demonstrates. He comically displays to the jury each witness's poor vantage point, misperception, lack of reliability, and stupidity. Vinny's technique in discrediting witnesses in this manner, as opposed to character and conduct impeachment allowed under Federal Rule of Evidence 608, is a wise move given this intimate courtroom in Beechum County, Alabama. Putting into question the vantage points and sensory perception of eyewitnesses does more to raise reasonable doubt than digging up dirt on good ol' boys and their elderly neighbors. The Beechum County folks likely expected the leather-donning loudmouth from Brooklyn to be much more offensive. For the most part, he was gracious, and he was effective.

? Exam Tips

Vinny does a good job in showing that the state's evidence was merely circumstantial, as opposed to direct evidence. Be able to distinguish between direct and circumstantial evidence. Do not assume, however, that direct evidence is automatically "better" than circumstantial evidence. For instance, consider direct evidence in the form of testimony from Sister Mary Margaret that she sat looking out the window overlooking the churchyard watching it snow all night long, and she never saw anybody enter upon the yard. With all due respect to the Sister, this direct evidence is less compelling than circumstantial evidence in the form of fresh footprints in the snow on the church grounds.

Expert Testimony

Vinny becomes better footed on solid ground when the subject matter turned to automobiles. In Scene 19, an automobile expert takes the stand and provides what appears to be indisputable evidence that the defendants' car tires left the tread marks in front of the crime scene. Out of sudden hope, Vinny causes a stir in the courtroom when he calls his fiancée to the stand. Enter Mona Lisa Vito. This is Marissa Tomei's most famous scene, as Mona Lisa, a hairdresser/auto mechanic, cleverly withstands the prosecution's challenging her qualifications as an expert witness (Scene 21).

The requirements for qualifying as an expert witness under Rule 702 of the Federal Rules of Evidence (below) is very similar to that of most other states, including Alabama:

Rule 702. Testimony by Experts: If scientific, technical, or other specialized knowledge will assist the trier of fact to understand the evidence or to determine a fact in issue, a witness qualified as an expert by knowledge, skill, experience, training, or education, may testify thereto in the form of an opinion or otherwise, if (1) the testimony is based upon sufficient facts or data, (2) the testimony is the product of reliable principles and methods, and (3) the witness has applied the principles and methods reliably to the facts of the case.

FED. R. EVID. 702. Leading Supreme Court cases on the admissibility of expert testimony under Federal Rule 702 include *Daubert v. Merrell Down Corporation*, 509 U.S. 579 (1993) and *Kumho Tire Co. v. Carmichael*, 526 U.S. 137 (1999). Both cases set forth the relevant factors used in determining whether or not a person qualifies as an expert, and whether their "expert" testimony may be admitted into evidence. Such factors include the need for expert testimony, the expert's qualifications in the subject area, whether the testimony is based on sufficient facts, and the use and reliability of the expert's principles, data, and methods.

Based on Rule 702, the Supreme Court's interpretation of the Rule (set forth in *Daubert* and *Kumho*), and the responses to the prosecutions "voir dire," does Mona Lisa qualify as an expert in the general automotive area? Would the testimony she provides about the cars and the tread marks be admissible as expert opinion?

LEGAL BRIEFS & MOVIE EXTRAS

*The American Bar Association Journal ranked *My Cousin Vinny* #3 in its August 2008 cover story and listing of *"The 25 Greatest Legal Movies."* Most of the movies included in this book are listed on the ABA's top 25 list. Others, I would argue, are noticeably and inappropriately absent from the ABA's list.

*Is there anything wrong with the prosecutor's voir dire, other than the fact that he made an idiot out of himself? Is it permissible that he got within an inch or so of Mona Lisa's face and roared: "you don't know do you?" *See* FED. R. EVID.

611(a) ("the court shall exercise reasonable control over the mode and order of interrogating witnesses and presenting evidence so as to … protect witnesses from harassment or undue embarrassment."); *See also* FED. R. CIV. P. 26(c) ("a court shall take actions to protect a party or person from annoyance, embarrassment, oppression, or undue burden or expense."). That behavior would not fly in front of any judge before whom I've ever appeared. Witnesses are entitled to respect, dignity, and personal space.

*The Alabama jury in *My Cousin Vinny* was told that both defendants would get the death penalty if the jury found them guilty. Is that true? Under the Federal Sentencing Guidelines, does accessory to murder carry the same penalty as murder? What about under your state's law? In researching the accessory crime in your jurisdiction, be mindful of the distinction between an accessory before the fact and an accessory after the fact.

Generally, an accessory before the fact is one who aids, abets, counsels, or encourages the commission of a felony but is not actually present at the scene. In such cases, accessory defendants can be punished to the same extent as the principle perpetrator. To be an accessory after the fact, the prosecution must prove three elements:

-a completed felony must have been committed;

-the accessory defendant must have known of the commission of the felony; and

-the accessory defendant must have personally given some aid or assistance to the felon.

In accessory after the fact cases, the general rule is that the accomplice is not guilty for the substantive crimes committed by the felon assisted.

*Query whether the prosecution would be allowed to call an expert witness mid-trial, without prior notice. *See* FED. R. CRIM. P. 16(a) and (b) (Discovery and Inspection/Disclosures). When Vinny objects to the prosecution's expert, the judge responds:

"Mr. Gambini, that is a lucid, well thought-out, intelligent objection …. OVERRULED!"

-Judge Chamberlain Haller, Beechum County, Alabama, portrayed by Fred Gwynne in his final performance (he passed away in 1993). Gwynne was most famous for his role as Herman Munster – a Frankenstein-like character in the 1960s sitcom *The Munsters*.

(Note that such a ruling is judicial error, given the prosecution's duty to disclose its incriminating evidence and all of its witnesses, and the defendants' constitutional rights to properly question all witnesses before trial.).

GUILTY AS SIN
(Hollywood Pictures 1993)

Starring: Rebecca De Mornay; Don Johnson; Jack Warden

Lesson: Ethics

Plot: Rebecca De Mornay plays Jennifer Haines, an attractive young criminal defense attorney working as an associate in a top law firm. Jennifer takes on a murder defense for a wealthy business client of the firm, David Greenhill (Don Johnson). Mr. Greenhill is a good-looking and charming businessman accused of murdering his rich society wife, Rita. Initially, Jennifer and her law firm partners assume she will be able to obtain a full acquittal for their rich client. Greenhill claims his wife framed him for her own murder, and Haines believes him, for a few minutes anyhow. Relying on the attorney/client privilege, however, Greenhill begins to show Haines his true colors, and Haines begins to have second thoughts about her beliefs, and about representing Greenhill. After an unsuccessful attempt to withdraw as counsel, Haines begins her own investigation of her client, placing both her life and her career in jeopardy.

ETHICS

The integrity of the attorneys, the judge, the FBI, and the criminal justice system itself are immediately placed under a cloud of doubt in this crime thriller. In Scene 1, Haines learns that an FBI agent is working undercover with the mobster she is presently defending in federal court. She strikes a deal with the prosecutor and the judge and gets her client a directed not-guilty verdict in exchange for her not revealing the agent's identity to the Mafia. What ethical violations did the judge, the prosecutor, and the defense attorney commit here? Could you argue that their actions should be excused or privileged under the circumstances?

Withdrawal of Attorneys

Another ethical question raised in this movie: under what circumstances may an attorney withdraw from a criminal case? After a scary confrontation between David and Jennifer at his apartment, Jennifer decides her client is fixated on her and she wants to withdraw. She admits to her firm's partners that she made a mistake in taking the case, and asks that they allow her to drop it. David had not paid over $29,000 in fees at that point; they readily agreed. The judge does not, however.

In Scene 5, Jennifer is before the court on her motion to withdraw, which she loses on the spot. She was ordered to continue the representation and uphold her ethical duty to defend Greenhill to the best of her abilities. She offered as grounds to withdraw the fact that he did not pay the fees and that he misrepresented his ability to pay. Is this a basis for withdrawal? Under ABA Model Rule 1.16 (Declining or Terminating Representation), there are two types of situations dealing with attorney withdrawal: mandatory withdrawal (shall) and permissive withdrawal (may). Note the circumstances below in which it is mandatory that an attorney withdraw. At any point in the representation, did Jennifer come into a situation where withdrawal became mandatory? Rule 1.16(a) provides that a lawyer ... **shall** withdraw from the representation of a client if:

> (1) the representation will result in violation of the rules of professional conduct or other law;
>
> (2) the lawyer's physical or mental condition materially impairs the lawyer's ability to represent the client; or
>
> (3) the lawyer is discharged.

Did there come a point during the criminal proceedings that

Jennifer had additional grounds she could have taken back to the Judge to support permissive withdrawal? Rule 1.16(b) provides that a lawyer **may** withdraw from representing a client if:

(1) withdrawal can be accomplished without material adverse effect on the interests of the client;

(2) the client persists in a course of action involving the lawyer's services that the lawyer reasonably believes is criminal or fraudulent;

(3) the client has used the lawyer's services to perpetrate a crime or fraud;

(4) the client insists upon taking action that the lawyer considers repugnant or with which the lawyer has a fundamental disagreement;

(5) the client fails substantially to fulfill an obligation to the lawyer regarding the lawyer's services and has been given reasonable warning that the lawyer will withdraw unless the obligation is fulfilled;

(6) the representation will result in an unreasonable financial burden on the lawyer or has been rendered unreasonably difficult by the client; or

(7) other good cause for withdrawal exists.

Note that these sentences are connected by the word "or," not "and." Note also that (7) provides a "catchall" ground for withdrawal. What facts from the movie support one or more of the above-stated reasons for permissive withdrawal? Can Jennifer show good cause?

Attorney/Client Communications

In Scene 6, Greenhill asks his lawyer to reassure him further about the nature of the attorney/client privilege. She said she would lose her license to practice law if she revealed his confidential communications, and that what he revealed would not be admissible in court anyhow. Note that Jennifer articulated two separate rules: the first is an ethical rule, prohibiting lawyers from revealing anything their clients tell them in confidence; the other is an evidentiary rule.

The ethical rule is found in ABA Model Rule 1.6(a) (Confidentiality of Information) ("a lawyer shall not reveal information relating to the representation of a client unless the client gives informed consent, the disclosure is impliedly authorized in order to carry out the representation or the disclosure is permitted by paragraph (b)."). An attorney who breaks ethical rules can lose her license, as Jennifer correctly noted. The other rule, as Jennifer tells her client, governs the admissibility in court of certain communications between an attorney and her client. This is an evidentiary rule, separate from the ethical rule requiring attorneys to keep their clients' confidences.

Did Jennifer properly analyze the ethical rule and its relevant exception? She tells her client that she would *have to* reveal a client's plans for future crimes. Is that accurate? The exception to the confidentiality rule that Jennifer refers to is Rule 1.6(b)(2): "a lawyer *may* reveal information relating to the representation of a client to the extent the lawyer reasonably believes necessary … to prevent the client from committing a crime or fraud that is reasonably certain to result in substantial injury to the financial interests or property of another and in furtherance of which the client has used or is using the lawyer's services." Note that this rule provides that an attorney *may* reveal a client's plans for future crimes; this is not a requirement. Some state rules are different, however.

Of course, Jennifer would be disbarred if it ever came to light that she planted evidence against her own client. She could also be sued for malpractice and, given the intentional nature of her actions, her firm's malpractice insurance carrier would likely deny coverage (malpractice policies are generally for protection against liability based on negligence). In addition to the obvious ethical violations and civil illegalities of framing your own client, did she commit any federal crimes when she planted evidence against him? *See* 18 U.S.C. §1503(a) ("Whoever corruptly … influences, obstructs, or impedes, or endeavors to influence, obstruct, or impede, the due administration of justice, shall be punished as provided in subsection (b)).") Subsection (b) provides for punishment of up to 20 years in prison plus a fine. Research whether your state's law is similar.

? Exam Tip

Despite the contrary suggestion from some of these movies, the legal profession has a broad and stringent ethical system, unlike most other industries. In addition to the state and multi-state bar exams, most states require lawyers to pass the Multi-State Professional Responsibility Examination (MPRE) before they can become licensed attorneys. The MPRE tests the ABA Model Rules of Professional Conduct and the ABA Model Code of Judicial Conduct. The MPRE consists of sixty multiple-choice questions that need to be completed within a two-hour timeframe. States vary in terms of when the MPRE must be, or can be, taken. States also vary in the scores they require for passing the MPRE. Do not expect that the professional responsibility or ethics course you take in law school will ready you for the MPRE.

Regardless of your ethics education in law school, you will need to do some extra studying and preparation before sitting for the MPRE. Gather information about your state's MPRE requirements early on in law school, and obtain some practice exams with answers and explanations.

LEGAL BRIEFS & MOVIE EXTRAS

*The jury was hung after 6 days of deliberations. The state moves for a new trial. We never find out if that would have been granted; Attorney Haines had other plans to bring down David Greenhill. Did the state have proper grounds to move for a new trial? What is the likelihood that such a motion would have been granted?

*Jack Warden appears in *Guilty as Sin*, as Jennifer Haines's friend, Moe. The ubiquitous Jack Warden also plays in *12 Angry Men*, *And Justice for All*, and *The Verdict*. All of these movies were also directed by Sydney Lumet.

PHILADELPHIA
(TriStar Pictures 1993)

Starring: Tom Hanks; Denzel Washington

Lesson: Employment law

Plot: This time Denzel Washington gets to be the lawyer (plaintiffs' attorney Joe Miller) instead of the criminal defendant sentenced to life in prison (*The Hurricane*). He accepts an employment discrimination case on behalf of plaintiff Andrew Beckett (Tom Hanks), also an attorney. Beckett's conservative Philadelphia law firm fired him once they discovered he had AIDS, transmitted from a gay lover. Tom Hanks is at his best in this role, and the movie successfully portrays the prejudices and homophobia that permeated the late 1980s and early 1990s. *Philadelphia* really gets to the heart of issues and prevailing attitudes about homosexuality, AIDS, and disability during this time period. The movie also provides trial scenes and legal strategies for law students to explore.

EMPLOYMENT LAW
Federal Americans with Disabilities Act

What current laws provide Andrew Beckett with causes of action for this type of discrimination in the workplace? One federal anti-discrimination statute that he may look to is the Americans with Disabilities Act of 1990. 42 U.S.C. §12101 et seq. Title I of the ADA prohibits disability discrimination in the workplace. Does he qualify for protection under the ADA? In order to be covered under the ADA, a person must prove that he is substantially limited in a major life activity. Then, that person has to prove that, despite the substantial limitations, he is able to perform the essential functions of the job. 42 U.S.C. §12102(2)(A) ("disability means a physical or mental impairment ... that substantially limits one or more major life

activities."); 42 U.S.C. §12111(8) ("qualified individual …
means an individual with a disability who, with or without
reasonable accommodation, can perform the essential functions
of the employment position that such individual holds or
desires."). Under these definitions, how would you argue he
qualifies? Is he substantially limited in major life activities? If
so, which ones? How would you argue that the ADA does not
protect him?

State Law Protections

Historically, ADA cases have had a 95% fail rate, which is
primarily because the plaintiff is unable to prove disability. *See*
Amy L. Allbright, *2004 Employment Decisions Under the ADA
Title I, - Survey Update,* 29 MENTAL & PHYSICAL
DISABILITY L. REP. 513 (July/August 2005). That is why
many state laws provide additional protections that cover people
who cannot prove they are disabled enough to fall within the
protection yet not so disabled that they cannot perform the
essential functions of their jobs. For example, Maine's anti-
disability discrimination statute does not require substantial
limitation in a major life activity; further, the Maine statute
specifically includes HIV in the per se list of conditions covered
under the anti-discrimination statute. Other state disability laws
also have broader protections than the ADA, including
Connecticut, Illinois, New Jersey, New York, California,
Maryland, Massachusetts, and Rhode Island. Webbert, David
G., *In Defense of Whitney,** MAINE BAR JOURNAL, Vol. 22,
No. 2 (Spring 2007), Note 22.

There may also be state law protections against sexual
orientation discrimination. *See, e.g.,* 5 M.R.S.A. §4552. If
Pennsylvania had such protections back then, Beckett's attorney
may have had better evidence to prove that the firm
discriminated against him not simply because of a disability, but
because of his sexual orientation. Recall that another employee,

who contracted AIDS from a blood transfusion, was not terminated - a fact the firm can use as a defense to show that it does not discriminate against AIDS patients. What would be unfavorable evidence in trying to show that he was discriminated against because of AIDS would become helpful in a sexual orientation discrimination case: one who gets AIDS from homosexual conduct is terminated, but one who gets AIDS from a blood transfusion is not. Beckett would still need to show that the employer's stated reason for terminating him – the alleged loss of an important complaint – was pre-textual (i.e., a lie), and that the real reason for termination was discriminatory.

? Exam Tip

State bar examiners like to test on laws unique to the state. If, for example, your state has embarked on one of the nation's first or most expansive civil rights laws, or has pioneered legislation involving issues of national controversy, be aware of such laws, and do not be surprised to see them pop up on a state bar exam essay question.

LEGAL BRIEFS & MOVIE EXTRAS

Whitney is Maine's landmark case that changed the law on disability and resulted in a cutting edge statutory definition of disability that includes a per se list of conditions automatically protected. *See Whitney v. Walmart,* 2006 ME 37, 895 A.2d 309; 5 MRSA §4553-A(1)(B). The per se list under Maine's Human Rights Act includes:

absent, artificial or replacement limbs, hands, feet or vital organs; alcoholism; amyotrophic lateral sclerosis; bipolar disorder; blindness or abnormal vision loss; cancer; cerebral palsy; chronic obstructive pulmonary disease; Crohn's disease; cystic fibrosis; deafness or abnormal hearing loss; diabetes; substantial disfigurement;

epilepsy; heart disease; HIV or AIDS; kidney or renal diseases; lupus; major depressive disorder; mastectomy; mental retardation; multiple sclerosis; muscular dystrophy; paralysis; Parkinson's disease; pervasive developmental disorders; rheumatoid arthritis; schizophrenia; and acquired brain injury.

5 M.R.S.A. §4553-A(1)(B). In 2008, Congress passed an amendment to the ADA, in part to model Maine's law. The amended ADA will make it easier for employees to prove they are protected individuals with disabilities. The stated purpose of the ADA Amendments Act of 2008 is to redress court decisions that have "created an inappropriately high level of limitation necessary to obtain coverage under the ADA." Under the new ADA, effective January 1, 2009, the court cases will focus, not on the employee's medical condition and associated limitations, but instead on the more important issue of whether the employer adequately accommodated the employee, or whether illegal discrimination occurred.

*As set forth in the movie's end credits, the story is based on the true story about Geoffrey Bowers, an attorney who sued his firm, Baker & McKenzie, for discriminatory termination. This 1987 case was one of the first AIDS discrimination cases in the country. The case was filed with the New York State Division of Human Rights, because most civil rights and employment cases must first be taken to a state administrative agency before a suit can be filed in court. In other words, employment discrimination plaintiffs must typically "exhaust administrative remedies" before seeking redress in court. In the *Bowers* case, this process took about seven years. Ultimately, the New York State Division of Human Rights awarded Mr. Bowers $500,000 in compensatory damages and back pay. Mr. Bowers died from his disease before the case was resolved, however. For more on the story, see Mireya Navarro, *Vindicating a Lawyer With AIDS, Years Too Late; Bias Battle Over Dismissal Proves Costly Not*

Only to Worker, but to Law Firm, N.Y. TIMES, January 21, 1994, available at:

http://query.nytimes.com/gst/fullpage.html?sec=health&res=9B0DE5DC1530F932A15752C0A962958260 (last visited October 27, 2020).

*Tom Hanks received his first Oscar for his brilliant portrayal of Andrew Beckett.

"This is the essence of discrimination: formulating opinions about others not based on their individual merits but, rather, on their membership in a group with assumed characteristics."

-Andrew Beckett's Attorney, Joe Miller

THE FIRM
(Paramount Pictures 1993)

Starring: Tom Cruise; Jeanne Tripplehorn; Holly Hunter

Lessons: Employment Law; Ethics; Criminal Law

Plot: A Harvard Law graduate, Mitch McDeere (Tom Cruise), takes a position at a mid-sized Memphis law firm, Bendini, Lambert, & Locke. Mitch is given the most competitive associate salary, and he and his wife Abby (Jeanne Tripplehorn) are provided with a house loan, a car, and other perks. It looks as though Mitch's career is off to an impressive start, with a top-notch firm. The firm's client base, however, consists mostly of the Mafia. The firm also seems to have a high accidental death rate for its associates. Mitch becomes suspicious after an encounter he has with the FBI, following the death of two young lawyers. He hires a private investigator to learn the firm's and its clients' secrets. The investigator is assassinated, and Mitch soon finds himself caught between the mob and the FBI. Just recently having passed the bar exam, his fresh knowledge of federal crimes, and the help from the dead P.I.'s secretary (played by an entertaining Holly Hunter), allows him to outsmart the FBI and avoid becoming another "accident-prone" associate. Although the book is better, *The Firm* is action-packed and star-studded; like all Grisham films, it is worth watching for that reason alone.

EMPLOYMENT LAW
Pre-employment Inquiries

In Scene 1, during Mitch's interview with the firm, were any inappropriate questions asked or comments made? That he is a top-notch Harvard graduate is a given; his academic qualifications are clear. The interview thus focuses on Mitch's familial background. What are the partners of Bendini, Lambert

& Locke saying, when they tell Mitch during his initial interview that they advocate "traditional family values?" Keep in mind that he volunteered the fact that he was married, in stating that when he gets "tongue-tied" it is with his wife, Abby. The bias toward "traditional family values" is therefore displayed in positive terms – the firm is glad he possesses this asset.

Consider, however, the converse. If he were unmarried, or gay, or of non-traditional family values, could the comment be construed as discriminatory? If the job candidate were a woman, how might the firm's favoritism toward "traditional family values" affect the partners' perception of her value to the firm? As the Supreme Court has recognized, gender-based stereotypes about traditional family values and female domestic responsibilities tend to "create a self-fulfilling cycle of discrimination." *Nevada Dept. of Human Resources v. Hibbs*, 538 U.S., 721, 736 (2003). *See also, Phillips v. Martin Marietta Corp.,* 400 U.S. 542, 544 (1971) (finding evidence showing that the employer defendant had a policy of not hiring women with young children, but had no such policy with respect to men with young children).

The Firm highlights a form of gender discrimination and preconceptions about family roles that remains a problem for women who want to be both moms and lawyers. *See, e.g.,* Joan C. Williams & Nancy Segal, *Beyond the Maternal Wall: Relief for Family Caregivers Who are Discriminated Against on the Job*, 26 HARV. WOMEN'S L.J. 77 (2003); Lauren Stiller Rikleen, *Ending the Gauntlet: Removing Barriers to Women's Success in the Law* (Thomson LegalWorks 2006). For further discussion on the issue of juggling career and family, as well as a useful reference guide about career options for lawyer-parents, see *Balancing Law and Parenthood: Part Time Careers in the Law*, Plonsky, Kathryn A., (West Hartford, Graduate Group, 1999).

ETHICS

One of Mitch's many concerns about what the FBI was asking him to do was his risk of being disbarred for revealing the Mafia's crime secrets, in violation of ABA Model Rule 1.6 (Confidentiality of Information). An exception to the confidentiality rule, at Rule 1.6(b)(2), allows an attorney to breach client confidences to prevent *future* crimes. Here, however, the FBI wants Mitch to help them nail the Mafia for acts already committed. Do any of the other exceptions under Rule 1.6(b) apply? *See* ABA Model Rule 1.6(b)(1) ("A lawyer may reveal information relating to the representation of a client to the extent the lawyer reasonably believes necessary ... to prevent reasonably certain death or substantial bodily harm.") What, if any, information could Mitch provide to the FBI that would alleviate the risk of imminent death or bodily harm?

ABA Model Rule 1.6(3) allows a lawyer to reveal a client's information if reasonably necessary "to prevent, mitigate or rectify substantial injury to the financial interests or property of another that is reasonably certain to result or has resulted from the client's commission of a crime or fraud in furtherance of which the client has used the lawyer's services." Does this rule help Mitch at all? How about ABA Model Rule 1.6(6), allowing for revelation of confidential information when necessary "to comply with other law or a court order?"

CRIMINAL LAW: FEDERAL CRIMES
Mail Fraud

The federal "mail fraud" statute, 18 U.S.C. §1341 ("Frauds and Swindles"), provides:

> Whoever, having devised or intending to devise any scheme or artifice to defraud, or for obtaining money or

property by means of false or fraudulent pretenses [and] for the purpose of executing such scheme ... places in any post office or authorized depository for mail matter ... such person shall be fined not more than $1,000,000 or imprisoned not more than 30 years, or both.

In other words, to prosecute for mail fraud, the government would have to prove that, in padding associate time entries and mailing out bills, the firm and its partners knowingly created a plan to defraud clients in terms of the amount of time spent on their cases, used false material representations in billing the clients with the specific intent of defrauding them, and then used interstate mail to send their clients the hiked-up bills. Under this statute, who can be charged with mail fraud? Only the partners? All of the partners? The folks in the billing department? Those who work the mailroom?

Conspiracy

Even if the government could not prove mail fraud for each Bendini, Lambert, & Locke defendant, it might still be able to show that each was involved in a conspiracy. The federal crime of conspiracy, set forth in Title 18 U.S.C. §371, provides that:

If two or more persons conspire either to commit any offense against the United States, or to defraud the United States, or any agency thereof in any manner or for any purpose, and one or more of such persons do any act to effect the object of the conspiracy, each shall be fined under this title or imprisoned not more than five years, or both.

Although the crime is punishable by no more than five years, each separate use of the mail in furtherance of a scheme to defraud constitutes a separate offense, punishable by five years each. *Milam v. United States*, 322 F.2d 104, 110 (5th Cir. 1963). Mitch utilizes the federal crime to get the FBI off of his back without risking his law license by breaching client confidentiality.

Could Mitch have been a co-defendant to mail fraud and/or conspiracy, as the FBI suggested, had he not appeared to cooperate with the FBI? In the *Milam* case, the Fifth Circuit held that "it is not necessary that a defendant actually do any of the mailing so long as there is sufficient evidence to tie him to the fraudulent scheme which involves the use of the mails." *Id.* at 107. Recall that Mitch did not even see the bills; he merely submitted his timesheets. In interpreting both 18 U.S.C. §371 and 18 U.S.C. §1341 (covering mail fraud and conspiracy to commit mail fraud), the federal courts have held that a defendant's knowing participation in a scheme to defraud is an essential element of mail fraud and of conspiracy to commit mail fraud. *See, e.g., Windsor v. United States,* 384 F.2d 535, 536 (1967) (citing 18 U.S.C. §§371; 1341). This essential element of the two crimes "cannot be based on so-called 'constructive' knowledge because of facts known to others with whom appellant was involved." *Id.* at 537. Did Mitch have the requisite knowledge? Even if he did, it is a "cardinal rule of conspiracy law that one does not become a co-conspirator simply by virtue of knowledge of the conspiracy and association with conspirators." *United States v. Grass*, 616 F.2d 1295, 1301 (5th Cir. 1980). For more information about the federal mail fraud statute and conspiracy crimes, see 72 C.J.S. Postal Service §58.

Racketeering

As Mitch points out, the partners' over-billing scheme may also constitute racketeering. Racketeering is prohibited under the Racketeering Influenced Corrupt Organization Act ("RICO") (discussed in the chapter regarding *Find Me Guilty*). RICO contains criminal and civil penalties for profiting from illegal means that affect interstate commerce, including mail fraud.

18 U.S.C. §1961(1). RICO contains conspiracy crimes as well. 18 U.S.C. §1962(d).

? Exam Tip

Whenever a fact pattern presents a criminal incident planned or perpetrated by more than one person, consider whether conspiracy or racketeering crimes are involved, and discuss the elements of those crimes in addition to the underlying crimes committed. Other joint conduct crimes include aiding and abetting and solicitation.

LEGAL BRIEFS & MOVIE EXTRAS

*The firm informs Mitch, after two of his colleagues are tragically and "accidentally" killed, that he should not be burdened with student loans; the firm will pay them. I warn against delusions of grandeur caused by this scene. This benefit is so rare that, if your firm offers to pay off your student loans before you have even taken the bar exam, you should probably hire your own private investigator and you should definitely avoid diving trips to the Cayman Islands. That being said, if you do not find a legal job right after law school, before even taking the bar exam, do not worry about it! I graduated from law school as the country started to dip into recession. Even during times of recession, when law firms are cutting back on their hiring, there are always people retiring, moving out of state, etc. For a person with a law degree, opportunities are always out there.

*Gene Hackman, star of *Class Action,* appropriately portrays Attorney Avery Tolar, one of Mitch McDeere's senior partners at Bendini, Lambert & Locke. Gene Hackman also appears in another great legal movie based on a John Grisham book, *Runaway Jury* (Regency Enterprises 2003).

"Here's a multiple choice: The difference between tax avoidance and tax evasion is: (a) whatever the IRS says; (b) a smart lawyer; (c) ten years in prison; or (d) all of the above."

-Says Avery Tolar to Mitch McDeere, as Mitch was studying for the bar exam

A TIME TO KILL
(Warner Brothers 1996)

Starring: Morgan Freeman; Matthew McConaughey; Sandra Bullock

Lesson: Evidence

Plot: Attorney Jake Tyler Brigance (Matthew McConaughey) represents Carl Lee Haley (Morgan Freeman) who is on trial for shooting and killing the two men who raped and beat his ten-year-old daughter. The judge presiding over Haley's trial is Judge Omar Noose - an interesting last name for a judge in a movie involving racial tensions and the Ku Klux Klan. Sandra Bullock plays Ellen Roark, a brilliant young Harvard Law student who offers Jake her pro bono law clerking assistance. This is another must-see John Grisham story that is rich with evidentiary and criminal analysis.

EVIDENCE
Expert Witnesses

Given Haley's insanity defense, the most important evidence in the trial is expert medical testimony. Both sides employ an expert psychiatrist for purposes of diagnosing Carl Lee Haley's mental condition at the time of the shootings. The state's expert says he was "without defects" of any kind. He mentions the McNaghten Rule. The McNaghten rule comes from the 1843 trial Rex v. McNaghten, 8 Eng. Rep. 718 (1843). Daniel McNaghten was a Scottish woodworker who killed the Prime Minister's Secretary (thinking it was the Prime Minister) under the belief that the government was plotting against him. He was tried for murder and acquitted on the grounds of insanity.

Did the good doctor properly state the McNaghten Rule? The Rule provides an insanity defense if:

(a)   at the time of committing the act,

(b)   the accused was laboring under such a defect of reason, from disease of the mind,

(c)   as not to know the nature and quality of the act he was doing, or

(d)   if he did know it,

(e)   that he did not know he was doing what was wrong.

Id. In other words, it is a defense to murder if Haley was so far out of reason due to his daughter's attack that he did not know killing the attackers was wrong, or that he could not comprehend the nature and quality of the shootings. How would you argue for the state that this defense does not apply? How would you argue for the defense that sufficient mental defect existed?

Consider the lesser crime of manslaughter. Under the Model Penal Code, manslaughter is defined as: "a homicide which would otherwise be murder … committed under the influence of extreme mental or emotional disturbance for which there is *reasonable* explanation or excuse." Model Penal Code §210.3(1)(b). If Jake felt he lacked evidence of Haley's insanity, he could have focused more on evidence of Haley's extreme anger to at least reduce his charge to manslaughter, showing that he was adequately provoked due to his daughter's attack.

The prosecution likewise might have considered manslaughter charges, as an alternative to bringing murder charges against Haley, to avoid the risk of Haley's being found not guilty of murder by reason of insanity. The prosecution could have focused on evidence showing that Haley's anger was unreasonable, and that he was not adequately provoked when the crimes were committed. The jury would be instructed on the lesser crime of manslaughter either way, but the evidence and the entire trial can take a different course depending on the initial charges and defensive strategies.

? Exam Tips

Many criminal law courses cover both the Model Penal Code and state criminal laws. Do not be afraid to interrogate your professor about which you should focus on come exam time, and whether or not you will be responsible for distinctions between the two. For the bar exam, be sure you know where your state follows the Model Penal Code and where your state law deviates from the national norm.

Evidence of Prior Convictions

In this trial, we see another discrediting of the witness technique employed: impeachment with a prior conviction. The defense's expert witness (the doctor who said the defendant was insane at the time of the murders) is impeached when asked about his being convicted for statutory rape, years ago. How could this evidence have been kept out? First of all, the extent to which a witness may be impeached by prior crimes is limited by Federal Rules of Evidence 609(a) and 609(b). Under Rule 609(a), a witness's crime "shall be admitted, *subject to Rule 403*, if the crime was punishable by death or imprisonment in excess of one year [a felony] ... [or] if it involved dishonesty or false statement, regardless of the punishment." Rule 609(b) puts a time restriction on impeachment with prior convictions. Such convictions are inadmissible "if a period of more than ten years has elapsed since the date of the conviction or of the release of the witness from the confinement imposed for that conviction." Is the good doctor's rape conviction admissible under Rule 609?

The questions become: 1. was the crime punishable by more than one year in prison (i.e., was it a felony)? 2. If not, was it a crime involving dishonesty? 3. When was the conviction or release from jail? Statutory rape is not automatically a felony; the criminal record would show whether he was convicted of a felony or a misdemeanor (which is punishable by less than one year in prison). If the crime were a misdemeanor, it would come in only if it were considered a crime involving dishonesty. Although one could argue that just about any crime has some *semblance* of dishonesty, in this doctor's case, it is unlikely that the incident *involves* dishonesty. In any event, if the doctor's conviction or his release from jail occurred more than ten years prior, the crime would be too old to be admitted.

Further, as Rule 609 suggests, when all else fails, a Rule 403 argument should be made. Rule 403 of the Federal Rules of Evidence provides that even relevant evidence "may be excluded if its probative value is substantially outweighed by the danger of unfair prejudice, confusion of issues, or misleading the jury." Assuming the conviction did come in under Rule 609, what arguments would you make that the defense would be highly prejudiced if the jury were to hear about the defense's star witness's very old crime?

Closing Arguments

Does Jake do anything improper during his closing argument? He made an announcement to the jury: "what if I told you Dr. Bass's conviction was when he was 23 and he had a relationship with a 17-year-old whom he wound up marrying?"

This is not proper closing. If evidence came in through the doctor's re-direct examination that established this fact, it would be proper for the attorney to remind the jury about it. The manner in which he raises the point during his closing suggests otherwise, however. Jake should have rehabilitated the good doctor and brought these facts out on re-direct; a jury could not have heard them for the first time during closing.

Perhaps most helpful in the jury's reaching a "not guilty" verdict was the defense attorney's statement in his closing argument "imagine she was white." Was this proper closing material? Some courts have found such tactics impermissible in opening or closing arguments. Lawyers are not allowed to make references designed to inflame the passions and prejudices of the jury, or use arguments that would lead the jury to decide the case on considerations other than the evidence. *Arrieta-Agressot v. United States,* 3 F.3d 525, 527 (1st Cir. 1993). Nor may a lawyer inject personal opinion into opening statements or closing arguments. *United States v. Young,* 470 U.S. 1, 8-9 (1985). Additionally, a lawyer may not open or close using the "golden rule argument," that is, asking the jurors to put themselves in the position of one of the parties to determine the proper verdict. *Lioce v. Cohen,* 149 P.3d 916, 929 (Nev. 2006); *Cassim v. Allstate Ins. Co.,* 94 P.3d 513, 522 (Ca. 2004); *United States v. Moreno,* 947 F.2d 7, 8 (1st Cir. 1991); *Ivy. v. Security Barge Lines, Inc.,* 585 F.2d 732, 741 (5th Cir. 1978). Along these same lines, a lawyer may not play upon a jury's emotional reaction to crimes other than the specific one being charged. *State v. Procopio,* 88 F.3d 21, 31 (1st Cir. 1996). Is that what Jake did? How would you argue that the statement "now imagine she was white" is a "golden rule statement" or that it is otherwise improper? How would you argue that it is permissible? For more on this subject, see 75A AM. JUR. 2D *Trial* §547.

LEGAL BRIEFS & MOVIE EXTRAS

*The movie *Primal Fear* (Paramount Pictures 1996) also involves the *McNaghten* defense. Richard Gere defends a young man accused of brutally murdering an archbishop. Initially, Gere sincerely felt he was defending an innocent person, to whom he was beginning to become attached. A tantalizing motive presents itself, however, and nothing is as it seems.

*Carl Lee Haley approaches Jake *before* he committed any crime, suggesting he may need an attorney after he carries out his revenge. ABA Model Rule 1.6(b)(2) (Confidentiality) provides that "a lawyer may reveal information ... to the extent the lawyer reasonably believes necessary ... to prevent the client from committing a crime." Should Attorney Brigance have called the sheriff and revealed his conversation with Haley? *Could* Jake have called the sheriff about the talk?

*Attorney Brigance likes the limelight and has no trouble talking to reporters about his case. Does he face any risks, divulging information to the media during the trial? ABA Model Rule 3.6 permits "extrajudicial publicity" so long as the attorney does not make any "extrajudicial statement that the lawyer knows or reasonably should know will be disseminated by means of public communication and will have a substantial likelihood of materially prejudicing an adjudicative proceeding in the matter." Given the vague language in this rule, an attorney should be careful. The Supreme Court has held that a criminal defense attorney could be reprimanded for public comments that create a "substantial likelihood of materially prejudicing" a trial. *Gentile v. State Bar of Nevada*, 501 U.S. 1030, 1033 (1991). The Court did make it clear, however, that "a defense attorney may pursue lawful strategies to obtain dismissal of an indictment or reduction of charges, including an attempt to demonstrate in the court of public opinion that the client does not deserve to be tried." *Id.* at 1043.

"Until we can see each other as equals, justice is never going to be even-handed. It will remain nothing more than a reflection of our own prejudices."

-Attorney Jake Tyler Brigance

IRRECONCILABLE DIFFERENCES
(Warner Bros. 1984)

Starring: Ryan O'Neal, Shelley Long, Drew Barrymore

Lesson: Family Law

Plot: Drew Barrymore stars as Casey Brodsky, the daughter of Albert Brodsky (Ryan O'Neal) and Lucy Brodsky (Shelley Long), two high-profile screenwriters. Lucy and Albert were more involved with their careers than with their daughter. Frustrated with her parents' anger and their dramatic Hollywood lifestyle, Casey hires an attorney and fights to have her nanny, Maria Hernandez (Hortensia Colorado), appointed as her legal guardian. As a result of their daughter's bold and desperate moves, the Brodskys find themselves at the center of a newsworthy courtroom battle resulting in mutual disparagement and divulgence of personal struggles and bad behavior. The format of this screenplay tells their story in flashback fashion as they recount their problems through open-court testimony.

The acting in this movie is nothing short of phenomenal. It is hard to believe Drew Barrymore was only nine years old when she starred in this role. When Casey testifies about her parents in court, it is hard to imagine any judge not ruling in her favor. Casey understands her parents no longer love each other, but she feels ignored, and she feels as though her parents refuse to "recognize [her] rights as a human being."

This movie highlights the need for all parents - all adults - to stop and think about how the drama in their lives might impact the children in their lives.

Emancipation of Minors

The movie begins with a media frenzy outside the courthouse where a reporter tells viewers about the legal issue on the table: The Emancipation of Minors Act of California, which is "what this trial is all about." That is not quite accurate. In the real world, with a child as young as Casey, an adult would need to step up. In this case, we have Maria, Casey's hired nanny. The process would be for Maria to petition for guardianship. Typically, laws enacted for the benefit of youngsters to be allowed early separation from their parents are designed for older children, petitioning on their own. Even in California, minors must be at least 14 years old before they can petition the court for emancipation. For the sake of discussion, however, this chapter focuses on the emancipation of minors, even though that is the incorrect process in Casey's situation.

The Emancipation of Minor's Act was enacted in California to "permit an emancipated minor to obtain a court declaration of the minor's status." California Emancipation of Minors Law Div. 11, Part 6, Chap. 3, Art. 2, §7001. Of course, the best interest of the child standard still applies: "[t]he court shall sustain the petition if it finds that the .... emancipation would not be contrary to the minor's best interest. *Id.* at §7122

Determining if a young person's best interests warrant emancipation depend upon the context, purpose, and the effect of emancipation if it were declared. The issue finds its way into courtrooms in a variety of settings. None of them resemble Casey's situation. Her situation was one of legal guardianship, not emancipation. In other contexts, however, a "tween" may have good reason - an actual legal need - for an emancipation decree.

In 1973, for example, 20-year-old male Frederick E. Berger petitioned against the Syracuse, New York, City Clerk, to compel the Clerk to issue the young man a marriage license. *Berger v. Ardornato*, 350 N.Y.S.2d 520. The Clerk had refused, in compliance with a local law that required parental consent for males under 21 to be issued a marriage license. *Id.* Fred's parents had refused such consent. *Id.*

The New York statute was problematic, not for its setting an age requirement on marriage licenses, but because it differentiated between the genders in determining the appropriate legal age for the age requirement. A female was allowed a license at age 18 without parental consent, but, males were not allowed to marry without parental consent until they turned 21. The Court found the law to violate "the Equal Protection Clause by discriminating in a manner that is arbitrary in its effect." *Id.* at 524. The New York Supreme Court said that, although, a state may establish a minimum age for marriage, "if a state chooses to discriminate as to age based upon sex, it must meet the test raised by the Equal Protection Clause." *Id.*

Later, in 1980, New York had revised its statute to set the age requirement for obtaining a marriage license without parental consent to 18, for both males and females. *Moe v. Dinkins*, 635 F.2d 1045. Ms. Maria Moe challenged the statute. *Id.* The Court cited the *Berger* case for its discussion about the concept and impact of emancipation. In *Moe*, the Court said of *Berger* that his status as "mature and emancipated" did not exempt him from a statute regulating age: "[t]he [Berger] Court did not embrace the opportunity to impute "reasonableness" into the parental consent requirement and allow the plaintiff to marry on that ground; instead, it declared the age differential [based on gender] totally unconstitutional. *Id.* at 1049. Unlike Fred, Maria was not emancipated, and was stuck with the statute requiring her parents' consent. *Id.*

In short, although an interesting concept from a wide range of angles, emancipation of minors law had nothing to do with Casey Brodsky's situation in *Irreconcilable Differences*. Thankfully, the guardianship process would have resulted in the same happy ending.

Citations to other state emancipation laws can be found at: **https://www.law.cornell.edu/wex/table_emancipation**

SPOILER ALERT: Casey gets to live with Maria and her family, with Lucy and Albert both granted (separate) visits with Casey at Maria's house. The end of the movie shows the Brodskys eating out together, all seemingly at peace with themselves and each other, despite the brokenness of their family. This is necessary for the viewer to enjoy a satisfying ending. In the real world, however, bitterness and anger can sometimes interfere with such healthy multi-family dynamics. Mediators, lawyers, judges, guardians, social-workers, extended family members, and others involved in children's lives can help to ensure smooth transitions in cases of "broken" families.

MOVIE BRIEFS & LEGAL EXTRAS

*When Drew Berrymore was 14, she herself petitioned the court for emancipation. She had her mother's full support for her to be considered an adult. This is a true emancipation, as opposed to what was really a guardianship petition in the movie. She probably needed adult status in order to properly enter into her many acting, modeling, and real estate contracts.

*Another way in which emancipation of minors enters into the courtroom is when biological parents seek such a determination for purposes of avoiding child support. In Casey's situation, of course, money not being an issue, Maria would have been awarded substantial child support for her guardianship over Casey.

"I'm just a kid, and I don't know what I'm doing sometimes. But I think you should know better when you're all grown up. I think you should know how to act, and how to treat people. And I think if you once loved someone enough to marry them, you should at least be nice to them, even if you don't love them anymore.
...
Mother, you and dad for a long time did not recognize my rights as a human being. You both treated me like chattel. You cannot do with me as you please anymore.
We have irreconcilable differences.

-Casey Brodsky

WAR OF THE ROSES
(20TH Century Fox 1989)

Starring: Michael Douglas; Kathleen Turner; Danny DeVito

Lesson: Family Law

Plot: Some divorces are amicable. Some are (spoiler-alert!) deadly. Oliver and Barbara Rose started out hot and heavy and had some wonderful married years while they struggled to put Oliver through law school while raising two children on a budget. Once Oliver's legal career became successful, the kids were grown, the Roses tired of each other. When Barbara files for divorce, Oliver does not take it well. Mrs. Rose wants the house "she created." She is even willing to forgo alimony in exchange for the house. "No," says Mr. Rose, out of spite, or pain, or some other mix of emotions that should not guide decisions in divorced situations, but often do. He decides he wants the house too, and he plans to fight for it. Soon, both Roses are out for vengeance.

Their story is told through Mr. Rose's divorce lawyer, Gavin D'Amato (Danny DeVito). Attorney D'Amato tells their story to a potential client, stating that, when a lawyer who charges $400 per hour wants to give you some free advice, you take it. After telling the would-be divorce client the story of the Roses, his advice was for him to go home and find some shred of the love he had for his wife when they met.

It goes without saying that lawyers do not typically turn business away in this manner, but the narration provides a clever backdrop for the troubling story about the nastiness that can creep into divorces and ruin families.

Marital Property

As a starting point, the house is easily classified as marital property because they acquired the property during their marriage. This is the general rule in most states. Exceptions include, without limitation, when property acquired during a marriage was a gift or an inheritance to one spouse alone. Here, the Roses started out together with essentially nothing and built their wealth – including their real estate - during the marriage. Each was equally entitled to the marital real estate and the law requires that it be equitably divided.

Not only did they both want to own the house, the both wanted to remain living there pending their divorce. That way, Oliver could avoid the risk of Barbara laying out some sort of possession claim to the house, or selling household possessions and fixtures piecemeal, or whatever other spiteful action she may have up her sleeve. Attorney D'Amato finds a loophole in a statute allowing Mr. Rose to stay living in the house pending the divorce. In a case like the Roses, that might be a long period of time, while they sort out all of the various financial issues in their divorce case. This is unfortunate; ultimately the Roses deprived viewers of any court determination, awarding the house to either Oliver or Barbara Rose. Had it played out, the value of the house would have been a part of the equitable division of all assets analysis. Often, the parties decide it is best to sell the house and split the proceeds – walk away, start anew.

Spousal Support

Mrs. Rose offered to give up her rights to alimony, more commonly known now as spousal support. Was that a valuable offer to provide in negotiations for the house? Should Oliver have listened to Attorney D'Amato's advice?

Should he have accepted the offer, divorced Barbara and moved out of the house for good? Probably.

States vary in terms of what factors are considered when deciding if and how much alimony to award a spouse. In Barbara's case, most of the common factors weigh in favor of her receiving sizable spousal support from Mr. Rose.

Although state court judges have great discretion in awarding support, the Uniform Marriage and Divorce Act, which many state statutes follow, in whole or in part, recommends that courts consider the following factors in determining whether spousal support should be awarded and in what amount:

1. The age, physical condition, emotional state, and financial condition of the former spouses.

Here, the Roses were middle-aged, and Mrs. Rose had very little earning power as compared to Mr. Rose, with his Harvard law degree and years of legal experience. This factor weighs in Barbara's favor.

2. The length of time the recipient would need for education or training to become self-sufficient.

Although her cooking business (selling pâté to fellow housewives) is off to a good start, to have any earning potential matching that of Mr. Rose, significant investment in education and training would be needed. This factor weighs in Barbara's favor.

3. The couple's standard of living during the marriage.

Bumpy at first, the Roses ultimately enjoyed fine living standards in their huge Boston house with their fine Baccarat.

It would be extremely difficult, if not impossible, for Mrs. Rose to maintain this type of lifestyle on her own. This factor weighs in Barbara's favor.

4. The length of the marriage.

The Roses were married for approximately 18 years; their two children had fully launched. Rose was a stay-at-home Mom all of those years. Many states regard ten years as the length of time for which spousal support to the lesser-earning spouse is presumed. *See, e.g.,* 19-A M.R.S.A. §951-A(2)(A)(1). This factor weighs in Barbara's favor.

5. The ability of the payer spouse to support the recipient and still support himself or herself.

If Mr. Rose can afford $400 per hour attorneys, he should be well able to fund a sizeable support award to his long-term wife and mother of his adult children. This factor weighs in Barbara's favor.

Unif. Marriage and Divorce Act §307, 9A U.L.A. 612 (1987). Based on these factors, Mrs. Rose's offer to decline spousal support was no small concession. Had the Roses not fallen to their death when the chandelier went down, Mrs. Rose may have been able to get the house and spousal support. Oliver could keep his 1960 British-made Morgan (albeit somewhat mangled) and the fancy stemware.

MOVIE BRIEFS & LEGAL EXTRAS

*Michael Douglas has played a lawyer in several movies. He has also co-starred with Kathleen Turner and Danny DeVito in *The Jewel of Nile* and *Romancing the Stone.* Such chemistry among this trio.

*Once things got severely nasty, could a protection from abuse order have been issued against one or the other Rose, requiring one of them to vacate the property? Locking someone in a sauna until they are within an inch from dying of heat stroke might justify an order.

"A civilized divorce is a contradiction in terms."

-Gavin D'Amato

MRS. DOUBTFIRE
(20ᵗʰ Century Fox 1993)

Starring: Robin Williams; Sally Field

Lessons: Family Law

Plot: Daniel and Miranda have three children and a big house in San Francisco. Miranda wants a divorce after Daniel throws his son an over-the-top birthday party on the same day he loses his job. Miranda decides this means Daniel is a bad influence on the children and a bad father. Based solely on a snapshot of the situation, which is often the case in family hearings, the court agrees. Miranda convinces a judge that Daniel should only be allowed limited and supervised visitation with his three kids, the loves of his life. With Daniel out of the house, and Miranda's busy and serious career, she needed to hire a nanny. Enter Mrs. Doubtfire. Daniel's brother, a make-up artist, convincingly costumes Daniel into the kids' new nanny, British widow, Euphegenia Doubtfire. Hilarious movie moments occur.

Underlying the comedy, the movie gets to the heart of some of the complexities of divorce law and family dynamics post-divorce. Despite the deception and anger (two very common themes in divorces) Mrs. Doubtfire helped the children cope with the divorce and, especially, missing their Dad. Mrs. Doubtfire also helped Daniel spend time with the kids. Ultimately, Mrs. Doubtfire helped Miranda recognize that Daniel was a good father, even if he was not a good husband for her any longer. Viewers are reminded that, even after divorce, the kids will still be well, as long as the parents retain or regain the perspective and priorities that Daniel and Miranda found in the end.

Supervised Visitation

In most states, trial courts have significant discretion in deciding whether or not to impose supervision upon a non-custodial parent's right to visit his or her children and maintain a meaningful relationship with them. They are guided by the overriding "best interests of the child" standard. *Unif. Marriage and Divorce Act* §407, 9A U.L.A. 612 (1987) ("[t]he general rule implies a 'best interest of the child' standard" for visitation rights, and that "[v]isitation rights should be arranged to an extent and in a fashion which suits the child's interest rather than the interest of either the custodial or noncustodial parent."). A parent's right to visitation needs to be balanced with the other parent's concerns that the kids are in some sort of danger, such as serious abuse or neglect. Even in those cases where there is actual danger, instead of terminating a parent's visitation rights altogether, supervised visits can strike that balance. *Mullen v. Phelps,* 647 A.2d 714, 723-24 (Vt. 1994) (holding that a custodial parent's interest in protecting children from abuse by noncustodial parent could be satisfied with supervised visitation as opposed to terminating the father's parental rights). Some states have statutes on point addressing the factors a court may consider in ordering supervision.

With respect to Daniel and Miranda, were the allegations severe enough to warrant imposing supervision? Was Miranda's evidence sufficient to prove the kids would be in danger if left with their father unsupervised? There was no abuse and certainly no neglect. In the real world, Daniel likely would not have been subject to supervision. In fact, they are likely excellent candidates for 50/50 residency and shared parental rights and responsibilities, discussed below.

Shared Parental Rights and Responsibilities

The concept of shared rights and responsibilities is not the same as "joint physical custody." Joint physical custody means that the actual, physical care of the child (lodging, feeding, etc.) is shared according to a court-ordered or agreed-upon schedule between the parents divided (sometimes equally, sometimes not). Shared parental rights and responsibilities relates to communication between the parents regarding major decisions regarding their kids. This is true regardless of which parent has primary residency/custody of the children. It is about decision-making. The law takes the view that, absent extraordinary circumstances, both parents should have a say in things like their child's religion, education, medical care, and extracurricular activities. Most states define "shared parental rights and responsibilities" within their family law statutes. Maine, for example:

> Shared parental rights and responsibilities. "Shared parental rights and responsibilities" means that most or all aspects of a child's welfare remain the joint responsibility and right of both parents, so that both parents retain equal parental rights and responsibilities, and both parents confer and make joint decisions regarding the child's welfare. Matters pertaining to the child's welfare include, but are not limited to, education, religious upbringing, medical, dental and mental health care, travel arrangements, child care arrangements and residence. Parents who share parental rights and responsibilities shall keep one another informed of any major changes affecting the child's welfare and shall consult in advance to the extent practicable on decisions related to the child's welfare.

19-A M.R.S.A. §501(5).

This arrangement allows both parents to share the ability to make decisions about the child, regardless of which parent is providing the day-to-day, physical care.

In terms of "physical custody," many states start with the presumption that, unless there is evidence to the contrary, shared parenting is in the best interest of the children, and splitting physical time between parents *and* sharing in decision-making is the preferred option when the parents live close enough to each other to make shared custody practical and feasible.

In guiding a court's determination of a shared custody arrangements and the allocation of parental rights and responsibilities, generally, state statutes set forth various factors for the best arrangement in any particular case where the parents cannot seem to work it out themselves. Michigan, for example, sets forth twelve distinct factors for determining the best interests of the child:

Sec. 3. As used in this act, "best interests of the child" means the sum total of the following factors to be considered, evaluated, and determined by the court:

(a) The love, affection, and other emotional ties existing between the parties involved and the child.

(b) The capacity and disposition of the parties involved to give the child love, affection, and guidance and to continue the education and raising of the child in his or her religion or creed, if any.

(c) The capacity and disposition of the parties involved to provide the child with food, clothing, medical care or other remedial care recognized and permitted under the laws of this state in place of medical care, and other material needs.

(d) The length of time the child has lived in a stable, satisfactory environment, and the desirability of maintaining continuity.

(e) The permanence, as a family unit, of the existing or proposed custodial home or homes.

(f) The moral fitness of the parties involved.

(g) The mental and physical health of the parties involved.

(h) The home, school, and community record of the child.

(i) The reasonable preference of the child, if the court considers the child to be of sufficient age to express preference.

(j) The willingness and ability of each of the parties to facilitate and encourage a close and continuing parent-child relationship between the child and the other parent or the child and the parents. A court may not consider negatively for the purposes of this factor any reasonable action taken by a parent to protect a child or that parent from sexual assault or domestic violence by the child's other parent.

(k) Domestic violence, regardless of whether the violence was directed against or witnessed by the child.

(l) Any other factor considered by the court to be relevant to a particular child custody dispute.

M.C.L.A. 722.23. Most other states use similar factors (I picked Michigan because it is one of the most inclusive of the common considerations for determining what living arrangement is in the best interest of the children.)

In Daniel and Miranda's case, several factors support shared custody, or equally share rights and responsibilities and a 50/50 schedule with the kids. Both parents clearly have the capacity to give love, affection, guidance, and to provide basic needs to the three kids. They live in close proximity to one another, presumably the same school district. Both parents enjoy moral and physical fitness. Domestic violence is not a factor. The children are old enough and seemingly intelligent enough to adapt to their parents sharing time with them, and they can afford to hire help.

An ideal arrangement might even be if the kids stayed in the big house 24/7 while the two parents travelled back and forth. They could even share time at Daniel's new apartment. This arrangement is not uncommon. The concept of the children staying in the marital home with the parents sharing time there with them, is known as "bird nesting." For more information about nesting pros and cons, see:

https://www.psychologytoday.com/us/blog/co-parenting-after-divorce/201307/birds-nest-co-parenting-arrangements

LEGAL BRIEFS AND MOVIE EXTRAS

*Early on in the movie, when the pair initially splits, both bash each other in front of the children. As a former family law attorney and mediator, this is the worst thing one can do and is in the least interest of the children.

"Dear, I always say, a flawed husband is better than none at all."

-Mrs. Doubtfire

LOSING ISAIAH
(Paramount Pictures 1995)

Starring: Jessica Lange; Halle Barry; Samuel L. Jackson

Lesson: Family Law

Plot: Young Khaila Richards (Halle Barry) was a crack addict with an infant son. Desperate for her next fix, she leaves her baby in an ally full of trash while she goes on a drug buy. She had planned to come back and get her child, but, she passes out on drugs and leaves him there overnight. He was thankfully rescued, and Khaila assumed he had died. One of the dedicated social workers at the hospital he is taken to, Margaret Lewin (Jessica Lange), decides to adopt the child, and happily raises him until he was four, Khaila being none the wiser.

After "losing Isaiah," Khaila hits rock bottom. She is sent to rehabilitation after being arrested on shoplifting charges. Khaila takes her rehab seriously, and when she is released, she lands a job as a housekeeper and childcare provider and focuses on staying sober. Three years pass, and Khaila confides in a caseworker that she abandoned Isaiah. Confident and clean, Khaila enlists the help of a lawyer (Samuel L. Jackson) and fights to regain custody of the child. In a hotly contested courtroom battle, things get ugly. Racial tensions are at the forefront of this movie, as well as the dynamics between birth parents and non-parents who serve as custodial caregivers. The movie raises the question of just how important it is to a child to be brought up by his or her natural birth parents, regardless of their history. Although we are left with a "feel-good" ending, there are some difficult, emotional scenes throughout.

Non-Parent Custody

When a person other than a biological parent wishes to obtain custody of a minor, he or she can petition the court for either a guardianship or non-parent custody. A petitioner must show either:

1. that they are for all intents and purposes the child's guardian, financially, physiologically, etc., or

2. That the biological parents are deemed unfit and that it is in the best interest of the child to have the petitioner appointed the custodial non-parent.

Courts are commonly asked to consider whether a parent is unfit. Grounds for such a finding include abuse, neglect, abandonment, severe or long-term mental illness or substance abuse, inability to provide essential care and affection, or any other factor that suggests a parent should not be raising a child.

State laws differ but, again, all are grounded in the best interests of the child standard. If appropriate, "unfit" legal parents can consent to a petition for custody of their child by a non-parent, either permanently or on a temporary basis. Without the consent, a non-parent attempting to gain custody of someone else's child has a high burden of proof. One must overcome a legal presumption that it is in the child's best interest to be with his natural parent. The evidentiary standard to rebut this presumption is "clear and convincing evidence" of the following:

-awarding custody to a legal parent is not in the child's best interests.

-The petitioner stands in loco parentis to the child.

-That it would be detrimental to have the child remain or be placed in the custody of the child's living legal parents.

-A court of jurisdiction has not entered or approved an order concerning the child's custody within one year before the person filed the petition unless there is a reason to believe the child's present environment may seriously endanger the child's physical, mental, moral or emotional health.

Or if one of the following applies:

-That one of the legal parents is deceased.

-The child's legal parents are not married to each other at the time the petition is filed.

-There is a pending proceeding for dissolution of marriage or legal separation of the legal parents at the time the petition is filed.

See:
https://www.lawfirms.com/resources/child-custody/custody-during-divorce/who-gets-custody.htm

In this case, social worker Lewin relies on the first set of factors, particularly, that she stands in locis as the parental guardian, and that it would be in Isaiah's best interest to continue living with her because the biological mother is unfit such that it would be detrimental to have her take custody of her son. The judge disagrees, overturns the adoption that had already legally occurred, and returns Isaiah to Khaila. The transition does not go smoothly. Khaila enlists Margaret's help in returning peace to Isaiah. At the end, it is clear both women will be a part of Isaiah's life, which is certainly in his best interest.

LEGAL BRIEFS AND MOVIE EXTRAS

*The process and factors described above mirror the standard for involuntary termination of parental rights, generally, whether by a petition of a guardian or by state intervention These factors are discussed below in the discussion of *I Am Sam*.

*Both the film and the novel highlight racial issues that are beyond the scope of this chapter or this book. When viewing this film from 1995, pay particular attention to the questions the judge asked the Lewins in connection with their fight to avoid losing Isaiah. "Do you read him bedtime stories featuring people that look like him?" Are such questions relevant? Are they warranted? Should any weight be given to their answers and, if so, how much? And why?

"Any animal can give birth. That doesn't make it a mother."

-Margaret Lewin

LIAR LIAR
(Universal Pictures 1997)

Starring: Jim Carrey; Maura Tierney

Lessons: Evidence; Contracts; Ethics

Plot: A somewhat less than ethical trial attorney played by Jim Carrey ("Fletcher Reede") loses his keen ability to lie – for just one day – due to the birthday wish of his five-year-old son. The problem for Fletcher Reede is that, the one day he cannot lie, he is scheduled to represent an important client of the firm, Mrs. Cole, in her divorce proceedings. Mr. Cole, a millionaire, has brought a bench (non-jury) proceeding to enforce a prenuptial agreement, under which Mrs. Cole gets nothing if she commits adultery. The case is worth "a truckload of money" to Fletcher's firm and he stands to make partner if he wins. Because Mrs. Cole had in fact committed adultery, he had relied extra heavily on his lying skills that day. Some silly courtroom scenes ensue. Aside from the obvious improprieties, even absurdities, there are some more subtle problems during Jim Carrey's trial scenes that should raise question to the trained legal eye.

Maura Tierney provides excellent support to Jim Carrey's role, playing Fletcher's ex-wife. The film provides a truckload of laughs and a handful of real legal issues. Also, its underlying theme of the father/son relationship is heartwarming, and we are left with a sufficiently feel-good ending.

EVIDENCE
Offers of Compromise

In Scene 5, when the parties first appear in court, the judge asks whether there is any chance of settlement. Mr. Cole's attorney states: "I don't think so, Your Honor, my client has already offered Mrs. Cole $2,000,000." Is there anything wrong with this revelation? Federal Rule of Evidence 408 (Compromise and Offers of Compromise) provides:

Evidence of ...compromising or attempting to comprise a claim which was disputed as to either validity or amount, is not admissible to prove liability for or invalidity of the claim or its amount. Evidence of conduct or statements made in compromise negotiations is likewise not admissible.

The public policy behind settlement negotiations being inadmissible is to encourage good faith settlements. If offers of compromise could be used against parties, people would be reluctant to make any settlement offers, fearing that knowledge of prior offers may prejudice the factfinder's assessment of liability. *Fahrbach v. Diamond Shamrock, Inc.*, 928 P.2d 269, 274 (1996); *Martin v. Johns,* 78 So.2d 398, 399 (Fla. 1955). A juror might assume, for instance, that because a party was willing to pay money to resolve the dispute out of court, he or she must have something to hide. In this case, there is no jury. The prejudicial impact is probably low with this judge; after all, he asked about settlement and expected an answer before scheduling the trial for later that day. Mr. Cole's attorney was probably not out of line under these circumstances. Had it been a jury trial, however, the risk of prejudice is heightened. A judge may even instruct the jury to disregard the attorney's comment about a prior settlement offer. *See, e.g., Poythress v Poythress*, 102 S.E.2d 607, 610 (Ga. 1958) (ruling that a trial judge properly protected the interests of the parties by instructing the jury to disregard references to settlement discussions).

Leading Questions

In Scene 13, Fletcher Reede is unable to ask his client's lover a specific question because he knows the answer would be a lie. He attempts: "Would you describe your relationship with Mrs. Cole as strictly platonic?" Aside from the obvious ethical violation of offering evidence known to be false, does the movie properly depict how Reede's examination of Mrs. Cole's lover would play out? *See* FED. R. OF EVID. 611(c) ("Leading questions should not be used during direct examination except as may be necessary to develop the witness's testimony."). Should Mr. Cole's attorney have objected to this question as leading?

A leading question is one that suggests the desired answer. Leading questions are "generally disallowed during direct examination because such questions may elicit the desired response irrespective of actual memory." *State v. Merced*, 933 A.2d 172, 175 (R.I. 2007) (internal quotations and citations omitted). Here, Reede is questioning his own witness, and this is a direct examination. He asks substantive questions that go directly to the merits of the case; he is not just developing the witness's testimony. Attorney Reede was leading the witness with a question that suggested the desired answer: that he and Mrs. Cole had a platonic relationship. There are some instances in which an attorney is permitted to lead a witness toward a desired answer. *See State v. Cox*, 472 S.E.2d 760, 762 (N.C. 1996) ("Leading questions are permissible when the witness has difficulty understanding questions because of immaturity, age, infirmity, or ignorance."). Attorney Reede's questioning is not one of these permissible instances, however. There is no objection, of course, because only the leading question could have brought out the funny conflict in the movie: because of his sweet son's birthday wish, Reede cannot ask a question if he knows the answer is a lie.

Witness Impeachment

Later in Scene 13, when Reede realizes his client lied about her age to get married, he begins to ask her rude and embarrassing questions. His opponent objects, stating that he is badgering the witness. The judge responds: "it's his witness!" Is the fact that

Mrs. Cole was Fletcher's own witness relevant? Federal Rule of Evidence 611(a), Control by Court, requires the court to "exercise reasonable control over the mode and order of interrogating witnesses ... so as to ... protect witnesses from harassment or undue embarrassment." Should the judge have exercised control over Reede's interrogation? Regardless of whether or not it was appropriate for Reede to badger his own witness, is it at least permissible that he impeach her? *See* FED. R. EVID. 607 (Who May Impeach).

? Exam Tip

When an evidence exam presents a highly offensive or outrageous piece of trial evidence, such as the sexually explicit audio tape in Scene 11, keep Rule 403 in mind and do not forget to discuss a balance between prejudicial effect and probative value. Typically, Rule 403 should be discussed only after analyzing any other possible grounds for inadmissibility or exclusion that may apply to the given fact pattern. For instance, with respect to the audio recording of Mrs. Cole's marital affair, authentication could be an issue.

CONTRACTS
Contractual Capacity/Minors

Mrs. Cole lacked contractual capacity because she was a minor, so, as Fletcher Reede points out, the prenuptial contract was void. But was it? Void means the contract is invalid automatically, without action by the courts or even the parties to the contract. "A void contract is ... 'incapable of confirmation or ratification.'" *Nature's 10 Jewelers v. Gunderson,* 2002 SD 80, ¶ 12, 648 N.W.2d 804, 807, *quoting* Black's Law Dictionary 1573 (6th ed. 1990). An example of a contract that is void automatically upon being entered into is a contract for a criminal act. Unlike void contracts, voidable contracts, such as those in which one party lacks contractual capacity, require action to be become void. The party who lacked capacity has the right to disaffirm the contract, or seek court declaration that the contract should be voided. Without such action, the contract is enforceable.

A minor lacks contractual capacity. Thus, when a minor enters into a contract, the contract is not *void*. It is *voidable*. *See* RESTATEMENT (SECOND) OF CONTRACT, §14 (providing that, "[u]nless a statute provides otherwise, a natural person has the capacity to incur only voidable contractual duties until the beginning of the day before the person's eighteenth birthday.") This means that the minor may reaffirm or ratify the contract upon reaching majority age by either performing or expressly approving the contract or by letting a reasonable period of time lapse, after turning eighteen, without disaffirming. *MacGreal v. Taylor*, 167 U.S. 688, 693-94 (1897). Or, the minor can void or disaffirm the contract by words or conduct inconsistent with the validity of the contract, or by expressly showing an intention to cancel the agreement. A minor must act to void a contract while he is still a minor or within a reasonable period of time after reaching majority. *Id.* at 698. Otherwise, the contract is deemed ratified. With respect to the Coles' prenuptial agreement, the lack of contractual capacity issue first arose that day in court. She never voided that contract while it was still voidable. She never showed any sign of disaffirming the contract within a reasonable period of time after reaching majority age. She therefore ratified, or affirmed, the contract by being aware of the prenuptial agreement and allowing it to exist for years after she reached majority age. *See Fletcher v. Marshall*, 632 N.E.2d 1105, 1107 (Ill. App. 1994) (holding that a minor ratifies a contract by taking distinct and decisive action clearly showing an intent to abide by the contract after reaching majority age).

Could you make any straight-faced arguments that there was no ratification? Does it matter that Mrs. Cole lied about her age? Does it matter whether age was even discussed prior to signing the prenuptial agreement? *See MacGreal v. Taylor*, 167 U.S. 688, 694 (1987) (finding a minor's contract voidable even though age was not discussed at the signing of the contract). In fairness to the adult party to the contract, who may not have known the other party was a minor, most courts require that the minor disaffirming a contract pay for any value the minor retains, or reimburse the non-minor party for expenses or incidental damages suffered. As the *MacGreal* Court stated: "courts will do justice to the adult if it can be done without disregarding or impairing the principle that allows an infant, upon arriving at majority, to disaffirm his contracts made during infancy." *Id.* at 700.

The distinction between void versus voidable also comes up in situations where minors enter into marriages – as Mrs. Cole did. In most states, the marriage is not void; it is voidable. If, shortly after reaching majority, the minor does not bring an action to have the marriage declared invalid, the marriage is considered valid, as Mrs. Cole's apparently was in the movie. *See, e.g., Brown v. Imboden*, 771 S.W.2d 312, 313 (Ark. 1989) ("equity can ... require that parties be estopped from denying the validity of a marriage"). So, the movie dealt with the void/voidable distinction correctly as to marriage but incorrectly as to the prenuptial agreement.

? Exam Tips

When an exam fact pattern presents a contract that seems to be void, voidable, or otherwise unenforceable (e.g., a lack of capacity, a failure of consideration, or a statute of frauds problem), do not disregard equitable principles that may nevertheless provide for relief. Keep these key terms in mind: promissory estoppel, laches, quantum meruit/quasi-contract, unjust enrichment, partial performance, etc., particularly when presented with a situation in which someone has relied to his or her detriment on somebody else's promise.

ETHICS

How many ethical violations can you find by how many attorneys in *Liar Liar*? Keep the following in mind:

ABA Model Rule 1.5 (d)(1) (Fees) ("A lawyer shall not enter into an arrangement for, charge, or collect ... any fee in a domestic relations matter, the payment or amount of which is contingent upon the securing of a divorce or upon the amount of alimony or support, or property settlement in lieu thereof."). When Fletcher is speaking with his supervisor about the Cole case, it seems apparent that the partner is banking on a win in order for the truckload of money to be delivered from Mr. Cole. Any such arrangement would be a contingent fee arrangement, which is not allowed in divorce cases.

ABA Model Rule 3.3(a)(3) (Candor to the Tribunal) ("A lawyer shall not knowingly ... offer evidence that the lawyer knows to be false."). Obviously, this is the whole point of the film: Fletcher's plan was to introduce false evidence, but the birthday wish would not allow that to happen.

ABA Model Rule 3.4(b) (Fairness to Opposing Party and Counsel) ("A lawyer shall not ... falsify evidence, [or] counsel or assist a witness to testify falsely."). See above.

ABA Model Rule 3.4(c) (Fairness to Opposing Party and Counsel) ("A lawyer shall not ... knowingly disobey an obligation under the rules of the tribunal."). "One more word and I'll hold you in contempt." (Judge). "I hold myself in contempt!" (Fletcher Reede).

ABA Model Rule 3.5(d) (Impartiality and Decorum of the Tribunal) ("A lawyer shall not ... engage in conduct intended to disrupt a tribunal."). Comes to mind the scene in the bathroom where he kicks his own ass in an effort to obtain a continuance.

ABA Model Rule 4.1(a) (Truthfulness in Statements to Others) ("In the course of representing a client a lawyer shall not knowingly ... make a false statement of material fact or law to a third person."). See above.

ABA Model Rule 5.1 (Responsibilities of a Partner or Supervisory Lawyer) ("A partner in a law firm, and a lawyer who individually or together with other lawyers possesses comparable managerial authority in a law firm, shall make reasonable efforts to ensure that the firm has in effect measures giving reasonable assurance that all lawyers in the firm conform to the Rules of Professional Conduct."). *See also,* ABA Model Rule 5.2 (Responsibilities of a Subordinate Lawyer) ("A lawyer is bound by the Rules of Professional Conduct notwithstanding that the lawyer acted at the direction of another person [but] does not violate the Rules of Professional Conduct if that lawyer acts in accordance with a supervisory lawyer's reasonable resolution of an arguable question of professional duty."). Here, Fletcher's partners were the very people encouraging him to be Liar Liar in order to win.

ABA Model Rule 8.3(a) (Reporting Professional Misconduct) (a/k/a the "Rat Rule") ("A lawyer who knows that another lawyer has committed a violation of the Rules of Professional Conduct that raises a substantial question as to that lawyer's honesty, trustworthiness or fitness as a lawyer in other respects, shall inform the appropriate professional authority."). The lawyer who was first offered the Cole trial, who refused it because he did not want to lie, may have made a report. Or not.

ABA Model Rule 8.4 (Misconduct) ("It is professional misconduct for a lawyer to ... violate or attempt to violate the Rules of Professional Conduct, knowingly assist or induce another to do so, or do so through the acts of another; [or] commit a criminal act that reflects adversely on the lawyer's honesty, trustworthiness or fitness as a lawyer in other respects; [or] engage in conduct involving dishonesty, fraud, deceit or misrepresentation."). See above.

? Exam Tips

Keep in mind that one action can give rise to multiple ethical rule violations, due to the overlap among the rules. For instance, any rule violation constitutes attorney misconduct, a violation of ABA Model Rule 8.4 (Misconduct). When another attorney is involved, ABA Model Rule 8.3 (Reporting Professional Misconduct) may be invoked, as well as rules regarding an attorney's duty to supervise subordinates.

LEGAL BRIEFS & MOVIE EXTRAS

*When Mrs. Cole's lover, Kenneth Falk, was called to the witness stand, he was already in the courtroom. In real life, Mr. Falk would have been sequestered so that he would not have heard the witnesses before him. (This occurs in *Jagged Edge* too). Witness sequestration is the norm, especially in cases like the Cole case, where witness corroboration could significantly impact the result.

*When Fletcher notices that his car was scratched while being towed, he complains to the towing agent, who asked Fletcher, sarcastically, what he is going to do about it. Fletcher has to admit that he will do nothing. He explains, and he mentions small claims court: "if I take it to small claims court, it will just drain 8 hours out of my life and you probably won't show up and even if I got the judgment you'd just stiff me anyway!" This is a common frustration when it comes to small claims. Small claims courts, however, can be great forums for resolving disputes where the dollar amount in controversy is not enough to warrant hiring an attorney. I often refer cold callers to my law firm to small claims court for this very reason. The dollar limits for small claims courts range from $1,500 to $10,000. Research your state's small claims court limits and procedures.

NIGHT FALLS ON MANHATTAN
(Paramount Pictures 1997)

Starring: Andy Garcia; Richard Dreyfuss; also featuring the star of the former HBO hit series *Soprano's*, James Gandolfini.

Lesson: Criminal Law

Plot: Sean Casey (Andy Garcia) is a young police officer who goes to law school and somehow manages to come out with an idealistic sense of justice. He becomes a New York Assistant District Attorney and kicks his career off to a great start when he is asked to prosecute drug dealer Jordan Washington. Washington is charged with murdering two cops and injuring a third cop - the third being Sean's father. Richard Dreyfuss plays Sam Vigoda, Jordan Washington's hotshot defense attorney. Casey gets his conviction and the trial is over fairly early in the film. But the law student still gets a good glimpse of the underside of criminal law. The publicity from the trial is a boon to Sean's career. The problem, however, is that Attorney Vigoda's defense strategy involved making accusations of police corruption implicating Sean's father. Sean begins to question his sense of justice and his career. The remainder of the film explores these conflicts.

It seems every class entering law school has at least one police officer. I graduated with two police officers and one county sheriff. I felt I had to include *Night Falls on Manhattan* largely for this reason. It is much more of a "cop opera" than a legal drama, but it does present some good trial scenes (Scenes 13-19). If you are not a huge fan of cop dramas, you could simply watch the court scenes.

This movie is directed by Sidney Lumet, who also brilliantly directed *12 Angry Men, The Verdict, Find Me Guilty,* and *Guilty as Sin*, among many other blockbuster hits.

CRIMINAL LAW
Opening Statements

 The trial scenes are from Scene 13 to Scene 19, beginning with the opening statements. The opening statements would never be that short in most criminal trials, especially in high profile cases where the defendant is a drug dealer and the victim is a police officer. (Granted, Vinny's opening statement in *My Cousin Vinny* is probably the shortest of any murder trial in history: "everything that guy just said is bullshit. Thank you."). Sometimes in jury waived trials, opening statements might be very short or even omitted altogether. Often, in these cases, the attorneys have submitted trial briefs outlining how the evidence will show they are entitled to judgment and an opening statement is simply a waste of judicial time (assuming the judge reads the briefs). But, given the nature of this jury trial and the interests at stake, the opening statements would be longer and less exciting.

The prosecutor's brevity allows Richard Dreyfuss's character to focus his opening statement on all of the interesting details the prosecution omitted (police corruption and facts supporting self-defense). Alerting jurors to the fact that the prosecution is dubious from the outset can be an effective way to establish reasonable doubt. But does Dreyfuss argue or otherwise cross the line during his opening statement? *See United States v. Young*, 470 U.S. 1, 8-9 (1985) (addressing inappropriate personal interjections in opening statements). *See also State v. Procopio*, 88 F.3d 21, 31 (1st Cir. 1996) (holding that an attorney may not play upon a jury's emotional reaction to crimes other than the specific one being charged).

Cross-Examination

Pay attention to Richard Dreyfuss's cross-examination, noting improprieties. For instance, he screams at a police officer on the stand: "finally someone gives me a straight answer!" Should such courtroom conduct be allowed? For guidance, see both the Federal Rules of Evidence (Rule 611(a)) and the Federal Rules of Civil Procedure (Rule 26(c)). An outrageous moment during cross-examination is when a witness for the defense has to be dragged out of the courtroom by a half dozen courtroom officials.

Miraculously, there is only one objection to analyze, in the final courtroom scene (Scene 19), the overruling of which allows a line of questioning on cop corruption, which sets up some comical testimony from the drug ring about their "biz" dealings and "operations" with crooked cops. The jury's "guilty" verdict very soon followed.

LEGAL BRIEFS & MOVIE EXTRAS

*I am told that if you live in New York City, you may appreciate this movie a little more than I did, particularly if you are or were a New York City police officer!

*This movie is loosely based on the real case of Larry Davis, a drug dealer who shot three police officers in an attempt to escape, and then accused the police force of accepting bribes. Source: Edward Levine, N.Y. TIMES, January 21, 1994, *The Laureate of Police Corruption*, available at: http://www.nytimes.com/1997/06/08/nyregion/the-laureate-of-police-corruption.html?_r=0 (last visited October 27, 2020).

"In a city of nine million people is there room for one honest man?"

A CIVIL ACTION
(Buena Vista Pictures 1998)

Starring: John Travolta; William Macy; Robert Duvall; Tony Shalhoub

Lessons: Civil Procedure; Ethics

Plot: The civil action that is the subject of this movie is a class action environmental lawsuit. Played by John Travolta, Jan Schlichtmann is a personal injury lawyer representing small town, working class families living in a low-income neighborhood in the Town of Woburn, Massachusetts. The Woburn neighborhood borders factories owned by corporate giants W.R. Grace and Beatrice Foods. Many of the local residents became ill, including several children who died of cancer. Jan Schlichtmann causes himself and his law firm partners financial and emotional downfall trying to prove that the two deep-pocket corporate defendants caused his clients' illnesses by dumping pollutants into their local water source.

CIVIL PROCEDURE
Rule 11

Very soon after Schlichtmann files his complaint, Cheeseman, the less experienced defense lawyer, who represents the smaller of the two defendant corporations, suggests requesting dismissal and Rule 11 sanctions. Rule 11(b) provides that an attorney, in signing a complaint, represents to the court that, "to the best of the person's knowledge, information, and belief, formed after an inquiry reasonable under the circumstance," the claims are warranted by existing law or by the non-frivolous argument for new law. *See Business Guides, Inc. v. Chromatic Communications Enters., Inc.,* 498 U.S. 533, 551 (1991) (holding that Rule 11 applies to a represented party who signs a pleading, motion, or other papers, as well as to attorneys). Both

Schlichtmann and the judge admit they "had to look it up." The judge brushes it off, but Rule 11 does help to protect against frivolous cases and may impose serious penalties on attorneys who fail to make a "reasonable inquiry." *See Atkins v. Fischer,* 232 F.R.D. 116, 126 (D.D.C. 2005) ("the court has an arsenal of options at its disposal" as possible sanctions pursuant to Rule 11). *See also,* ABA Model Rule 3.1 (Meritorious Claims and Contentions) ("A lawyer shall not bring or defend a proceeding, or assert or controvert an issue therein, unless there is a basis in law and fact for doing so that is not frivolous.").

Do you agree with the judge's decision? What steps did Schlichtmann take in making his reasonable inquiry? After all, he soiled his $400 shoes when he himself observed employees of the large corporate defendants operating dump trucks along a waterway near his prospective clients' homes. He found deep pockets, but did he pass Rule 11? What evidence does he need to support his clients' cause of action? Did he have enough, or was further inquiry required?

Did Cheeseman do anything wrong in bringing the Rule 11 motion to dismiss? His motion is subject to Rule 11 as well as ethical rules. Did he make a reasonable inquiry to ensure his motion was sufficiently grounded? By filing a Rule 11 motion, did Cheeseman set a noncollegial tone for the case? Worse, might Cheeseman's motion have left a lasting sense of annoyance on the part of the judge? *See* American College of Trial Lawyers Code of Pretrial and Pretrial Conduct, Rule 6(a) (Motion Practice) ("before setting a motion for hearing, a lawyer should make a reasonable effort to resolve the issue without involving the court."). Although this Code is not binding, there are plenty of judges who support this principle quite strongly. Cheeseman got his defense off to a bad start by bringing the motion to dismiss. The denial of the motion may even have served to validate the plaintiffs' claims.

For Jan Schlichtmann, this early victory sparked the sense of pride that proved disastrous for him later in the case.

Rule 42(b)

Jerome Facher (Robert Duvall), the older and more experienced lawyer, is uninterested in joining co-defendant's Rule 11 motion, suggesting they hit "him where it really hurts." He ultimately does. His weapon: civil procedure. Facher foreshadows his procedural plans when he tells Jan, following a deposition of some of the plaintiffs, that the plaintiffs can never testify to a jury. Jan responds: "well, I don't see how you can stop them." Facher simply tells Jan: "of course you don't." What is Jan missing here?

Rule 42(b) of the Federal Rules of Civil Procedure and most state rules allow for separate trials when the court, "in the furtherance of convenience or to avoid prejudice, or when separate trials will be conducive to expedition and economy, may order a separate claim of any claim, cross-claim, counterclaim, third-party claim, *or of any separate issue.*" The testimony of those injured is not relevant to the issue of liability; it is relevant only to the separate issue of damages. The plaintiffs would only have to rehash their sad stories in court testimony if the first trial finds liability. The defendants feared, as well they should, that a jury would be influenced by the severity of the injuries and would want to hold *somebody* responsible - why not the deep-pocket defendant companies? In fact, Schlichtmann was *banking* on his clients' being able to win over a jury's sympathies. He figured, after hearing about the illnesses and deaths of children, the jurors would want to find the big bad corporations liable. His plan backfired. The jury would only hear of the illnesses after sitting through days of testimony about water contamination, full of boring statistics and scientific data.

The defense's techniques teach the art of thinking procedurally and utilizing the rules of civil procedure to your client's benefit at every stage of litigation.

? Exam Tips

Most of your law school classes will focus on reading appellate cases and analyzing the black letter law that they created. In a course about civil procedure, however, do not underestimate how important it is to simply read the federal and/or the state rules that you will be required to buy. This will allow you to see the big procedural picture as you learn the cases in your Civil Procedure textbook. Also, be sure you know where your state's civil rules of procedure differ from the Federal Rules of Civil Procedure. An essay question on your state bar exam may test you on these distinctions.

ETHICS

As Jan's monologue at the beginning of the film points out, a lawyer's trial-hungry pride can get in the way of reaching a fair settlement for his clients. That's what happened to Jan. When Jan and Attorney Facher are in the hallway waiting for the jury to decide the liability issue against the defendants, Attorney Facher offers Jan $20,000,000. Jan immediately turns down the settlement offer. Aside from bad judgment, is there anything wrong with Jan's declining this settlement so quickly? *See* ABA Model Rule 1.2(a) (Scope of Representation and Allocation of Authority between Client and Lawyer) ("A lawyer shall abide by a client's decision whether to settle a matter."). *See also,* Comment 2 to ABA Model Rule 1.4 (Communication) ("[A] lawyer who receives from opposing counsel an offer of settlement in a civil controversy ... must promptly inform the client of its substance unless the client has previously indicated that the proposal will be acceptable or unacceptable or has authorized the lawyer to accept or reject the offer."). So, unless

Jan knew all of his clients would think $20,000,000 was too low, or they all had previously authorized Jan to reject any offer that did not meet a threshold amount, Jan made an ethical violation in addition to a stupid mistake.

The duties of an attorney with respect to communicating settlement offers to clients become more complicated where, as here, the lawyer represents a number of clients in the same or similar matter. Each client must consent to the settlement "after being advised of the existence and nature of all the claims involved in the proposed settlement, of the total amount of the settlement, and of the participation of each person in the settlement." American Bar Association Model Code of Professional Responsibility 5-106. Jan Schlichtmann's duty of properly communicating this settlement offer required that he engage in complex conversations with his large group of clients. Thus, ethically, there is no way Attorney Facher could have resolved the claims against his client through a last-minute hallway run-in with opposing counsel.

LEGAL BRIEFS & MOVIE EXTRAS

A Civil Action is based on Jonathan Harr's true-story novel of the same name. Several civil procedure professors have utilized Mr. Harr's book in their courses.

*The movie ends with Jan Schlichtmann a broken, bankrupt man, having foolishly rejected a $20,000,000 settlement offer from a deep-pocket defendant that was ultimately found not to be liable. But Attorney Schlichtmann did bounce back and still practices law in Beverly, Massachusetts. This story shows the ups and downs of being a trial attorney. The high points can be glorifying but the low points can be gut-wrenching. Sound a bit like law school?

"Pride has lost more cases than lousy evidence, idiot witnesses and a hanging judge all put together. There is absolutely no place in a courtroom for pride."

-Jerome Facher

MISS SLOANE
(FilmNation Entertainment 1999)

Starring: Jessica Chastain; Sam Waterston

Lesson: Constitutional Law

Plot: Elizabeth Sloane (Jessica Chastain), a high-powered lobbyist, works for a firm hired by gun manufacturers to lobby Congress in opposing a bill that would expand background checks prior to purchasing firearms. Governed by her own ego as opposed to any allegiance to a certain political view, she decides to root for the other side after her boss (Sam Waterston) rustles her feathers. She starts her own lobbying firm and leads the efforts in support of the bill. A woman with serious character flaws, this leads to a world of trouble for Elizabeth. They do show her being released from prison at the end of the film though.

The story is told in back flash. We see that Elizabeth is testifying before a Senate subcommittee, setting the scene for two years earlier, and how she got there. I do not have much more to say about the movie itself; I did not like the characters and thought the message about lobbying, generally, was extremely negative. Some lobbyists do great work.

At the heart of the debate over the bill is of course the Second Amendment. The right to bear arms.

Second Amendment: Right to Bear Arms

The Second Amendment provides simply for the right to bear arms. Like all fundamental rights, they are unalienable, but they are not without certain limits. When the Second Amendment was written, our forefathers could not have foreseen the technology that would result in militia style firearms becoming commonly held self-defense weapons. Mass shootings across the nation have occurred when these guns find themselves in the wrong hands. The National Rifle Association has one of the strongest lobbies in the nation, and gun reform laws have been faced with heavy challenge. As a result, the Supreme Court has had to grapple with balancing the Second Amendment rights with the need to protect citizens from the dangers of unregulated or under-regulated access.

The Supreme Court has been rather shy in terms of granting cert. in gun cases over the last decade or so. In 2008, however, the Supreme Court struck down provisions of the Firearms Control Regulations Act of 1975 as unconstitutional. The Court determined that handguns are "arms" for the purposes of the Second Amendment, and found that the portion of the Regulations Act that required all firearms including rifles and shotguns to be kept "unloaded and disassembled or bound by a trigger lock." *District of Columbia v. Heller,* 554 U.S. 570 (2008). Writing for the majority, Justice Scalia was worried that allowing the regulation would render the Second Amendment extinct. *Id.* at 636.

The Court also stated that the right to bear arms is not unlimited and that guns and gun ownership would continue to be regulated. The *Heller* case was the first Supreme Court case to decide whether the Second Amendment protects an individual right to keep and bear arms for self-defense, or if the right was intended for state militias.

In June 2020, the Supreme Court declined to hear 10 gun-related cases next term. One such case involved a challenge to a Maryland law requiring that gun permit applications state a "good and substantial reason" to carry outside the home. The challengers (the Maryland State Rifle and Pistol Association) lost and tried to appeal. The law remains in place in light of the Supreme Court's denial of the appeal. See https://wamu.org/story/20/06/15/scotus-2a-denied-gun-rights-cases/

In August 2020, however, the Ninth Circuit struck down a California law barring citizens from owning "large capacity magazines" that can contain more than ten rounds of ammunition. *Duncan v. Becerra,* ___ 3 F.3d ____ (2020 WL 4730668; federal citation not yet available). California citizens and residents brought action to challenge the law, arguing that the ban resulted in too broad of a burden on the right to self-defense. *Id.* at *2. The Ninth Circuit agreed. *Id.* In a three-judge panel decision, the court ruled that "[e]ven well-intentioned laws must pass constitutional muster" and that the magazine ban "strikes at the core of the Second Amendment" and is therefore unconstitutional. *Id.* at *2. After all, the court reasoned, this type of ammunition comes standard in Glocks and Berettas, and they are some of the most popular handguns. *Id.* at *9. It is not yet clear whether the California Attorney General will ask for a full court review or appeal the decision, or if the Supreme Court will grant cert.

LEGAL BRIEFS & MOVIE EXTRAS

*The Fifth Amendment was also invoked in this movie, actually several times, by Miss Sloane, when questioned about ethics violations surrounding her arranging a trip for a senator to Indonesia to research the feasibility of a tariff on palm oil.

*If you want to see a documentary regarding the balance between Second Amendment rights and protecting against gun violence, albeit with a highly liberal slant, see *Bowling for Columbine* (2002), in which filmmaker Michael Moore explores gun violence and blames past administrations for its prevalence. I could not get through the first few minutes. Too violent.

THE HURRICANE
(Universal Pictures 1999)

Starring: Denzel Washington as "The Hurricane"

Lesson: Criminal Law/Procedure (Constitutional Law)

Plot: Starring Denzel Washington, this is the story of "The Hurricane." Rubin "Hurricane" Carter was a talented young boxer with a promising career, until he was convicted of the infamous Lafayette Grill murders of 1966. Based on true events, this movie traces Hurricane's convictions and his 20-year fight for freedom. He wrote his memoirs from his cell. His autobiography may have been the impetus that finally freed him from prison. A young boy and some social activists happened to come across Hurricane's book. They became convinced that he was innocent – a victim of racial discrimination and wrongful prosecution. They crusaded to reverse his convictions. Watch how Hurricane makes his way through the justice system, and consider these controversial questions: does Hurricane's story have a happy ending? Was there a justice system failure? If so, was there redemption and vindication? Or can a justice system failure be remedied if one wrongfully loses 20 years of his life? Would things have turned out differently for Hurricane had he not enjoyed some boxing fame? Even more controversial is the fact that some feel Hurricane was guilty of the murders, and that the justice system failure was his ultimate release from prison. What do you think? To form a solid opinion about The Hurricane, I encourage readers to go beyond Hollywood's rendition of the story.

CRIMINAL LAW/PROCEDURE
Criminal Appeals (Constitutional Law)

This movie, as well as the real life story, highlights a complete utilization of the appellate process in criminal proceedings. At least five appeals were filed in Hurricane's 20-year fight. Hurricane was convicted of murder twice - by two different New Jersey juries. He appealed both convictions on the ground that he did not receive a fair trial by an impartial jury, in violation of the Sixth Amendment. The first conviction was from an all-white jury. He was granted a new trial on appeal. At the second trial, only two black people sat on the jury, which again convicted Hurricane. That conviction was affirmed on appeal. Hurricane's last hope was to appeal in federal district court, by writ of habeas corpus, claiming unlawful detention based on a deprivation of the Sixth Amendment right to a trial by an impartial jury. 28 U.S.C. §2254(a) (habeas corpus) (providing that federal courts "entertain an application for a writ of habeas corpus on behalf of a person in custody pursuant to the judgment of a State court only on the ground that he is in custody in violation of the Constitution or laws or treaties of the United States."); *Heck v. Humphrey*, 512 U .S. 477, 481 (1994) ("habeas corpus is the exclusive remedy for a state prisoner who challenges ... his confinement" based on the Constitution.). Hurricane's argument was that he would not be in prison but for a constitutional violation – in the form of a failure to provide an impartial jury. Hurricane's argument was that he was in custody due to the constitutional law violation by way of the Sixth Amendment: that he was denied an impartial jury. It was this third appeal that finally freed Hurricane. His convictions were set aside and he was entitled to a new trial.

The prosecution filed two unsuccessful appeals of this ruling, first to the Third Circuit, which affirmed, and then to the United States Supreme Court, which denied cert. The government has a right to appeal only in limited situations. *See, e.g.,* Rule 3(c) of the Tennessee Rules of Appellate Procedure (enumerating only six instances in which the state may appeal in criminal matters); *See also*, 18 U.S.C. §3731 (disallowing government appeals in criminal matters where the Double Jeopardy Clause would prohibit further prosecution). What grounds allowed the prosecution to appeal the granting of the writ of habeas corpus? What grounds exist under your state's law?

Defeated, the State of New Jersey apparently chose not to re-try Hurricane a third time. What factors might have affected the prosecution's decision not to re-try the case? The Dylan song?

? Exam Tip

When answering an essay exam, be sure you understand the position from which you are to respond. For instance, you may be asked to write from the standpoint of the defense, the prosecution, or an appellate judge. Or, you simply may be asked to "discuss" a given situation. Read the question and the instructions carefully and then frame your answer from the proper perspective. This is particularly true when the fact pattern presents controversial issues. Your conclusion is less important than your explanation of how you got there. *See* Richard Michael Fischl and Jeremy Paul, *Getting To Maybe: How to Excel on Law School Exams* (Durham, Carolina Academic Press 1999).

LEGAL BRIEFS & MOVIE EXTRAS

*This movie was based on two different books: the first was Hurricane's memoirs, *The Sixteenth Round: From Number 1 Contender to #45472*. Written from prison, Carter published this autobiography in 1974. The other book, *Lazarus and The Hurricane,* was written by Sam Chaiton and Terry Swinton, the two social activists that helped the young boy (Lazarus) in his crusade to free Hurricane.

*Hurricane's story is also told in a famous Bob Dylan song of the same name. Written in 1975, Hurricane was still in jail when Dylan sang of his plight. Dylan roared: *"It won't be over till they clear his name."* Did they? Was justice done in The Hurricane's case? Some people believe that The Hurricane's guilt or innocence remains an unanswered question.

"This is the story of The Hurricane. The one the authorities came to blame, for something that he'd never done!"

-Bob Dylan, *The Hurricane*, 1975

ERIN BROCKOVICH
(Universal Pictures 2000)

Starring: Julia Roberts; Albert Finney

Lessons: Civil Procedure; Ethics

Plot: A cluster of illnesses in Hinckley, California come to light while a paralegal, Erin Brockovich (Julia Roberts), investigates a pro bono real estate matter for her law firm. She discovers that the nearby corporate giant, PG&E Company, has been polluting the water with a deadly form of chromium, which causes a host of illnesses including all types of cancer. She persuades her boss to take on the case for the many plaintiffs affected – a number that seemed to keep growing. Although Erin had very little legal training, she befriends the plaintiffs and becomes an integral component of the lawsuit and a key reason for its success. Also based on a true story, there are many parallels to *A Civil Action* in this movie, though moviegoers enjoy a much happier ending with Erin Brockovich's story.

CIVIL PROCEDURE
Rule 23: Class Action v. Direct Action

The Hinckley case was the largest settlement in a direct action toxic tort lawsuit. Why was this action brought as a direct action as opposed to a class action? Rule 23 of the Federal Rules of Civil Procedure governs class actions. Rule 23(a) sets forth the threshold prerequisites for class certification:

> (1) the class is so numerous that joinder of all members is impracticable;

> (2) there are questions of law or fact common to the class;

(3) the claims or defenses of the representative parties are typical of the claims or defenses of the class; and

(4) the representative parties will fairly and adequately protect the interests of the class.

Would it have been possible for the Hinckley plaintiffs to be certified as a class? What are the pros and cons of proceeding with a class action instead of a direct action? What additional steps would the team have needed to take in order to bring the case to court as a class action? *See* FED. R. OF EVID. 23(b)-(f).

Alternative Dispute Resolution

Two major types of alternative dispute resolution (ADR) are mediation and arbitration. Both involve the parties' sitting down with a third-party neutral who acts as a factfinder and a decision maker. The difference between the two is that, typically, an arbitrator's decision is binding, whereas a mediator's decision is more likely a recommendation. Both forms of ADR can be effective means of resolving a case without the continued escalation of attorneys' fees and judicial resources.

Many state statutes and/or court rules of civil procedure contain mandatory ADR provisions in certain types of cases. A few of those states include Maine (Rule 16B, Maine Rules of Civil Procedure: alternative dispute resolution), Massachusetts (Mass. Gen. L. Title I Chapter 211B: Section 19: mandatory alternative dispute resolution program), Montana (M.R. App. P., Rule 7: mandatory appellate alternative dispute resolution), New York (N.Y. Ct. Rule 3405. arbitration of certain claims), and Ohio (74 Okl. St. Ann. §840-6.1: alternative dispute resolution program). Some state legislatures have given their courts the authority to mandate ADR. *See, e.g.,* the Illinois statute (IL ST CH 735 §5/2-

1009A), providing that "the Supreme Court of Illinois, by rule, may provide for mandatory arbitration of such civil actions as the court deems appropriate."). Some local district court federal rules also have mandatory ADR provisions.

The Federal Rules of Civil Procedure encourage ADR through Rule 16, entitled "Pretrial Conferences; Scheduling; Management." Rule 16 contains provisions authorizing courts to order parties to appear before the court for settlement conferences or to engage in private ADR aimed at resolving disputes through agreement rather than trial. So, under the Federal Rules, a federal judge has the discretion to make ADR mandatory in the particular cases that come before her court. For more information about the history of ADR, see Thomas J. Stipanowich, *ADR and the "Vanishing Trial": The Growth and Impact of "Alternative Dispute Resolution,"* Journal of Empirical Legal Studies, Vol. 1 Issue 3, page 843-912, November 2004.

? Exam Tip

Find out what, if any, alternative dispute resolution provisions are contained in your state's rules and statutes; you may need to be familiar with these ADR requirements for your state's bar exam.

ETHICS
Fee-Splitting with Other Law Firms

When Attorney Ed Masry and Erin teamed up with another law firm, they must have taken certain steps to ensure ethical compliance with respect to the fee-splitting arrangement. ABA Model Rule 1.5(e) (Fees) provides that:

A division of a fee between lawyers who are not in the same firm may be made only if:

(1) the division is in proportion to the services performed by each lawyer or each lawyer assumes joint responsibility for the representation;

(2) the client agrees to the arrangement, including the share each lawyer will receive, and the agreement is confirmed in writing; and

(3) the total fee is reasonable.

Complicating the fee-splitting issue further is the fact that the two firms represent multiple clients in the same case. Each client must agree to the fee arrangement and the manner in which any award will be distributed to the various plaintiffs. Here, the parties agreed to allow the arbitrator to determine how best to divide the settlement award among the numerous plaintiffs, depending upon the severity of the plaintiffs' illnesses and losses and other factors.

Fee Splitting with Non-lawyers

At the end of the movie, Attorney Ed Masry gives Erin a $2,000,000 bonus for her good work. ABA Model Rule 5.4 (Professional Independence of a Lawyer) provides:

(a) A lawyer or law firm shall not share legal fees with a nonlawyer, except that:

(1) an agreement by a lawyer with the lawyer's firm, partner, or associate may provide for the payment of money, over a reasonable period of time after the lawyer's death, to the lawyer's estate or to one or more specified persons;

(2) a lawyer who purchases the practice of a deceased,

disabled, or disappeared lawyer may, pursuant to the provisions of Rule 1.17, pay to the estate or other representative of that lawyer the agreed-upon purchase price;

(3) a lawyer or law firm may include nonlawyer employees in a compensation or retirement plan, even though the plan is based in whole or in part on a profit-sharing arrangement; and

(4) a lawyer may share court-awarded legal fees with a nonprofit organization that employed, retained or recommended employment of the lawyer in the matter.

Does the $2,000,000 "bonus" that Attorney Ed Masry gives to Erin violate Rule 5.4? How might Ed have dealt with this rule in awarding Erin?

Unauthorized Practice of Law

Paralegals are bound by the same ethical rules as the attorneys for whom they work. ABA Model Rule 5.5 (Unauthorized Practice of Law; Multi-jurisdictional Practice of Law) particularly applies to paralegals in that it prohibits the practice of law by unlicensed professionals. Code and canons of the paralegal professional also prohibit the unauthorized practice of law (UPL). For instance, the National Association of Legal Assistant (NALA) Code of Ethics and Professional Responsibility include several canons regarding the unauthorized practice of law, including Canon 3, which provides:

A legal assistant must not (a) engage in, encourage, or contribute to any act which could constitute the unauthorized practice of law; and (b) establish attorney/client relationships, set fees, give legal opinions or advice or represent a client before a court or agency unless so authorized by that court or agency; and (c) engage in conduct or take any action which would assist or involve the attorney in a violation of professional ethics or give the appearance of professional impropriety.

Similarly, the National Federation of Paralegal Associations (NFPA) has a Model Code of Ethics and Professional Responsibility and Guidelines for Enforcement, which states, at Section 1.8 "a paralegal shall comply with the applicable legal authority governing the unauthorized practice of law in the jurisdiction in which the paralegal practices."

Do any of Erin's actions or communications with clients, witnesses, or others constitute the unauthorized practice of law? Several other well-meaning paralegals have found themselves in trouble for crossing the UPL line. *See, e.g., Furman v. Florida Bar,* 376 So.2d 378 (Fla. 1979) (in which the Florida Bar Association took action against a former legal secretary who helped low income people complete routine divorce forms); *see also, In the Matter of Arons,* 456 A.2d 867 (Del. 2000) (in which Marilyn Arons and others were accused of engaging in the unauthorized practice of law in connection with Arons's running the Parent Information Center of New Jersey, which provided services to parents of disabled children in due process hearings before administrative agencies). These cases show just how important it is that paralegals be careful not to engage in the unauthorized practice of law.

In addition, supervising attorneys need to ensure that their legal assistants do not cross ethical lines. ABA Model Rule 5.3 (b) (Responsibilities Regarding Nonlawyer Assistants) provides that "a lawyer having direct supervisory authority over the non-lawyer shall make reasonable efforts to ensure that the person's conduct is compatible with the professional obligations of the lawyer."

See also RESTATEMENT (THIRD) OF THE LAW GOVERNING LAWYERS §11.

Did Attorney Masry follow this rule with respect to Erin?

For a case highlighting the risks attorneys face for failing to comply with their supervisory duties, see *Attorney Grievance Commission v. Smith,* 116 A.2d 977 (Md. 2015). Among other misconduct that resulted in disbarment, the attorney's "virtual abandonment of his practice to the charge of his non-lawyer assistant, with little or no supervision to such an extent that she engaged in the unauthorized practice of law and was able to misappropriate client monies for almost four years constitutes conduct prejudicial to the administration of justice." *Id.* at 992.

? Exam Tips

Whenever an ethics exam fact pattern involves a paralegal who seems to be over-stepping her boundaries, consider both ABA Model Rule 5.3 (b) (an attorney's duty to supervise non-lawyers) and ABA Model Rule 5.5 (regarding the unauthorized practice of law by non-lawyers).

LEGAL BRIEFS & MOVIE EXTRAS

*The employees of PG&E have their own claims against the company for illnesses they sustained because of the toxic chromium that PG&E used in an attempt to save a few dollars. State and federal workers' compensation laws allow victims of work-related injuries to be compensated for injury or illness sustained during the course of their employment, as well as lost wages. In cases of death, the employee's heirs receive income and burial benefits.

*This movie is not only based on a true story, but, according to Erin, "the movie was true and probably 98% accurate," from the clothes, to the trash mouth, to the biker dude. Hollywood "took very few creative licenses," says Erin Brockovich on her personal website. Julia Roberts won an Academy Award for her portrayal of Erin Brockovich. Erin has won several of her own awards for her excellent work as a consumer rights advocate and many other accomplishments.

"Do they teach lawyers to apologize? 'Cause you suck at it."

- Says Erin Brockovich to Attorney Ed Masry

I AM SAM
(New Line Cinema 2001)

Starring: Michelle Pfeiffer; Sean Penn

Lessons: Family Law

Plot: Sean Penn brilliantly portrays Sam Dawson, a man with an intellectual disability who finds himself raising his 7-year-old daughter, Lucy, as a single parent. Lucy's mother had abandoned her and Sam when Lucy was born. He gets by all right the first six years, with the help of a lonely recluse of a neighbor and an energetic support group of those similarly situated with Sam – high-functioning men with intellectual disabilities. Sam and Lucy remain under the state's radar. Once Lucy's learning and reading capabilities began to exceed her father's, the officials begin to take notice. That he and his daughter had the same level of intelligence raised concerns for human services and the state decided to petition to terminate his parental rights and allow foster parents to adopt Lucy. Neither Sam nor Lucy were on board with this plan. When Sam was asked whether he thinks it would be better for Lucy to live with him or with the foster family, where he could visit her, he states that he thinks it would be better if Lucy lived with him and the "Fosters" could come visit them at their house.

If anybody ever needed a lawyer, it was Sam. Luckily, he catches high-powered family law attorney Rita Harrison Williams (Michelle Pfeiffer). At a weak moment, Rita agrees to take his case pro bono. He does not make it easy for her to represent him. The problem for Rita was that Sam was inclined to tell the truth. There are some funny and heart-warming scenes carried out beautifully by fabulous actors. The courtroom scenes are deep and emotional – much like family courtrooms all over the country. Through the journey, Rita and

Sam both teach each other some valuable life lessons, about what is important in life, and about what it truly takes to be a "good" parent. The movie raises the question: is love enough? Or is there some level of intelligence that a human must surpass in order to avoid state intervention in their parenting roles?

Termination of Parental Rights

As discussed in *Losing Isaiah,* there is a very high threshold for an involuntary termination of a parent's right to raise his own child. This is true whether a guardian is petitioning for custody, as in *Losing Isaiah,* or by state intervention, as was the case for Sam. The Court requires "clear and convincing evidence" to terminate a natural parent's rights to his or her child. The U.S. Supreme Court, in *Santosky v. Kramer,* balanced the rights of natural parents against the state's legitimate concerns regarding child welfare. 455 U.S. 745 (1982).

The Court essentially affirmed its ruling that "the interest of parents in their relationship with their children is sufficiently fundamental to come within the finite class of liberty interests protected by the Fourteenth Amendment." *See id., quoting Smith v. Organization of Foster Families,* 431 U. S. 862-863 (Stewart, J., concurring in judgment).

The Court compared parental rights to the state's interest: The Court acknowledged that the state has a parens patriae interest in preserving and promoting the child's welfare and a fiscal and administrative interest in reducing the cost and burden of such proceedings. *Id.* at 766-68. Such an interest deserves far less protection than the risk of unfairly terminating rights of parents in their natural child. "Due process requires that the State support its allegations by at least clear and convincing evidence." This sends a message to the fact-finders that they must have "subjective certainty about [their] factual conclusions necessary to satisfy due process." *Id.*

Mental illness is certainly a factor in certain termination cases. But Sam had an intellectual disability. Should a contrast be made? Is there a lesser degree of instability with respect to mental illness than to a life-long, functional but intellectually challenged adult? He struggles to brew coffee and has trouble traveling across town by bus. He also has a very supportive circle of friends and neighbors that assist him with Lucy. Compare Lucy with Casey in *Irreconcilable Differences.* Here, Lucy is Sam's life.

As a former family law attorney and mediator, I hope to assure readers that our justice system is not as bad as this movie portrays. First of all, Sam would not have had to luck out and get an attorney by chance. Because the right to raise one's own child is considered a fundamental right, Sam had a constitutional right to an attorney. The movie, seemingly in its desire to paint a dark picture of the family court system, failed to acknowledge this legal protection. Other protections exist too that were not explored in the film. For instance, Sam would have been afforded the opportunity to have his visitations with his daughter in his home, perhaps supervised initially, where state officials would see that Lucy enjoyed a safe and happy home. A guardian may have been appointed to undergo this task. The movie incorrectly shifted the burden onto Sam, presuming that a disabled man could not raise a child. In the real world, the state would have failed to meet its burden of showing complete unfitness.

The ending is left unclear. The "Fosters" appear at the Dawsons' apartment, apparently conceding to Lucy's need for her father. Like in *Losing Isaiah,* we are left with a sufficiently satisfying ending in that it appears Lucy will have the benefit of the Fosters as well as her Dad, although it is not clear where she will live.

Reinstatement of Parental Rights

Not discussed in the movie was the fact that some state laws provide for or actually require reunification efforts after terminating parental rights. The states with reinstatement of parental rights statutes vary significantly. Factors for granting a petition to reinstate can involve statutory timeframes. For example, to be eligible for reinstatement in California, three years must pass from the termination date. CA Welf & Inst Code § 366.26(i)(3)(2017). In New York, two years must pass. N.Y. Fam. Ct. Act §§ 635-637. States also differ in terms of the burden of proof that a party must meet in order to have parental rights reinstated. Although a high standard of "clear and convincing evidence" is required in most states with reinstatement or reunification statutes, some states have much lower evidentiary thresholds. In Nevada, the lower "preponderance of evidence" standard applies. Nev. Rev. Stat. Ann. § 128.190(3). North Carolina courts will accept any evidence that is "relevant, reliable, and necessary" to decide whether reinstatement is appropriate. N.C.G.S. Chapter 7B-1114(g). Some states require older children to consent to reinstatement of parental rights. See Maine, e.g., at 22 M.R.S.A. §4059.

In short, reinstatement of parental rights laws are all over the board. Nevertheless, foster care can be temporary and, in Lucy's case, should be temporary if necessary at all. Once Sam set into place the help he needed (tutors, cleaners, whatever), full reunification may have occurred and parental rights may not have been forever terminated as was suggested in the movie.

LEGAL BRIEFS & MOVIE EXTRAS

*For more information on the varied state laws involving reinstatement of parental rights, see **http://www.ncsl.org/research/human-services/reinstatement-of-parental-rights-state-statute-sum.aspx**.

*There are many movie references in *I Am Sam*, including a very obvious reference to *Kramer v. Kramer*. Sam gives the same speech in court that Mr. Kramer provided in his quest for custody of his son. This occurs to his lawyer's dismay. Although he started out making some good sense and clear arguments, it becomes evident that he is simply quoting a movie, and even refers to Billy - Mr. and Mrs. Kramer's son – as opposed to his daughter Lucy.

"Can you grasp the concept of manipulating the truth? Not lying, just a tweak here and there"?

- Rita Harrison Williams, to which her client, Sam, answers, after some thought: "No."

LEGALLY BLONDE
(MGM 2001)

Starring: Reese Witherspoon; Luke Wilson; Selma Blair

Lessons: Criminal Law/Procedure; Constitutional Law

Plot: A blonde and bold California sorority girl follows her college boyfriend to Harvard Law School after he dumps her for a "more serious" girlfriend, Vivian Kensington (Selma Blair), also a Harvard Law classmate. Elle winds up losing passion for her beau but finding passion in the law. Thoroughly entertaining and sufficiently "feel good," law students must temporarily suspend their disbelief because we all know that you cannot go from getting a 143 to a 179 on the LSATs after only a few practice sessions with the sorority sisters, no matter what cleverness lies beneath those golden locks. Elle not only gets accepted to Harvard Law, but she finds herself assisting her Criminal Law professor in the defense of an aerobics queen she idolizes, her sorority sister Brooke Taylor Windham. Brooke Windham is being tried for murder, accused of shooting her rich, 60-year-old husband. Elle believes in Brooke's innocence. After she loses respect for her perverted professor, Elle suddenly takes over Brooke's case, with the help and support of her new love interest, Emmett (Luke Wilson), a young attorney on the professor's staff.

CRIMINAL LAW/PROCEDURE

After the good professor proves to be a sleaze, his client fires him and Elle takes on Brooke Windham's defense (Scene 28). To support her right to represent Brooke, Elle cites a Massachusetts court rule allowing a law student to try criminal cases in some situations. Massachusetts does have such a rule, but it would never be applied in this case. Rule 3.03 (Legal Assistance to the Commonwealth and to Indigent Criminal

235

Defendants, and to Indigent Parties in Civil Proceedings) provides:

(1)   A senior law student in an accredited law school … with the written approval by the dean of such school of his character, legal ability, and training, may appear … on behalf of indigent defendants in criminal proceedings … provided that the conduct of the case is under the general supervision of a member of the bar of the Commonwealth.

(2)   The term "senior student" or "senior law student" shall mean students who have completed successfully their next to the last year of law school study.

Mass. R. S. Ct. 3.03. Based on the relevant sections of Rule 3.03, how many reasons can you find why Elle could not represent Brooke Windham in her murder trial, even under this rule? Consider the following (give-away) hints: Is the law student in question, "One Elle" Woods, a senior law student? Has the dean provided written approval? Would Ms. Windham pass a financial screening for indigence?

CONSTITUTIONAL LAW
Fifth Amendment: Self-Incrimination

The Fifth Amendment provides that "no person … shall be compelled in any criminal case to be a witness against himself." The Fifth Amendment's mandate was made applicable to the States through the Fourteenth Amendment in the 1969 Supreme Court case of *Benton v. Maryland*, 395 U.S. 784 (1969). In Scene 29, Elle's vast knowledge of hairstyling chemicals enables her to catch the murder victim's daughter, Chutney Windham, in a lie. Ultimately, Ms. Windham blurts out a confession on the witness stand. The judge then instructs the bailiff to take her into custody. Was this the proper Fifth Amendment protocol? What, if anything, should the judge have done to protect the constitutional rights of Ms. Windham? In a subsequent criminal prosecution against Ms. Windham for killing her father, would this courtroom confession hold up to the Fifth Amendment's protection against self-incrimination? Are any other constitutional amendments implicated with respect to Ms. Windham's confession?

? LSAT Exam Tips

Work a little fun into studying for the LSATs and other exams. For example, logic is heavily tested on the LSATs. Buy one of those Dell books of logic problems, bring it with you to the beach or on a canoe trip, and prepare for the logic section of the LSATs in your own relaxing way. Most of the problems you will find in these logic books are more extensive than the logic questions on the LSATs. Take a break from the practice exams, but stay in your LSAT state of mind and see how quickly you can figure out some of the more difficult problems. If you can do that, the LSAT problems will seem easier.

? Exam Tips

As Cosmo Girl Elle Woods would agree, your beauty rest is most crucial on nights before major exams. A good meal is critical before hitting the hay though. Remember that any type of fish makes a good "brain food." The day before a test like the LSATs or the bar exam, mix up some tuna, broil some fresh haddock, or grill up some salmon and enjoy a nice relaxing meal before turning in for a good night's sleep. In the morning, have a simple breakfast, which includes both protein and fiber. For most people, a little caffeine is probably in order as well! To avoid stomach upset during the test, try peppermint or green tea, as opposed to coffee, for your pre-test morning caffeine fix.

Also, when doing prep tests either for the LSATs or the bar exam, reward yourself after successfully completing each practice exam, with chocolate, a manicure, a movie, or an invigorating workout. Keep some reality and fun in your life during crazy law or pre-law exam preparation!

LEGAL BRIEFS & MOVIE EXTRAS

* Legally Blonde is based on the book by Amanda Brown, which was originally titled *One Elle*. Amanda Brown has since written a series of books featuring the character "Elle Woods." All of Amanda Brown's books are well-written and entertaining. In Amanda Brown's book, Elle Woods went to Stanford Law School, not Harvard. Perhaps the movie version was set at Harvard to parallel the *Paper Chase*; there are some references to the *Paper Chase* in *Legally Blonde* - can you spot them? Harvard also seems to be Hollywood's choice for its law students. Other Harvard law students from movies discussed in this book include James Hart, from the *Paper Chase*, Ellen Roark, from *A Time To Kill*, and Mitch McDeere, from *The Firm*. The real Bryan Stevenson from *13th* was also a Harvard Law graduate.

*In Scene 30, the court refers to the murder case of Brooke Windham as "the matter of *The State vs. Brooke Windham.*" Would this be the accurate case name? Keep in mind that the case is set in Boston, Massachusetts.

"The law is reason free from passion."

-immortal words spoken by Aristotle, but discredited by Elle Woods

REVERSIBLE ERRORS
(Lions Gate Entertainment 2004)

Starring: Felicity Huffman and her real-life husband, William Macy; also starring Monica Potter, Tom Selleck, and Glenn Plummer

Lesson: Constitutional Law/Criminal Procedure

Plot: *Reversible Errors* was actually a four-hour made-for-television mini-series, but I could not resist including another great story by Scott Turow (author of *Presumed Innocent*). The movie takes us through Rommy "Squirrel" Gandolf's (Glenn Plummer) 10-year appeal of a triple homicide conviction, all the while on death row. William Macy plays Arthur Raven, a successful corporate lawyer who is forced to handle the pro bono appeal in an effort to save Squirrel from death row. What makes Raven's job more difficult is the fact that Squirrel had "confessed" to the high-profile murders during a police interrogation nearly a decade earlier. Raven begins to believe Squirrel's innocence after meeting Gillian Sullivan (Felicity Huffman), a former judge who fell upon her own legal problems, but had information that may prove Squirrel's innocence.

On the other side of the law, Assistant District Attorney Muriel Wynn (Monica Potter), who made a name for herself by prosecuting Squirrel's case, fights to defend her guilty verdict. She teams up with her former lover, Detective Larry Starczek (Tom Selleck), who also worked on the original case. Full of surprises along the way, this film resembles an oversized Law and Order episode, complete with two sets of (often boring) lover conflicts. Turow's legal thrillers, like John Grisham's (author of *The Firm* and *A Time To Kill*), are rich with legal queries. Hollywood fills their stories with stars without trampling on their accuracy too much.

CONSTITUTIONAL LAW/CRIMINAL PROCEDURE
Fifth Amendment – Criminal Confessions

During Detective Starczek's interrogation (Scene 7), Squirrel had confessed to the murders, but was apparently confused and arguably coerced. Under current constitutional law, was Squirrel's confession obtained improperly, such that it should have been excluded from trial?

The Fifth Amendment provides that "no person ... shall be compelled in any criminal case to be a witness against himself." The Fifth Amendment's mandate was made applicable to the States through the Fourteenth Amendment via the 1969 Supreme Court case of *Benton v. Maryland*, 395 U.S. 784 (1969). The constitutional protection against self-incrimination prohibits coerced confessions from being admissible evidence at criminal trials. Coercion includes both psychological and physical pressure. Here, Squirrel's confession was admitted at trial, and was likely the crucial piece of evidence leading to his conviction. Based on the circumstances surrounding Squirrel's confession, what facts support constitutional arguments for excluding the confession from evidence at trial? Thinking procedurally, how might these arguments be used for purposes of a subsequent appeal? *See* 28 U.S.C. §2254(a) (habeas corpus) (providing that federal courts "entertain an application for a writ of habeas corpus on behalf of a person in custody pursuant to the judgment of a State court only on the ground that he is in custody in violation of the Constitution or laws or treaties of the United States."); *Heck v. Humphrey*, 512 U .S. 477, 481 (1994) ("habeas corpus is the exclusive remedy for a state prisoner who challenges ... his confinement" based on the Constitution.).

For more information about the Fifth Amendment and its line of cases about coerced confessions, see Mark Godsey, *Rethinking the Involuntary Confession Rule: Toward a Workable Test for Identifying Compelled Self-Incrimination.* 94 CAL. L. REV. 465

(2005). Available at http://ssrn.com/abstract=622961 (last visited October 27, 2020).

Note also that Squirrel did not have an attorney present during the interrogations. The Sixth Amendment (discussed below) affords a criminal suspect the right to counsel, and may be implicated with respect to confessions elicited during police interrogations without the presence of defense counsel. *Massiah v. United States,* 377 U.S. 201, 205 (1964).

When all else fails, one might make a Rule 403 evidentiary argument that the confusing nature of Squirrel's alleged admission or confession renders it more prejudicial than probative.

Sixth Amendment – Waiver of Right to Jury Trial

The Six Amendment provides that "[i]n all criminal prosecutions, the accused shall enjoy the right to a speedy and public trial, by an impartial jury." U.S. Const. amend. VI. The decision of whether or not your client will exercise his constitutional right to a jury belongs to the criminal defendant and not the attorney (just like whether or not the criminal defendant will take the stand in his defense). *See* ABA Model Rule 1.2(a) (Scope of Representation and Allocation of Authority between Client and Lawyer). Although the decision lies with the defendant, attorneys do not keep silent on the issue, of course. Attorneys who represent the most unpopular types of criminal defendant clients – those guilty of rape or murder – often recommend a bench trial. Experience tells them they will be hard pressed to find a sympathetic jury and their client's fate is probably better off in the hands of a "soft" judge. That was the case here. As Judge Sullivan tells us, Squirrel, based on the advice of his attorney, waived his right to a jury because he knew that the judge would not be inclined to invoke the death penalty. His attorney was so certain of a guilt finding based on Squirrel's "confession" that he looked past the verdict to the sentencing. His concern was not about a guilty verdict; he was worried about the death sentence.

If the insanity defense were tried, how might that have affected the defense's decision to have a jury trial? If a jury trial were elected, what types of citizens would you want on Squirrel's jury, in terms of background and life experience? Who might be most sympathetic?

? Exam Tips

On a multiple-choice exam, you may be required to select which constitutional amendment is violated based on a fact pattern setting forth questionable police conduct. Keep in mind that the Fifth Amendment has been interpreted more broadly than the Fourth Amendment or Sixth Amendments. Just remember: when all else fails, plead the Fifth.

Another tip for multiple-choice exams, generally, is to cover up the possible answers while reading the exam question. Try to anticipate the correct response before you are distracted by seeing all of the options. If you do not see your anticipated answer among the possible responses, you are back to the process of elimination, but you have not lost any time. If you feel as though you are spending too long trying to determine which answer is best, skip the question and come back to it if you have time. If you run out of time, guess, and color those circles in quickly. On the bar exam, you are not penalized for wrong answers, so no answer should be left blank. When you must guess, answer C unless you have already discarded C as clearly wrong. Statistics suggest that C answers are the most common. This is an absolute last resort.

LEGAL BRIEFS & MOVIE EXTRAS

*If you are considering criminal law, either for internships, clerkships, or careers, you should read as much Scott Turow as possible. Other books by Scott Turow include: *One L* (1977), *Burden of Proof* (1990), *Presumed Innocent* (1999), and *Pleading Guilty* (1993).

*What specifically were the various "reversible errors" that freed Squirrel? How would you "brief" the issues? What do the criminal appeal cases in your state say about what constitutes reversible error?

NORTH COUNTRY
(Warner Brothers 2005)

Starring: Charlize Theron; Frances McDormand; Michelle Monaghan; Woody Harrelson

Lesson: Employment Law

Plot: Josey Aimes (Charlize Theron) is a single mom and one of a handful of women able to get a good paying job at Eveleth Taconite Company, an iron mine in Minnesota. Almost everyone in Aimes' small Northern Minnesota community depends on the mine for household income. The iron mine is the only local employment opportunity that could allow Josey Aimes to properly care and provide for herself and her two children. On the job, Aimes becomes a victim of some of the most egregious acts of sexual harassment imaginable. When she reports this harassment, her boss tells her to "take it like a man." Instead, she fights for her and other women's rights to earn a good income like the men, without sexual harassment.

North Country is based on a true story, but Hollywood takes some liberties with its depiction of the trial, particularly in the final courtroom scene. The film does do a good job highlighting civil rights and workplace fairness. The characters are well-crafted and personal relationships are explored in a deep and realistic manner.

EMPLOYMENT LAW
Gender Discrimination in the Workplace

Historically, the workforce at the mine was predominantly male. When women began working at the mine in the 1980s, some men physically and verbally abused them. Some women simply put up with the men because they depended on the mine for income and they did not want to make waves. Despite odds against her, Aimes uses the legal system to fight back. The real case upon which *North Country* was based is *Jenson v. Eveleth Taconite Co.,* 130 F.3d 1287 (8th Cir. 1997). It was the first sexual harassment class action in the nation. The court defined the class as: "all women who have applied for, or have been employed in, hourly positions at Eveleth Mines at any time since December 30, 1983, and who have been, are being, or, as a result of the operation of current practices, will be discriminated against with regard to the terms and conditions of their employment because of gender." 139 F.R.D. 657, 667 (D. Minn. 1991).

The *Jenson* case included both state law claims and federal claims under Title VII of the Civil Rights Act of 1964 (42 U.S.C. §2000e-2, et seq.). Title VII prohibits employment discrimination on the basis of race, color, religion, sex, or national origin. Title VII of the Civil Rights Act provides, in relevant part, that "[i]t shall be an unlawful employment practice for an employer ... to discriminate against any individual with respect to his compensation, terms, conditions, or privileges of employment, because of such individual's race, color, religion, sex, or national origin." 42 U.S.C. §2000e-2(a)(1). Title VII also protects employees who oppose or report unlawful discrimination against retaliation by their employers. 42 U.S.C. §2000e-3. In Scene 11, the company tries to force Aimes to resign. Company officials tell her she should spend less time stirring up female co-workers and more time improving job performance. Does the company's conduct in this scene violate the anti-retaliation provisions of Title VII? What other forms of retaliation is Aimes subjected to for reporting sexual harassment? See Scene 20, the union meeting.

Since the *Jenson* case, the United States Supreme Court has decided a long line of Title VII cases, providing caselaw guidelines for proving and defending workplace sexual harassment cases under Title VII. The Supreme Court has stated that "[t]he phrase 'terms, conditions, or privileges of employment' evinces a congressional intent to strike at the entire spectrum of disparate treatment of men and women in employment, which includes requiring people to work in a discriminatorily hostile or abusive environment." *Harris v. Forklift Sys.*, 510 U.S. 17, 21 (1993) (internal citations and quotations omitted). Relying on *Harris*, the Supreme Court has also held that, "when the workplace is permeated with discriminatory intimidation, ridicule, and insult that is sufficiently severe or pervasive to alter the conditions of the victim's employment and create an abusive working environment, Title VII is violated." *Oncole v. Sundowner Offshore Servs.*, 523 U.S. 75, 78 (1998).

The Supreme Court's Title VII cases outline the tests a plaintiff must meet to succeed in an abusive or hostile work environment claim. A plaintiff must establish: (1) that she (or he) is a member of a protected class; (2) that she was subjected to unwelcome sexual harassment; (3) that the harassment was based upon sex; (4) that the harassment was sufficiently severe or pervasive so as to alter the conditions of plaintiff's employment and create an abusive work environment; (5) that sexually objectionable conduct was both objectively and subjectively offensive, such that a reasonable person would find it hostile or abusive and the victim in fact did perceive it to be so; and (6) that some basis for employer liability has been established. *See Faragher v. City of Boca Raton*, 524 U.S. 775 (1998) and the Supreme Court's line of case law following *Faragher*.

Often, the 6th factor is the most heavily litigated: employer liability for discriminatory conduct by its employees. The Supreme Court has ruled that, when the sexual harasser is "indisputably within the class of an employer organization's officials who may be treated as the organization's proxy," the unlawful sexual harassment is automatically imputed to the employer. *Faragher v. City of Boca Raton*, 524 U.S. 775, 789

(1998). Among the class of officials who may serve as an employer's proxy such that his actions are automatically imputed to the employer are supervisors who "hold a sufficiently high position in the management hierarchy of the company." *Id.* at 789-90. The question then becomes, is a harassing manager part of the group of officials that can impute the liability to the employer with the deep pockets?

In *Burlington Industries, Inc. v. Ellerth*, the Supreme Court set forth a two-tiered requirement for employers to assert an affirmative defense against imputed liability based on a manager's sexual harassment: (1) the employer must show that it exercised reasonable care to promptly prevent and correct the harassment; and (2) the employer must show that the employee unreasonably failed to take advantage of any preventive or corrective opportunities provided by the employer or to avoid harm otherwise. 524 U.S. 742, 765 (1998). As to the non-managers, many courts have held that a plaintiff may establish employer liability for a non-supervisory co-employee if the plaintiff demonstrates that the employer "knew or should have known of the charged sexual harassment and failed to implement prompt and appropriate action." *Crowley v. L.L. Bean*, 303 F.3d 387, 395 (1st Cir. 2002) (quoting *White v. N.H. Dept. of Corr.*, 221 F.3d 254, 261 (1st Cir. 2000)).

What specific facts from *North Country* would you use to show that management knew about, or that they themselves caused, the sexual harassment? See, for example, Scene 7, in which Josie reports harassment to a supervisor, who simply tells her she should "take it like a man."

From a preventative maintenance perspective, what advice would you give your corporate clients about sexual harassment training? How would you advise them to properly handle complaints about sexual harassment by managers, supervisors, or co-workers? A proper investigation of a sexual harassment complaint should be conducted by a neutral investigator, in a fair and professional manner. Key witnesses need to be questioned thoroughly, and the investigator needs to understand and apply the company's policies and procedures even-handedly. From the plaintiff's standpoint, counsel should be looking for any deficiencies in the investigation process, noting anything that suggests the investigation was not conducted in a timely, fair, consistent, and thorough manner.

Damages

The 8th Circuit opinion in *Jenson* provides an excellent analysis of damages and illustrates the importance of including state law causes of action, because state laws often provide remedies that are broader than those available under federal law. When the *Jenson* case was filed, in 1988, the remedies available under Title VII were limited to back-pay, injunctions, and other equitable relief. *See United States v. Burke,* 504 U.S. 229, 238 (1992); 42 U.S.C. §2000e-5(g). It was not until 1991 that Congress enacted 42 U.S.C. §1981a(b)(1), which allows plaintiffs to bring claims for punitive damages against private defendants who intentionally violate Title VII upon a showing that the defendant engaged in discrimination "with malice or a reckless indifference to the federally protected rights of an aggrieved individual." Luckily, the plaintiffs sought additional remedies, including punitive damages, under the Minnesota Human Rights Act, which provides for punitive damages in civil actions "upon clear and convincing evidence that the acts of the defendant show a willful indifference to the rights or safety of others." *Jenson v. Eveleth Taconite Co.,* 130 F.3d 1287, 1300 (8th Cir. 1997) (citing Minn. Stat. §549.20, subd. 1 (1988)).

To prove that punitive damages are appropriate, plaintiffs' attorneys should focus discovery on the employer's willful or reckless disregard for its employees' federally protected rights. For instance, can it be proven that the employer knew about the harassment but failed to take proper action? Did the employer fail to send the message to the plaintiff's co-workers that discrimination would not be tolerated? Based on the movie, what specific facts would you use to show the company's willful indifference about gender discrimination at the mine?

What other types of damages would you seek for this class of plaintiffs? For guidance, United States Supreme Court cases that discuss Title VII remedies include *McKennon v. Nashville Banner Publishing Co.*, 513 U.S. 352 (1995) and *Landgraf v. USI Film Products*, 511 U.S. 244 (1994).

? Exam Tip

There is a wide array of damages available in employment law cases. When analyzing damages for purposes of an essay exam, consider all possibilities: actual damages, incidental damages, emotional distress, lost wages, lost benefits, punitive damages, injunctions, and other equitable and monetary bases for relief.

Workers' Compensation Laws

In addition to the gender discrimination/sexual harassment claims, some of the class members may also have claims under state workers' compensation laws for any injuries suffered as a result of the extreme sexual harassment. In this case, some of the maltreatment constituting the hostile work environment involved physical contact (perhaps even criminal sexual assault). To the extent physical harm resulted, medical and lost wage benefits may have been required under Minnesota's workers' compensation laws.

Even where immediate physical injuries are minimal or absent, many states provide for workers' compensation coverage where injury at work manifests in the form of extreme stress. For instance, Josey was sexually attacked in the powder room by a male co-worker (Scene 15). Physically, she appeared fine; emotionally, however, her stress level had to have been extraordinary. Also, in Scene 13, Josey's co-worker, Sherry (Michelle Monaghan), was using the onsite port-a-potty, until her male co-workers flipped it over, causing her to fall off of the pot, flat on the ground. The fall itself may not have caused compensable physical injury, but the incident caused Sherry a level of humiliation I cannot even imagine. Such harm may rise to the level of extraordinary stress, beyond what any employee should be expected to endure. This is particularly true where the stress manifests itself in significant physical symptoms. Stress claims under workers' compensation laws, however, are much harder to prove than claims for more obvious physical injuries, such as those sustained at the nuclear power plant in *Silkwood*.

LEGAL BRIEFS & MOVIE EXTRAS

*Another great movie involving sexual harassment in the workplace is the Michael Douglas/Demi Moore thriller *Disclosure* (Warner Brothers 1994), based on a bestselling novel by Michael Crichton. The sexual roles are reversed from the norm in *Disclosure*. Michael Douglas plays Tom Sanders, a software executive whose boss, Meredith Johnson (Demi Moore), makes sexual advances towards him and threatens his job when he becomes apprehensive of the affair.

*For more information about the real case, see *Class Action: the Story of Lois Jenson and the Landmark Case that Changed Sexual Harassment Law*, Bingham, Clara, and Leedy Gansler, Laura (Doubleday, 2002).

*This movie briefly discusses the requirements for class certification. See Scenes 18 and 25-26. The judge told Aimes that the court would certify her class if she finds three other plaintiffs. Based on Rule 23 of the Federal Rules of Civil Procedure, was the judge's ruling proper? What else would

Aimes be required to show in order to proceed with her litigation as a class action? Why do you suppose it was important that the case be brought as a class action?

"Well, the good news is, all roads lead to lawyers."

-Woody Harrelson (as Josey's attorney, initially reluctant to take her case)

WEDDING CRASHERS
(New Line Cinema 2005)

Starring: Owen Wilson; Vince Vaughn

Lesson: Family Law

Plot: In terms of plot, the movie is shallow. But, how can you not laugh out loud watching Owen Wilson (who plays John Beckwith) and Vince Vaughn (who plays Jeremy Grey) perform their comical antics. For a profession, John and Jeremy are business partners. As divorce mediators, they try to keep divorces from crashing into litigation. For a hobby, John and Jeremy are also partners. As a best-buddies and as a team, they fake their way into the weddings of strangers, just to share in the food, fun, and festivities of the beginning of marriage instead of the ending of marriage. Their well-developed conspiracy is threatened when they get too close to certain guests at a politician's daughter's wedding. The plot of the movie is not really conducive to intelligent discussion about family law. In the opening scene, however, we see the guys working a case. They mediate jointly and actually do some good work. I have included it because there are some good examples of small things a good family law mediator can do to help the parties reach an agreement as opposed to litigating their divorce. Plus some of my Facebook friends said I had to include it because it is funny.

Family Law Mediation

Mediation is a forum in which a neutral mediator – or two - facilitates communication between parties to promote reconciliation, hopefully mutual understanding, and possibly full settlement without any stressful contested courtroom drama. Mediation is particularly suited to divorces and other family law proceedings because there is likely to be a continuing relationship between the parties, especially if minor children are involved, or if a family business is impacted. Many divorcing couples find mediation allows them to avoid the high financial and emotional costs of a litigated divorce; because settlement is generally quicker, costs are reduced.

As rightly noted in Scene 1, mediation provides an alternative to costly and time-consuming litigation. With mediation, costs are reduced and the parties can typically reach resolution faster than if they spend their time gearing up toward a vicious courtroom battle. Divorce mediation also allows couples to avoid the risks of such a trial. It can protect confidentiality, decrease stressful conflict, and may even help couples learn skills to resolve future conflicts. Mediation may also protect the children of a marriage from the pain of parental conflict and uncertainty about their schedules and their lives.

In *Wedding Crashers*, the two team up to offer a co-mediation format. Although for purposes of the comedic scene and the movie's need to show viewers the mediators' skills immediately, all parties sat at the same table, with both mediators, and complete resolution was achieved with the help of John and Jeremy. In the real world, mediation often requires the parties being separated during some portion of a mediation session, where the mediator goes back and forth between the parties. The period of time during which one party waits for the return of the mediator might be stressful and feel like wasted time and money. With a co-mediator format, mediators can meet separately with the parties, and then they can more quickly exchange notes and approach both parties with some common ground ideas. This format works especially well where, as here, the two mediators have a solid working relationship and are completely in sync with each other – just like John and Jeremy, who at times seem to share one brain.

Further, some cases may involve complex financial considerations. Some family law mediators are trained mostly in the human relationships side of family dynamics, and relevant state law on equitable division of assets, generally. Other mediators might have a stronger business or financial background. Where significant money is at stake, alternative dispute resolution might be more beneficial with the help of multiple professionals. This could be a co-mediation, or perhaps other professionals working alongside mediators, such as accountants, actuaries, business and real estate valuation professionals, market experts, etc.

In most states, mediation in family cases involving minor children is mandatory and is often offered by the courts at reasonable rates. Even if mediation is not required in certain family law cases, it is the most common mechanism for resolving disputes involving divorce and child custody.

MOVIE BRIEFS & LEGAL EXTRAS

*Of course, not all cases are ideal for mediation. There are some cases where the parties are not on equally playing fields, such as cases of domestic violence. A good mediator will know when a mediation should be concluded for lack of good faith, intimidation, fear, or for other good reasons that indicate a mediation would be non-productive at best.

"You know how they say we only use 10 percent of our brains? I think we only use 10 percent of our hearts."

–John Beckwith

WHAT HAPPENS IN VEGAS
(Regency Enterprises 2008)

Starring: Ashton Kutcher; Cameron Diaz

Lesson: Family Law

Plot: Jack Fuller (Ashton Kutcher) and Joy McNally (Cameron Diaz) meet up in Las Vegas. Coincidentally, they are both from New York City. Coincidentally, they are also both down on their luck and drunk. Jack had just been fired from his job – a job in which his father was his boss. Joy had just been dumped by her slimy boyfriend in front of a room full of people she had gathered together for a surprise birthday party for the jerk. Jack and Joy both head to Vegas with a friend. Rob Corddry and Lake Bell play their funny friends. After some drunken fun … oops, Joy and Jill get married. Their first fight as a married couple occurs the next morning. Realizing their grave mistake, Joy and Jack confront each other in the casino near the slot machines. They are both hungover and regretful. They angrily agree to the mutual mistake. They argue over who made the worse mistake (or something like that). Joy tries to ignore Jack, and she plays the slots. Jack takes her quarter and feeds it to a machine, pulls the level, and bam – he wins a three-million-dollar jackpot. Marital property! Diaz, claims, and she wants half. Only the first few minutes of this movie occur in Vegas. What happens in Vegas actually plays out mostly in New York.

Despite what the critics say, Cameron and Ashton have spot on chemistry and the audience wants to see them together by the end of the film. Spoiler Alert: you guessed it. He shows off his listening skills and remembers where she felt at peace: Fire Island New York.

Annulments

Back in New York, they mutually seek to dissolve the marriage and they fight about the slot machine money. Unlike a divorce, an annulment regards the marriage as if it never occurred. Cameron pressed for a divorce instead of an annulment; this way, she would be entitled to half of the jackpot money because it was marital property. Either way, Judge Whopper (Dennis Miller), giving some righteous rationale about the "sacred institution of marriage," sentences them to six months of marriage – that is, trying to live together as a married couple. The plot is funny and there is an undeniable chemistry and comic match between Cameron and Ashton. The movie is worth the watch for that reason alone. In terms of providing any accurate information for legal lessons regarding marriage and divorce, all I can say is, "no way." No way would the couple have been subjected to six months of "trying" their marriage. That might even fall within the Constitution's prohibition of cruel and unusual punishment. Vegas weddings are quite easily annulled. In fact, the law is quite clear on this point and has been in place as long as Sin City itself.

In Nevada, grounds for annulment include "want of understanding." This allows either party to a marriage to get their marriage annulled if either were incapable of understanding they were entering into a marriage; in other words, if either the bride or the groom lacked sufficient mental capacity at the time of the ceremony to willingly consent to the marriage. Intoxication is considered evidence of insufficient capacity to marry, such that the marriage is invalid. *Mahan v. Mahan*, 88 So.2d 545, 548 (Fla. 1956) (holding that marriages entered into while the parties were intoxicated is invalid unless later ratified by the parties).

The burden is on the party seeking the annulment to prove lack of mental capacity or want of understanding. *Hudspeth v. Hudspeth,* 206 S.W.2d 863, 870 (Tex. 1947). What proof existed for Joy or Jack to have satisfied the burden of proving grounds for annulment based on "want of understanding" or lack of capacity? Well, unfortunately or fortunately, their friends captured the whole drunken night on video. Any judge – in Nevada or New York or just about anywhere else in the country – would certainly find that the couple lacked the mental capacity to enter into a marriage the night of the nuptials. That being said, even in cases of lack of capacity, a marriage is not automatically void. It may only be voidable if the couple was intoxicated at the time of the ceremony. Voidable means it can be ratified once the intoxication wears off. In fact, I suspect many people are drunk at their own wedding ceremonies, and most of them engage in ratification quite soon thereafter. But I digress.

This void v. voidable distinction is also discussed in *Liar Liar.* Voidable means it can be ratified once the intoxication wears off. *See, e.g. Prine v. Prine,* 18 So. 781, 785 (Fla. 1895) (holding that it is "well established that a marriage, invalid at the time for want of mental capacity, may be ratified and made valid afterwards by any acts or conduct which amount to a recognition of its validity."). In *Liar Liar,* the marriage was ratified even though entered into by a minor. *In What Happens in Vegas,* Jack took immediately steps to ensure the drunken marriage was *not* ratified. Joy wanted a divorce, in order to be awarded half of Ashton's money. This is because if the marriage never happened, she would have no claim to it as marital property, although she could have made some other arguments. It was her quarter after all. But the point is that, due to affirmative steps taken, Joy and Jack did not ratify their marriage in the same way as in *Liar Liar.*

LEGAL BRIEFS & MOVIE EXTRAS

*Ashton and Cameron both were married in 2015. Not to each other though. Ashton married actress Mila Kunis and Cameron married musician Benji Madden.

*Is there any situation in which an American judge could render such an order? Is there anybody who has heard of anything even close? If so, please contact me because it might be a movie in the making.

"I've been married for twenty five years to the same wonderful, infuriating woman. And granted there are days when I want to light her on fire but I don't, because I love her. And that would be illegal. And you know something, and I might be old fashioned but when I said those vows, I meant them."

- Judge Whopper

UP IN THE AIR
(Paramount Pictures 2009)

Starring: George Clooney; Anna Kendrick

Lessons: Employment Law

Plot: George Clooney plays Ryan Bingham, a career "job transition" expert. That basically means he travels around the country doing the "dirty work" of overseeing company layoffs and terminations on behalf of employer clients. Natalie Keener (Anna Kendrick) is new to the industry but comes into it with efficiency ideas that Clooney feels loses the human touch. Natalie feels Skype or similar videoconferencing would better serve their clients' needs at a lower cost, eliminating the travel that essentially defines Ryan Bingham's life (hence the movie title). The company orders Ryan to take Natalie on his next trip to fire people. Human dynamics and relationship questions highlight the trip and the film. The acting is excellent but the ending does not provide for a very "feel-good" finish. Still, the employment law implications in the large-scale layoffs Ryan and Natalie conduct is worthy of note.

Reductions in force typically do not appear discriminatory on their face, in that they do not specifically target a protected group. Decisions are typically based on economic factors, salaries, department restructurings, and other "legitimate business decisions" not intended to impact people based on their membership in a protected class. If, however, the group of employees affected by the layoff suggests a disproportionate dismissal of older employees, females, employees with disabilities, or any other group protected by federal or state employment discrimination laws, discrimination claims could ensue. Such claims care couched in terms of "disparage impact" discrimination. Reductions in force can implicate several employment laws and other concerns due to the potential for affecting protected classes. This summary focuses on federal laws involving larger scale employer reductions in force.

Worker Adjustment and Retraining Notification Act

The Worker Adjustment and Retraining Notification Act ("Warn"), 29 U.S.C. 2101 et seq., requires most employers with 100 or more employees to provide a 60-day written notice of any "plant closings or mass layoffs of employees" (reductions in workforce). A "plant closing" is "the permanent or temporary shutdown of a single site of employment, or one or more facilities or operating units within a single site of employment, if the shutdown results in an employment loss at the single site of employment during any 30-day period for 50 or more employees excluding any part-time employees."

Any large employer planning major RIFs must comply with the Warn Act and give proper notice. Failure to do so could result in lawsuits by affected employees and a civil penalty of up to $500 for each day of violation. 29 U.S.C. § 2104(a). This penalty may be avoided if the employer satisfies the liability to each aggrieved employee within 3 weeks after the closing or layoff is ordered by the employer. *Id.*

The Age Discrimination in Employment Act

The Age Discrimination in Employment Act ("ADEA"), 29 U.S.C. § 621 et seq., prohibits discrimination on the basis of age in programs and activities receiving federal financial assistance. When it comes to reductions in force, disparate impact is a heavily litigated issue.

In *Meacham v. Knolls Atomic Power Laboratory*, a research laboratory engaged in a RIF. 554 U.S. 84 (2008). To determine whom to terminate, the company asked supervisors to rank employees based on three factors: performance, flexibility, and critical skills. *Id.* Of the thirty-one employees who were let go, all but one was over the age of forty. Twenty-six of these dismissed employees filed suit against Knolls for age discrimination under the ADEA. *Id.*

The United States Supreme Court ruled that exemption from liability for disparate impact claims under the ADEA for employer actions based on reasonable factors other than age creates an affirmative defense, on which employer bears both the burden of production of evidence and the burden of persuasion of its merits. *Id.* at 87. In other words, it is up to the employer to prove beyond a preponderance of the evidence that legitimate business reasons resulted in the termination decisions. All aspects of the termination decision-making process, especially with respect to deciding which employees to fire, should be clearly documented. All RIF policies and procedures should be followed precisely and without exception. When a layoff might result in older employees being let go, there is a potential for ADEA claims. This is another example of why hiring a consultant to assist with large layoffs might be a good idea.

Uniformed Services Employment and Reemployment Rights Act

Those men and women protecting our country constitute another class of employees that should be considered in terms of any reduction in force. Federal law protects military employees through the Uniformed Services Employment and Reemployment Rights Act (USERRA), 38 U.S.C. § 4301 et seq. The intent of USERRA is to ensure that employees do not lose their civilian employment status and benefits simply as a result of their service to our country. USERRA provides them with the opportunity to return to their civilian employment upon completion of their military service. Employers must reinstate returning military personnel to the same position and with the same benefits, pay, and seniority they would have enjoyed had they not left their civilian job to serve the country. Also, under USERRA, for the first 30 days of an employee's military leave, the employer must continue the employee's existing health, dental, and life insurance at no additional cost to the employee.

If a service-member becomes disabled due to military service and becomes unable to perform the job duties, an employer is required under USERRA to employ the returning soldier in a job that is the "nearest approximation to" the prior position. In addition, a service-member cannot be fired without cause for up to one year (depending on the length of military service) after reinstatement, regardless of most states' "employment at will" status or an employer's personnel policies. USERRA also contains anti-discrimination provisions, such that hiring, promotion, and termination decisions cannot be made solely on the basis of present or anticipated service membership.

USERRA does contain an exception for any reductions in the workforce that would have included the military employee; however, it is the employer's burden to prove that the defense applies. Complete and concise records for any reduction in force should be maintained to prove that the service member's position was part of the reduction.

Employment Leave and Reductions in Force

Employers should also be mindful of layoff decisions affecting employees in a job-protected leave status, such as under workers' compensation laws, FMLA, or USERRA. An employer is prohibited from considering an employee's absence on protected leave as a factor in deciding whether to lay off that employee. This does not mean, however, that such employees are protected from layoffs generally. An employee on leave is not protected from discharge if the employee would have been laid off regardless of his being out on leave. An employer must be able to prove that the employee would have been terminated had he or she not taken the leave. If, for example, the employee's entire department was let go, that might be an easier showing than if only she were impacted and none with similar positions, not on leave, were affected.

LEGAL BRIEFS & MOVIE EXTRAS

*Other RIF considerations include the typical legal requirements on employers when any employee terminates for any reason. For example, COBRA notification may apply. The Consolidated Omnibus Budget Reconciliation Act (29 U.S.C. § 1161 et seq.) is a health insurance program that allows eligible employees and their families continued health insurance benefits when the employees lose their job. Under COBRA, it is incumbent upon the employer to notify employees of their COBRA rights. Also, under wage and hour laws, certain employees may need to be paid for all accrued but unused vacation time. With so many employees terminating in a RIF situation, there is a high risk of noncompliance. Often, employers wish to utilize a professional consultant to assist them in working their way through a RIF. Might I suggest Ryan Bingham?

*Federal employers must have specific regulatory requirements governing reductions in force, which are codified at 5 C.F.R. § 351. Federal agencies must follow the procedures set forth in the Code of Federal Regulations when conducting a RIF.

*Union employees also have protections from layoffs within the provisions of their union contracts, or collective bargaining agreements ("CBAs"). The CBA between a union and the employer sets forth RIF rules that must be followed.

DELIVERY MAN
(Touchstone Pictures 2013)

Starring: Vince Vaughan; Chris Pratt; Cobie Smulders

Lesson: Family Law

Plot: I just had to include another Vince Vaughan movie. Here, Vince plays Davis Wozniak aka "Starbuck." David is a charming underachiever who is always looking for easy money schemes. His two main endeavors were serving as "delivery man" for his family's meat market and growing marijuana in his apartment. In the 1990's, however, he made a few extra bucks through anonymous donations to a fertility clinic. Twenty years later, he finds out he's fathered 533 children when he is served with court papers, in which 142 of his offspring file a class action lawsuit to compel him to reveal his identity, something he is not inclined to do. Luckily, he has an attorney buddy. Chris Pratt plays David's friend Brett - a stay-at-home frazzled father and in-active lawyer. Brett agrees to defend David in the class action, but Brett turns out to be highly incompetent.

Background conflicts throughout the movie include David's relationship with his girlfriend, Emma (Cobie Smothers), and his unstable financial situation. Emma announces she is pregnant and becomes non-committal toward David, convinced he would be a bad father. He aims to prove her wrong. Meanwhile, however, he needs to come up with $80,000 to repay loans from ruthless lenders who will drown him if he cannot pay the debt. The class action lawsuit could not have come at a worse time.

This movie explores the true meaning of fatherhood. Getting served with the class action lawsuit sparked David's interest and curiosity about some of these tweens and young adults that he "fathered." So he decides to stalk some of them. Conveniently, his lawyer Brett provides him with a legal file containing contact information for the plaintiffs. Brett tells David not to open the envelope, but, guess what? He opens the envelope. With his newfound knowledge, he manages to interject himself into the lives of some of his children, while still remaining anonymous. David considers himself their "guardian angel." Angel or not, David undergoes a change and (spoiler alert), by the end of the movie, he is ready for "real" fatherhood.

In terms of legal lessons, because of its comedic style, *Delivery Man* does not get to the heart of some of the issues the movie's themes raise. These include rights of fathers, rights of privacy, confidentiality agreements for sperm donors and their impact on the resulting children. A predominant question is whether or not a donor should have the right to permanent anonymity.

Sperm Donor Rights

As a starting point, Starbucks has no obligation to these young adults. The Uniform Parenting Act provides that any male who donates sperm under the guidance of a physician for purposes of artificial insemination is not the father unless he is married to the sperm recipient. Further, contract law applies to Starbuck's anonymity. The contract under which David and the sperm bank were operating apparently contained the very common confidentiality clause. Part of the agreement between sperm donors and fertility clinics was that the donor's parental rights and obligations are waived, and the clinic will keep the identity of compensated donors anonymous. In some cases, however, once a child turns 18, many of these sperm banks will make the donor's identity available to the tween/adult child upon request. By this time, there would no longer be any parental expectations or child support requirements, and therefore the donor is more inclined to finally have his identity revealed. David, however, still had reservations, and relied on the confidentiality contract he signed every time under the pseudonym Starbuck. The class action plaintiffs were seeking to declare the contract unenforceable as against public policy. As Brett tried to explain it to David, "they claim that your right to privacy should take a backseat to their basic human rights to know who their biological father is. It's very complex." I tried to find case law balancing the privacy rights of donors against public policy as to third parties to these such contracts. There is very little case law on the issue.

There is case law about disclosure of a biological father's identity for purposes of a lawsuit involving a medical condition of the child at issue – a condition found to be genetic. In *Johnson v. Superior Court,* a California court found that, notwithstanding confidentiality clauses in agreements between Cyrobanks and sperm donors, good case may void such contract clauses under public policy considerations. 80 Cal.App.4th 1050, 1066-67.

Courts may also refuse to enforce the waiver of parental obligation clause, which relieve sperm donors from having to pay child support. Similar to the *Johnson* case, the Supreme Court of Pennsylvania found that, contract or not, allowing a sperm donor to escape child support - purely by private contract with a mother with whom he had a relationship - would go against public policy. *Ferguson v. McKiernan,* 940 A.2d 1236 (Pa. 2007). In this case, the donor was known to the mother in advance of the decision and contractual arrangement, and there were allegations that their sexual relationship continued even after known conception. *Id.* at 1239. So that may have impacted the Court's decision.

The cases are very fact-specific in terms of how certain sperm donor contracts may be deemed against public policy. I have not found a case declaring such confidentiality clauses per se unenforceable. Freedom of contract is alive and well and if courts were inclined not to enforce these types of contracts, it might have a chilling effect on donors willing to assist women who choose this option for procreation. That being said, it is becoming difficult for clinics to guarantee anonymity to their donors, with advanced genetic testing, and with more state legislatures and sperm bank governance understanding the importance of a child's right to know his or her genetic makeup.

Washington has a unique state law concerning sperm bank donations. The state law makes "open" sperm donation the default, such that a donor needs to specifically request anonymity. The trend used to be the other way around: default is anonymity unless a donor chooses to have an open profile. It is typical that the fertility banks themselves set the rules and regulations, as state law guidance is minimal. They seem to be moving away from anonymity being the norm. A California Cryobank, for example, instituted a policy in 2018 under which "all new donors must agree to a policy that gives offspring access to the donor's name, donation location, last known address, and email address, when they turn 18." Finding the Lost Generation of Sperm Donors, The Atlantic, May 18, 2018 available at:
 https://www.theatlantic.com/family/archive/2018/05/sperm-donation-anonymous/560588/ (last visited October 27, 2020).

One thing not realistic in the movie (yes, because there is only one thing): it is quite difficult to become a sperm donor and David may not have been accepted. "Cryobanks tend to accept only about 1% of applicants, after screening for issues like medical history, disease genes, education, even height and hair color." 'There's no such thing as anonymity': With consumer DNA tests, sperm banks reconsider long-held promises to donors, *Statnews*, MEGHANA KESHAVAN, September 11, 2019. Available at:

https://www.statnews.com/2019/09/11/consumer-dna-tests-sperm-donor-anonymity/ (last visited October 27, 2020)

LEGAL BRIEFS AND MOVIE EXTRAS

*This film is actually an American remake of a slightly earlier Canadian film, called *Starbuck*. But I didn't see this version. It didn't have Chris Pratt. Both films are by Ken Scott and both are allegedly loosely based on a true story (or several true stories).

*Although there is a get-together among the 142 plaintiffs, none of their mothers appear in the film, nor are they even really addressed. The only real female role was that of Cobie Smulders, but I like her way better as Robin from *How I Met Your Mother*. Cobie is unable to shine in the unsubstantial role of Emma – not Robin's fault.

"No one but the father can decide if he is the father or not."

-Starbucks

DEEP WATER HORIZON
(Participant Media 2016)

Starring: Mark Wahlberg; Kurt Russell, John Malkovich

Lessons: Employment Law

Plot: This docu-drama tells the tragic story of the deadly explosion on the Deepwater Horizon oil rig in 2010, off the coast of Louisiana. Eleven workers on board the rig were kill and many more were injured. Millions of barrels of oil were spilled into the Gulf of Mexico. The disaster resulted in extensive litigation against British Petroleum, Transocean Ltd., and other companies responsible for operating the Deepwater Horizon rig. The extent of the damages to the workers and the culpability level of the defendants resulted in lawsuits seeking monetary awards well beyond the limits of the workers' compensation system. Also, notwithstanding "sole remedy" provisions in workers' compensation laws, the Deepwater Horizon defendants faced class action wrongful death claims by family members of the 11 deceased victims. Excellent acting, action-packed, fast-paced – this is a great movie – until you remember it actually happened.

Exceptions to Workers' Compensation Sole Remedy Rule

As discussed in *North Country*, the workers' compensation system presents a sort of compromise between injured employees and their employers for purposes of litigating claims. An employee does not have to prove negligence by his employer in order to receive medical and lost wage benefits under workers' compensation laws. Typically, however, the state worker's compensation system provides the sole remedy. Employees and surviving heirs are barred from civil suits against the employers for injuries sustained at work. Exceptions of course apply. In the context of complex litigation such as the Deepwater Horizon cases, employees and surviving family members allege "egregious conduct," or "intent" by the employer to overcome the presumption that workers' compensation is the sole remedy for workplace injury. Employees generally must meet a high burden of proof that their employers deliberately intended to hurt them. In most states, negligence is insufficient to sue for more than the limited workers' compensation benefits. In Arizona, for example, the employee must show that the employee "personally and purposefully acted with the direct goal of injuring a worker." Ariz. Rev. Stats. § 23-1022 (2018).

Some state laws allow lawsuits outside of workers' compensation - even where there is a lower threshold of culpability - when the employee dies due to a workplace accident. Even Texas allows lawsuits based on an employer's "gross negligence," omission, or intentional act when the employee died as a result. Tex. Lab. Code § 508.001 (2018). Surviving family members in these states can bring wrongful death or loss of consortium claims when they lose a loved one due to an accident on the job, particularly where the accident could have and should have been avoided.

Workers' compensation laws vary widely among states, and they are often changing with political climates and other factors. Workers' compensation claims can also overlap with other employment laws, such as discrimination, retaliation, accommodations, etc. Lawyers, human resource professionals, and business owners need to keep apprised of these laws and their interaction with other torts, insurance issues, and risk factors. Most importantly, employers and employees alike need to be mindful of the illness or injury risks within their industry and take all precautions to mitigate these risks so that workers can be safe and healthy – and so can the economy.

WHO GETS THE DOG?
(Epic Pictures Group 2016)

Starring: Alicia Silverstone; Ryan Kwanten

Lesson: Family Law

Plot: Pretty simple plot here: couple with no kids are divorcing. They both want the dog – a beloved yellow Labrador Retriever named Wesley. They fight over the dog through divorce proceedings. (Spoiler alert!) They wind up back together and Wesley lives happily ever after. The plot is thin and the acting is only fair. But the legal theme invokes cutting edge discussion about how pets are treated in divorce proceedings, and whether it is time for a national change to the archaic approach of simply regarding pets no differently than other personal property to be equitably divided, just like furniture, cars, or Christmas ornaments.

Pets in Divorce

Despite that fact that most Americans come to regard their cats and dogs as members of the family, the law is clear that pets are regarded as personal property. Often, our beloved animals are marital property, assuming the pet was acquired during the marriage (and was not a gift to one of the spouses, etc.). Modern legislation has moved slightly toward a hybrid standard for answering the question: Who gets the dog? A 2017 Alaskan statute at least provides that a court, in awarding property rights with respect to a jointly-owned pet, may "take into consideration the well-being of the animal." Alaska Stat. Ann. §25.24.160. Similarly, a 2018 law in Illinois provides for the court to consider the future well-being of companion animals when determining "who gets the dog."

California, however, in 2019, went further in providing statutory guidance for treating pets differently from typical "personal property" in divorce proceedings. The new California law is cutting edge, in that it allows judges to consider, not merely the well-being of pets, but also the "care" of the pet in general. In deciding who should be awarded the "pet animal … the court, at the request of a party to proceedings for dissolution of marriage or for legal separation of the parties, may assign sole or joint ownership of a pet animal taking into consideration the care of the pet animal." Cal. Fam. Code § 2605(b) (West 2018). The law also allows the court to enter an order upon request that assigns a divorcing party the duty of "care for the pet animal prior to the final determination of ownership of the animal." § 2605(a). This way, while the parties continue their divorce battle, the court could determine where the pet will live in the interim. The law went into effect January 1, 2019. So far, I could not find any case citations addressing the statute (nor did I find any in Alaska or Illinois), but the hope is that other states are taking similar measures and modeling bills after California's more progressive law. Family law parties, advocates, and courts are likely to wrestle with these issues more and more.

Under the statutory definition, care includes, without limitation, "the prevention of acts of harm or cruelty [as described in California's Penal Code] … the provision of food, water, veterinary care, and safe and protected shelter." § 2605(c). The "well-being" and "care" of a "pet animal," hopefully, can easily be proven by either party, under this definition, provided the party is keeping the pet alive and not inflicting harm upon the animal that would rise to the level of criminal conduct. Geez. Should the court's analysis go further? Should a "best interests of the dog" standard apply, under which the full living situation of each party is examined in deciding "who gets the dog"?

For now, at the very least, California's law is a step in the right direction and other states should enact similar legislation. Interim hearings could be held to ensure the pet's well-being as divorces and separations head down whatever course they may, some being long and nasty. "Who gets the dog" might also be a good topic for discussion at mediation in any family matter. Early decisions about the continuing care and well-being of pets in divorce cases is in the best interests of all involved – two-leggers and four-leggers alike.

What about if the couple jointly owning a pet are not married? The split of their "personal property" would not be governed by family law; it would instead be subject to personal property recovery actions, such as forcible entry and detainer actions for possession of personal property held by another. A replevin action is also recognized in state common laws as a means to recover personal property one claims is being wrongly detained by another. Those types of statutes and state common laws focus on who has the better right to possession of the property. Often times these are brought by creditors in repossession actions when debtors do not cooperate in, say, returning the cars they are not able to afford. But cases can arise between two individual pet owners who lived together and are parting ways and fighting over the dog. Might laws be added to personal property FED statutes that also take the welfare of the pet into consideration in determining who gets the dog when non-married people are separating?

LEGAL BRIEFS AND MOVIE EXTRAS

* For additional reading about pets in divorce, see https://www.divorcemag.com/blog/who-gets-the-pets-in-a-divorce (last visited April 26, 2020)

FIND ME GUILTY
(Yari Film Group 2006)

Starring: Vin Deisel; Ron Silver; Annabella Sciorra

Lessons: Criminal Law; Criminal Procedure/Constitutional Law

Plot: *Find Me Guilty* is based on the true story of "Fat" Jack DiNorscio, who was serving a jail sentence already when he is indicted for federal RICO charges. Angry at his attorney for charging him hundreds of thousands of dollars so he could spend the better part of his life in jail, he decides to defend himself this time - from his jail cell - in the largest and longest Mafia trial in American history (20 defendants, 76 charges; over two years of testimony). Vin Diesel fabulously portrays Jack DiNorscio.

Much of the dialogue comes straight from the actual trial transcripts. Because the filmmakers were focusing on the most outrageous, fit-for-the-movie scenes featuring Fat Jack himself, we see only scattered portions of the actual courtroom presentations. Although the facts of the case are not always coherently presented, the movie nevertheless presents plenty of courtroom perspective and ammunition for legal analysis.

CRIMINAL LAW
Racketeer Influenced Corrupt Organizations Act

Fat Jack and his "family" are brought up on, among other things, violations of 18 U.S.C. §1961 et seq., more commonly known as "RICO," an acronym for Racketeer Influenced Corrupt Organizations Act. RICO makes it "unlawful for any person who has received any income derived, directly or indirectly, from a pattern of racketeering activity ... to use or invest, directly or indirectly, any part of such income, or the proceeds of such income, in acquisition of any interest in, or the establishment or operation of, any enterprise which is engaged in, or the activities of which affect, interstate or foreign commerce." RICO is broad in that it prohibits profiting from just about any illegal activity. Racketeering includes any "act or threat involving murder, kidnapping, gambling, arson, robbery, bribery, extortion, dealing in obscene matter, or dealing in a controlled substance; [or] any act which is indictable under any of the following provisions of Title 18, United States Code [listing close to 50 federal crimes]." 18 U.S.C. §1961(1).

Conspiracy is prohibited under RICO. 18 U.S.C. §1962(d) ("It shall be unlawful for any person to conspire to violate any of the provisions of [RICO]"). In Scene 6, one of the other defense attorneys warns Jack that his representing himself could be hazardous to him and the other 19 defendants. He seems most worried about the conspiracy charges, telling Jack it is "not hard to prove…two of you in the same room, that's conspiracy." Perhaps the defense attorney's concern was the fact that the government does not need to prove the underlying crimes in order to make conspiracy charges stick. The inchoate offense of conspiracy and the completed substantive offense that is the object of the conspiracy are separate crimes. *United States v. Felix,* 503 U.S. 378, 390 (1992). In other words, for a conspiracy conviction, the government does not even have to prove that the criminal objective was completed. *See Garrett* v. *United States,* 471 U.S. 773, 778 (1985) (holding that "[c]onspiracy is a distinct offense from the completed object of the conspiracy" such that completion is not required).

Although conspiracy law can be broad, the Fifth Circuit has made it clear that "[c]onspiracy law is not a dragnet for apprehending those with criminal dispositions." *United States v. Grass,* 616 F.2d 1295, 1301 (5th Cir. 1980). Perhaps the prosecutors could have saved taxpayers hundreds of thousands of dollars and over two years of judicial resources had they viewed conspiracy in a manner similar to that of the Fifth

Circuit's view in the *Grass* case instead of embarking on such an overzealous and futile quest.

CRIMINAL PROCEDURE
(CONSTITUTIONAL LAW: The Sixth Amendment)

Fat Jack tells the Judge he plans to represent himself, but the Judge cautions him against having a "fool for a client." Jack asks the judge if the old adage were true, to which the judge responds: "sometimes." As Jack rightly notes, "then that means sometimes it ain't." Jack is no fool after all - this is the same solid logic that can be used to establish reasonable doubt. Where there are two possible theories, even a slim possibility of the alternative theory creates doubt. Jack ultimately persuades the judge that he is exercising his constitutional right to represent himself, telling him his legal experience is that he was in prison half his life. For obvious reasons, many people in the legal profession generally discourage any criminal defendant's decision to exercise this right. That being said, was the judge's discouragement appropriate under the circumstances? What discretion did the judge have?

The Supreme Court has held that a trial judge may "terminate self-representation by an accused who deliberately engages in serious and obstructionist misconduct." *Faretta v. California*, 422 U.S. 806, 834 (1975) (citing the Sixth Amendment). The *Faretta* Court held that:

both the 'spirit and the logic' of the Sixth Amendment are that every person accused of crime shall receive the fullest possible defense; in the vast majority of cases this command can be honored only by means of the expressly guaranteed right to counsel, and the trial judge is in the best position to determine whether the accused is capable of conducting his defense. True freedom of choice and society's interest in seeing that justice is achieved can be vindicated only if the trial court retains discretion to reject any attempted waiver of counsel and insist that the accused be tried according to the Constitution.

Id. Is there any case law in your state on whether or not a criminal defendant who exercises his Sixth Amendment rights can succeed on an appeal based on inadequate counsel? For an interesting case highlighting the interface between the Sixth Amendment's guarantee of adequate counsel and its corresponding right to self-representation, see *Jones v. Walker,* 496 F.3d 1216, 1229 (Ga. 2007). Mr. Jones was a pro se criminal defendant who successfully appealed on ineffective counsel grounds and obtained a new trial. *Id.* The Court held that, for an effective waiver of the Sixth Amendment right to counsel and proper invocation of the correlative right to self-representation: "[t]wo requirements must be met. First, the defendant must 'clearly and unequivocally' assert his desire to represent himself thus waiving his right to counsel. Second, the court must determine that the defendant has made this election 'knowingly and intelligently.'" *Id.* (internal citations omitted). Given the judge's thorough discussion with Jack, these requirements were likely satisfied.

? Exam Tip

When facts present either an inadequate attorney or a pro se defendant and errors that result in a criminal conviction, be ready to write about Sixth Amendment implications. Of course, where an attorney is involved, ethical issues and malpractice claims might also need to be discussed, depending on the class and the test.

LEGAL BRIEFS & MOVIE EXTRAS

*According to wikipedia.com, Rico was the nickname of Caesar Enrico Bandelloin, the gangster featured in the 1931 organized crime movie *Little Caesar*. It is speculated (but not confirmed) that drafters of the original RICO bill created the acronym in reference to the character.

Find Me Guilty is another Sidney Lumet directed film. Sidney Lumet also directed *12 Angry Men, The Verdict, Night Falls on Manhattan*, and *Guilty As Sin*. Compared to most Lumet films, however, *Find Me Guilty* fared quite poorly at the box office.

*A famous adage from this movie is "a laughing jury is never a hanging jury." If your practice will involve jury trials and you've got the gift of good humor, use it! But only if you've also got the gift of good judgment!

MICHAEL CLAYTON
(Warner Brothers 2007)

Starring: George Clooney; Tom Wilkinson

Lesson: Ethics

Plot: The gorgeous and talented George Clooney is Michael Clayton, "special counsel" in the fictitious New York City law firm of Kenner, Bach & Ledeen. Clayton "cleans up" various messes facing the firm and its large, corrupt, corporate clients who cannot seem to focus on anything but their bottom line. *Michael Clayton* is not a courtroom drama; there are no trial scenes to analyze, nor are there any attorney styles or strategies to model. In fact, law students should view *Michael Clayton* as a lesson in how *not* to handle "messes!" In addition, this suspenseful film is rich with gripping dialogue and compelling characters. And...did I mention George Clooney?!?! The movie should not be missed for that reason alone.

ETHICS
Attorney Impairment

Michael Clayton brings out into the open controversial problems that can plague attorneys, including substance abuse and mental illness. In Scene 7, Clayton is sent to Milwaukee to handle a situation involving the firm's partner, Arthur Edens (Tom Wilkinson). Edens skips his medication and has a mental breakdown during a major deposition. Clayton reprimands Edens for missing his meds, and deals with the mess in his usual "clean up, cover up" manner. Clayton continues to cover for Edens, even after he complicates a class action lawsuit the firm was defending.

It is estimated that 10-20% of legal professionals will deal with an addictive disorder during their career and 33% will deal with short-term or chronic depression. Susan Daicoff, *"Asking Leopards to Change Their Spots: Should Lawyers Change?"* 11 GEO J. LEGAL ETHICS 547 (1998). Studies show that 60-85% of all legal malpractice actions stem from an attorney's impairment from substance abuse or mental illness. Rick B. Allan, *Alcoholism, Drug Abuse and Lawyers: Are We Ready to Address the Denial,* 31 CREIGHTON L. REV 265, 265-66 (1997) (citing studies of alcohol and drug abuse conducted in Washington, Wisconsin, and Arizona). These are serious diseases affecting attorneys and their law firms. More is required than periodic "clean ups" by a law firm "janitor."

Impairment of an attorney in a law firm raises ethical issues not only for the attorney, but also for the other members of the firm. ABA Model Rule 5.1 (Responsibilities of a Partner or Supervisory Lawyer) provides:

(a)   A partner in a law firm, and a lawyer who individually or together with other lawyers possesses comparable managerial authority in a law firm, shall make reasonable efforts to ensure that the firm has in effect measures giving reasonable assurance that all lawyers in the firm conform to the Rules of Professional Conduct.

(b)   A lawyer having direct supervisory authority over another lawyer shall make reasonable efforts to ensure that the other lawyer conforms to the Rules of Professional Conduct.

(c)   A lawyer shall be responsible for another lawyer's violation of the Rules of Professional Conduct if:

(1) the lawyer orders or, with knowledge of the specific conduct, ratifies the conduct involved; or

(2) the lawyer is a partner or has comparable managerial authority in the law firm in which the other lawyer practices, or has direct supervisory authority over the other lawyer, and knows of the conduct at a time when its consequences can be avoided or mitigated but fails to take reasonable remedial action.

When an attorney suffers from chronic addiction, depression, or other impairment, at some point, he will not be able to meet the standards of conduct required under the ABA Model Rules, including, without limitation, ABA Model Rule 1.1 (Competence) and ABA Model Rule 1.3 (Diligence). The American Bar Association has dealt with the issue of attorney impairment within a law firm and has issued ABA Formal Opinion 03-429 (June 10, 2003), which sets forth the obligations of partners and supervisory attorneys with respect to impaired lawyers within their law firms. In short, law firm partners cannot turn a blind eye to the impairment of an attorney in the firm and resulting ethical violations. *See also* RESTATEMENT (THIRD), OF THE LAW GOVERNING LAWYERS §11 (holding that the lack of awareness of another attorney's misconduct does not excuse a violation of the duty to supervise).

With respect to Arthur Edens, how many ethical rules were violated as a result of his impairment? Or was it an act of conscience, as opposed to impairment, that caused Edens to violate rules? Either way, can any of his actions be defended? What duties to his corporate client did Edens breach?

LEGAL BRIEFS & MOVIE EXTRAS

Reversible Errors also deals with issues of attorney impairment. There, even judges fall prey to the harms of substance abuse.

*For more information about substance abuse and mental impairment and the American Bar Association's efforts to curb its detrimental impact on the legal profession, visit the ABA's Commission on Lawyer Assistance Programs ("CoLAP") at its website:

http://www.abanet.org/legalservices/colap

Because of the ABA and state bar associations' heightened awareness of impairment and the need to reach out to peers affected, rules regarding the duty to report professional misconduct ("rat rules") generally exempt disclosure of information obtained about a lawyer during the course of an approved lawyer's assistance program.

FRACTURE
(New Line Cinema 2007)

Starring: Anthony Hopkins; Ryan Gosling

Lessons: Ethics; Criminal Law/Procedure (Constitutional Law)

Plot: Ted Crawford (Anthony Hopkins) is accused of attempting to murder his wife, who is in a coma after being shot in the head. Crawford's prosecution is assigned to Assistant District Attorney Willey Beachum (Ryan Gosling). Willey Beachum was in the process of winding up his ADA position and moving into a better paying job at a large law firm. When Crawford is freed on a technicality, however, Willey Beachum gives up his high paying new law firm position in his obsession to prove Crawford's guilt. Crawford thinks he is versed in constitutional law, but Beachum proves to be the more knowledgeable.

ETHICS

In Scene 5, Willey tells his new mentor and love interest about his sneaky way of snagging himself an interview with the firm. He essentially outsmarts a criminal defense attorney – a senior associate of the firm against whom he had a criminal trial. He negotiated himself an interview with the firm's hiring partner in exchange for his "throwing" the case against the senior associate's client. The defense attorney comes to court unprepared and, despite Willey's "throwing the case," the judge winds up finding the firm's client guilty and giving him the maximum penalty. His mentor laughs and tells Willey he really didn't do anything wrong. But did he? ABA Model Rule 8.4(e) provides that "it is professional misconduct for a lawyer to … state or imply an ability to influence improperly a government agency or official or to achieve results by means that violate the Rules of Professional Conduct or other law." Did Willey use his government position as ADA and his influence over the court to advance his personal career in violation of Rule 8.4(e)? Does Willey's conduct violate any other section of ABA Model Rule 8.4, regarding the integrity of the profession? *See, e.g.,* ABA Model Rule 8.4(d) (prohibiting a lawyer from engaging in conduct "prejudicial to the administration of justice.").

CRIMINAL LAW/PROCEDURE
(CONSTITUTIONAL LAW)
Fruit of the Poisonous Tree Doctrine –
Fourth & Fifth Amendments

In Scene 8, the judge determines that the defendant's confession was "the fruit of the poisonous tree" and therefore inadmissible. The propriety and admissibility of a criminal confession must comply with both the Fourth Amendment's protection against unlawful search and seizures and the Fifth Amendment's protection against self-incrimination. *See Brown v. Illinois,* 422 U.S. 590, 601 (1975). The Fourth Amendment reads, in part: "[t]he right of the people to be secure in their persons, houses, papers, and effects, against unreasonable searches and seizures, shall not be violated." U.S. Const. amend. IV. Under the Fifth Amendment, "[n]o person shall ... be compelled in any criminal case to be a witness against himself." U.S. Const. amend. V. Even where a confession is made voluntarily under the Fifth Amendment, the Fourth Amendment may nevertheless cause a "tainted" voluntary confession to be excluded. That is what happened in this case.

To protect the constitutional rights of the accused against improper police conduct, such as unlawful searches and arrests or coerced confessions, the Supreme Court has carved out the so-called "exclusionary rule" to keep any ill-gotten evidence out of trial. *Brown v. Illinois,* 422 U.S. at 599. The rationale is that, if the evidence cannot be used, the police will be less likely to resort to improper means to obtain such evidence. *See id.* The fruit of the poisonous tree doctrine is a subset of the exclusionary rule. If the illegal search, arrest, or post-arrest interrogation is "poisoned" by improper police conduct, any confession or other evidence obtained through the poisonous process is excluded as "fruit of the poisonous tree." For more information about the history of the doctrine, see Robert M. Pitler, *'The Fruit of the Poisonous Tree, Revisited and Shepardized,* 56 CALIF.L.REV. 579, 603-604 (1968).

Going back to Scene 3, what precisely was the poisonous tree that produced the tainted fruit that was Crawford's confession? In Scene 8, Crawford articulates the problem to the judge in layman terms. In short, the arresting officer, Lt. Robert Nunally, had a sexual relationship with the victim. The Supreme Court has held that the "presence of intervening circumstances … and, particularly, the purpose and flagrancy of the official misconduct are all relevant" in determining whether a police-procured confession passes Fourth Amendment muster. *Brown v. Illinois,* 422 U.S. at 604-05 (internal citations omitted). How would you argue for the defense that Lt. Nunally's relationship with the victim was an intervening circumstance with respect to the defendant's arrest and interrogation? What specific conduct by Lt. Nunally was an intervening circumstance that tainted the confession? In other words, what was the "purpose and flagrancy" of the Lt. Nunally's conduct with respect to Ted Crawford, and how does it affect Crawford's constitutional rights?

Now consider the facts from the other perspective. As Willey pointed out to the judge, Crawford dictated and signed his written confession at the police station, long after his arrest. How would you argue for the prosecution that this written confession should be admitted into evidence? In *Brown v. Illinois*, the Supreme Court held that the temporal proximity between the tainted arrest and the confession is relevant in determining if the confession should be excluded under the fruit of the poisonous tree doctrine. 422 U.S. at 604-05. Does the time that elapsed cleanse the confession of the taint from the poisonous tree? Could Crawford rely on the Sixth Amendment's right to counsel, in arguing that his confession was still tainted fruit?

Double Jeopardy

In Scene 15, Crawford incorrectly relies on the "double jeopardy" concept that one may not "be twice put in jeopardy of life or limb" for the same crime. The Double Jeopardy Clause is contained in the Fifth Amendment, made applicable to the States through the Fourteenth Amendment in *Benton v. Maryland*, 395 U.S. 784, 794 (1969). The United States Supreme Court recognizes three separate constitutional "double jeopardy" protections under the Fifth Amendment. The Fifth Amendment "protects against a second prosecution for the same offense after acquittal. It protects against a second prosecution for the same offense after conviction. And it protects against multiple punishments for the same offense." *North Carolina v. Pearce*, 395 U.S. 711, 717 (1969).

Note however that, by its express language, the double jeopardy concept only applies to the specific crime previously tried. Often, when new evidence presents itself post-trial, there are other crimes that the prosecution can bring against the acquitted defendant without running afoul of the Fifth Amendment. That is what happened here. Crawford was previously put in jeopardy for the offense of attempted murder. Subsequently, new evidence came to light about his actions: in bragging about his faulty double jeopardy trick, he admitted shooting his wife. After he pulled the plug and his wife died, the prosecution became free to put him in jeopardy for the offense of murder without running afoul of the Fifth Amendment.

This clever ending shows the limits to the constitutional protection against double jeopardy and a common misconception among laypeople about its scope. As the movie shows, separate prosecutable offenses can arise from essentially the same criminal conduct. For instance, the Supreme Court has invalidated double jeopardy defenses in many cases where criminal defendants are prosecuted for conspiracy and subsequently charged with carrying out the conspired crime. In *United States v. Felix*, the Supreme Court allowed the defendant to be tried twice for operating a methamphetamine facility – one trial for the offense of attempting to manufacture an illegal drug, and another trial for conspiracy to manufacture, possess, and distribute methamphetamine. 503 U.S. 378, 391-92 (1992). The Court held that "the conspiracy charge against Felix was an offense distinct from any crime for which he had been previously prosecuted, and the Double Jeopardy Clause did not bar his prosecution on that charge." *Id. See also Garrett* v. *United States*, 471 U.S. 773, 778 (1985) (holding that "[c]onspiracy is a distinct offense from the completed object of the conspiracy"); *Blockburger v. United States,* 284 U.S. 299 (1932) (defining "same offense").

Another limit to the Double Jeopardy clause stems from the "dual sovereignty" doctrine. Under the dual sovereignty doctrine, the Supreme Court has held that the Double Jeopardy Clause does not bar successive prosecutions by two states for the same conduct. *See Heath v. Alabama,* 474 U.S. 82, 87 (1985) (holding that a defendant who crossed the Georgia/Alabama state line in the course of a kidnapping and murder could be prosecuted for murder in both states without violating the double jeopardy principles). Additionally, a state can prosecute a defendant for murder, after which the federal government might try the same defendant for a federal crime arising out of the murder (e.g., terrorizing, kidnapping, etc.). An example of such a situation was the Oklahoma City bombings of 1995. Had the federal government not executed Timothy McVeigh for killing federal employees, the State of Oklahoma could have prosecuted him for other murders arising out of the explosions even if the federal case had resulted in a mistrial or an acquittal. Similarly, both state and federal courts may prosecute a bank robbery under their respective laws.

On the other hand, see *Harris v. Oklahoma*, 433 U.S. 682, 682 (1977) (holding that a conviction for felony murder acts as a bar to a conviction of the underlying felony); *Price v. Georgia*, 398 U.S. 323, 327 (1970) (holding that a conviction for a lesser offense bars retrial for a greater offense arising out of the same incident). For more on double jeopardy principles, see sections 1.08-1.11 of the Model Penal Code.

? Exam Tip

When a fact pattern suggests a double jeopardy situation, keep in mind its limitations and the potential for subsequent criminal charges where there are multiple jurisdictions or multiple crimes involved. For instance, you may be provided with a scenario in which a criminal defendant engages in illegal conduct in more than one state, which might be a clue that you are facing a double jeopardy question and a dual sovereignty situation.

LEGAL BRIEFS & MOVIE EXTRAS

*Anthony Hopkins gives another fine performance in *Fracture*. As Ted Crawford, Hopkins was almost as creepy as his character Hannibal Lecter from *Silence of the Lambs*.

*Another legal movie dealing with the Double Jeopardy Clause is (no surprise) *Double Jeopardy* (Paramount Pictures 1999), starring Ashley Judd and Tommy Lee Jones. Ashley Judd plays a woman imprisoned after being framed for killing her husband. While in prison, she discovers her husband is still alive. When freed from prison, she sets out to kill him and seek protection from re-prosecution under the Double Jeopardy Clause. The movie is well acted and entertaining, but it is almost entirely based on factual and legal errors. It is still worth watching, however. See if you can spot all of its legal inaccuracies and other problems.

"I appreciate your concern for the dignity of the court. ...Unfortunately, the man is a tax-paying citizen and entitled by our constitution to try and manipulate the legal system like everybody else!"

-Says Judge Pincus in response to Willey Beachum's concerns about Crawford's representing himself and turning the case into a "circus."

FLASH OF GENIUS
(Universal Pictures 2008)

Starring: Greg Kinnear; Alan Alda; Lauren Graham; Dermot Mulroney

Lesson: Intellectual Property

Plot: *Flash of Genius* is based on the true story of Dr. Robert Kearns, a professor and an owner of an auto parts store. Dr. Kearns invented a car feature that is now standard in most makes and models: the intermittent windshield wiper. Ford Motor Company tried to rob him of his "flash of genius" idea, and Ford had the resources to do so. Still, Dr. Kearns takes on the (then) corporate giant and fights for his patent rights to his invention. *Flash of Genius* is the story of his struggles and sacrifices along the way. In addition to the intellectual property law implications, the movie raises ethical issues and highlights some of the impediments people face when they must work their way through complicated legal processes. *Flash of Genius* does have some value for law students, although I thought parts of the movie were rather boring. The end of the film contains some decent courtroom scenes to analyze, and with the underdog *finally* attaining justice, we are rewarded with a happy ending. But it is difficult to watch Dr. Kearns's life fall apart throughout the years leading up to his ultimate victory.

INTELLECTUAL PROPERTY

There are four basic forms of protection for intellectual property (i.e., human ideas and invention): patents, trademarks, trade secrets, and copyrights. A **patent** is an exclusive right to an idea, given to the original inventor, for a certain period of time, under the condition that the inventor discloses the secrets after that time period elapses. A **trade secret** is the unique process or special formula used to create something that is not known to the general public and the "know how" is not publicly available. A **trademark** is a distinctive sign, symbol, design, or company logo that an individual or a business uses to identify the goods or services it produces. A **copyright** gives exclusive rights to the original author or creator of intellectual property for 70 years after the author's death, after which the property goes into the public domain.

Some inventions or creations have components that fall under all four protectable categories. For example, the components and designs for the windshield wiper unit at issue in this movie were patented. The process required for putting the unit together might be a trade secret. The name of the wiper unit or the package design might be a trademark. The advertisements and literature about the wipers may be copyrighted.

The intellectual property at the heart of Dr. Kearns's situation involves patent law. His intermittent windshield wiper unit, and the various components that comprise the unit, enjoyed the right to patent protections. These patents are governed by the United States Patent Act, 35 U.S.C. §§1-376. The Patent Act states that one who "invents or discovers any new and useful process, machine, manufacture, or composition of matter, or any new and useful improvement thereof, may obtain a patent therefor, subject to the conditions and requirements of this title." 35 U.S.C. §101. What went wrong for Dr. Kearns, in terms of the patents to his invention? What should he have done differently?

There is a good overview of the Patent Act on Cornell Law School's website:

www.law.cornell.edu/patent/patent.overview.html (last visited October 27, 2020).

? Exam Tips

An effective method to prepare for multiple-choice exams, such as the multi-state bar exam or the patent bar exam, is studying prior or model exams. These models typically give you the correct answer, as well as the reason why that answer is the best choice. Be sure you thoroughly understand why the answer is correct and why the other answers are incorrect. Also, for the patent bar, study the Manual of Patent Examining Procedure thoroughly, but do not expect to be able to memorize the thousands of pages of rules and regulations contained in the manual. Your patent bar study time will be much more productive if you focus on where to quickly find information within the manual, as you are provided a copy of the manual with the patent bar exam. Studying where to find the right information, as opposed to memorizing the right information, is also helpful for essay exams focusing on court rules of procedure, in which you are provided with a copy of the rules but you will not have time to search through them to find the answers. You need to know right where to look.

LEGAL BRIEFS & MOVIE EXTRAS

Flash of Genius highlights a complex area of law: patent law. Patent law is highly specialized. Normally, when an attorney chooses a practice area, the attorney is said to "focus her practice" in that area. The attorney cannot, however, say that she "specializes" in a particular area unless:

(1)   the lawyer has been certified as a specialist by an organization that has been approved by an appropriate state authority or that has been accredited by the American Bar Association; and

(2)   the name of the certifying organization is clearly identified in the communication.

ABA Model Rule 7.4(d) (Communication of Fields of Practice and Specialization). Patent law typically falls under this exception. *See* ABA Model Rule 7.4(d) ("A lawyer admitted to engage in patent practice before the United States Patent and Trademark Office may use the designation 'Patent Attorney' or a substantially similar designation."). For law students with science backgrounds, taking the patent bar and forming an intellectual property specialty may prove fulfilling and lucrative.

The Rainmaker (Paramount Pictures 1997), based on a John Grisham novel, presents a similar David v. Goliath-type legal victory for the underdog. There, an inexperienced lawyer successfully battles a large insurance company on behalf of a family being denied medical insurance coverage when one of the kids was in dire need of healthcare.

Joy (Fox 2000 Pictures 2015), starring Jennifer Lawrence, also has some of the same themes regarding intellectual property and invention. Based on a true story, Joy, too, is cheated out of her intellectual property, but fights back and becomes a leader in the niche of home shopping network products.

LINCOLN LAWYER
(Lionsgate Entertainment 2011)

Starring: Matthew McConaughey; Marisa Tomei

Lesson: Ethics

Plot: Mickey Haller (McConaughey) is a shady criminal defense attorney who practices law out of the back of his 1986 Lincoln Town car, driven by Earl, his chauffeur, friend, and confidant. He finds himself in an ethical conundrum and a conflict between two clients. He discovers that one of his clients, young, rich, playboy Louis Roulet, is a serial killer. The attorney-client privilege, Mickey feels, prevents him from disclosing this confidential information. The problem, however, is that the information could be exonerating for another of Mickey's clients, Jesus Martinez, who was wrongly incarcerated for one of the murders Roulet committed. Mickey had convinced Martinez to plead guilty in order to avoid the death penalty. Mickey needs to find a way to get the information out in the open without breaking his client's confidentiality.

Mickey uses another former client, Gloria, who was serving pretrial time with a jailhouse snitch, to get the information out about Roulet and his murders. Gloria leads the snitch to believe that, if he testifies against Roulet, he will enjoy more favorable treatment from the prosecution. Further, Mickey informs a prosecutor, who happens to be his ex-wife, Maggie, that he has uncovered evidence that would exonerate Martinez, but that would also implicate Roulet in the murder for which Martinez was charged.

In using Gloria to relay confidential information, and in telling his ex-wife about the evidence against Roulet, Mickey Haller breaks client confidentiality and breaks the attorney-client privilege he owed to Roulet. Leaving aside the fact that

Mickey's use of the snitch is a criminal conspiracy to commit perjury, the question is: do the exceptions to the client confidentiality rule save Haller?

Client Confidentiality – Exceptions

As discussed in prior chapters, the exception to the client confidentiality requirement, ABA Model Rule 1.6(b)(2), states that "a lawyer *may* reveal information relating to the representation of a client to the extent the lawyer reasonably believes necessary ... to prevent the client from committing a crime or fraud that is reasonably certain to result in substantial injury to the financial interests or property of another and in furtherance of which the client has used or is using the lawyer's services." In short, a lawyer may – but is not required to – breach confidentiality in order to stop a crime or fraud from happening in the *future*. That Mickey Haller's client was a serial killer, Haller may have had a reasonable belief that his client would kill again.

Haller also had a reasonable basis to be concerned for his own safety, having been threatened by this client to keep his mouth shut. There was likely sufficient basis for Haller to invoke an exception. There were, however, risks, both in terms of his and his family's safety and with respect to the Professional Rules of Conduct. The situation is heightened by the fact that another of Haller's clients who would benefit from Haller's breaching the attorney/client confidentiality rule with respect to Roulet. Louis Roulet would go to jail, but, Haller might be able to reopen the Martinez case and exonerate him. It makes for an interesting movie that most lawyers will not be able to watch simply for the story and may result in nightmares about the bar exam.

Another exception to the confidentiality rule stems from Rule 1.6(b)(4). A lawyer is permitted to seek counsel from another lawyer, in a particular case, allowing her to disclose enough information to secure professional advice, including how to proceed with a potential ethical dilemma. This exception does not include divulging a client's identity and providing the full information to an ex-wife/prosecutor.

Even if Haller may have been able to disclose the information under Rule 1.6(b)(2) or 1.6(b)(4), the manner in which he proceeded was not in line with the Model Rules.

LEGAL BRIEFS & MOVIE EXTRAS

*Aside from the attorney client privilege and confidentiality breaches, Mickey Haller violates almost as many rules as Vincent Gambini and Fletcher Reede. Consider for example his lie to a judge, claiming he needed a continuance in order to locate a fictitious witness. The real reason was that he refused to go to trial until his client paid him, but he could not admit that to the judge. This violates the rules regarding candor and decorum. What other ethical violates does Mickey Haller commit? Would bribing jail security for quicker access to your clients count?

*The Lincoln Lawyer is based on a novel of the same name by Michael Connelly.

THE JUDGE
(Warner Bros. 2014)

Starring: Robert Downey, Jr.; Robert Duvall

Lesson: Criminal Law

Plot: Judge Joseph Palmer (Duvall) and Hank Palmer (Downey, Jr.). Father v. son. Small town judge v. big city defense attorney. This film is as much a father-son "troubled relationship" exposition as it is a courtroom drama. Hank returns home after his mother passes away, despite his having been estranged from the "Judge," as even his sons were required to call him. He stays longer than anticipated, after his father is accused of running down an enemy, evidence of which seems apparent, to Hank, from the fender of his father's Cadillac.

Complicating the issue of whether the Judge is guilty or innocent is the fact that Hank is uncertain whether his father knows whether or not he committed the crime, given his age and mental infirmities and the fact that he had recently lost his wife. The victim was a man who, two years earlier, had been released from prison and had killed his girlfriend. The Judge regretted that he was responsible for his short prison sentence, and resented the man for taunting him in town and for disrespecting his wife's grave.

Hank, unimpressed with the small town lawyer who was hired to represent his father (Dax Sheppard), Hank steps up to defend his father. Dax gets to co-counsel, however, which provides some necessary comic relief.

For analysis about the appropriateness of a son representing a father in a capital murder charge, please refer to films regarding ethics in this book. The focus of this chapter is on two tools among the many in a criminal defense attorney's toolbox: jury selection and motions for change of venue.

Jury Selection

When the attorneys are selecting from the jury panel, pay attention to the small-town dynamics at play in terms of the desired audience for their big murder trial. The inexperienced lawyer asks the Palmer men: "Now, what exactly is our target juror?"

The Judge: "Intelligent people who will listen to instructions and follow the evidence."

Hank: "Crackpots. Those I can persuade to swallow their own tongues. Anyone whose seen a Sasquatch. Moon landing deniers. Those are our people."

For Hank's voir dire of the panel, he simply asks, "Bumper Stickers. Anybody got one on their car, truck, RV?"

Responses ranged from "Tolerance" (no way) to "Willie Nelson for President" (yes) to "Wife and Dog Missing. Reward for Dog" (hell yes!).

Importantly, the trial in this film does not have any racial undertones or need for a true cross-section of society in order for a fair and impartial jury (compare with the juries in *A Time to Kill* and *To Kill a Mockingbird*.). And as the presiding judge noted, in denying a change of venue (discussed below), there is likely an equal number of jurors who like the Judge as compared to those who dislike him. This preliminary jury selection step is portrayed as an unserious, light-hearted process in a criminal proceeding. As discussed elsewhere in this book and my other law books, the voir dire process and an attorney's ability to control his audience of factfinders is crucial. If a failure occurs in obtaining an impartial jury, a failure has occurred in the criminal process.

Change of Venue

The term "change of venue" refers to a transfer of a case from one court to another court, located in a different geographical area, of the same or similar jurisdiction. The reason a party requests a change of venue is directly related to the concept of an impartial jury. A change of venue request is often one of the first considerations for a criminal defense team. There are a host of reasons why a small town criminal defendant may wish for his trial to be heard outside of town. In *The Judge*, however, the preliminary request for a change of venue was made by the prosecution, not the criminally accused.

The concept of venue change is aligned with the constitutional right to a fair and impartial jury. The prosecution argued that the Judge should be tried outside of the very town in which he sat on the bench for 40 years. The presiding judge disagreed, reasoning that there would be just as many people in town who might hate Judge Palmer for locking them up. Venue remained in Judge Palmer's own court, where he sat in a different chair with a different title.

When a criminal defendant requests a change of venue, additional constitutional considerations are required to ensure that the defendant is afforded an impartial jury. The Sixth Amendment grants an accused the right to a speedy trial by an impartial jury of the state and district in which the crime is alleged to have been committed; no such right is afforded the prosecution under the Sixth. In granting a defendant's request for a change of venue, courts commonly examine five factors (taken from *Williams v. Superior Court*, discussed below):

1. **The nature and gravity of the offense**. The worse the allegations, the worse the potential punishment. A heightened vigilance of a defendant's constitutional rights must be afforded to protect the accused's liberties.

2. **The extent of news coverage**. If a defendant has essentially been "convicted" by public opinion based on local news reporting, a court would consider a motion to change venue to a location where there is less media coverage, perhaps in a place where fewer people know the story and the players involved.

3. **Community characteristics**. The smaller the town, the more difficult it might be to ensure impartiality among jurors. It might prove difficult to find a full jury where no members had any involvement with the defendant or the victim.

4. **Defendant's status in the community.** In *Williams v. Superior Court*, the defendant, a non-resident black man charged with "murder with special circumstances, rape, burglary, kidnaping, kidnaping for robbery and robbery," in a county where only 402 of its 117,000 residents were black. 668 P.2d 799, 803. (1983). The Supreme Court of California granted the motion to change venue. *Id.* at 806. In doing so, the court examined all of these five factors, but seemed to put much weight on the defendant's status, as compared to that of the victim's status (a beloved, strong, young white woman who was a well-known and well-liked member of the community). *Id.*

5. **The victim's status in the community.** Sometimes a victim is so beloved in or sympathetic to her community that it is near impossible to find a jury that would not already be rooting for the death penalty for an accused. Such were the facts in the tragic tale told in *Maine v. Superior Court*, 438

P.2d 372 (1968). In this murder / manslaughter / aggravated assault trial, one of the victims was a young girl, caught in a fray of bullets, found unconscious on the side of the road. *Id.* at 378-379. The community came together to raise funds for her parents to offset the medical costs for all of the procedures that would save her life. *Id.* Because, in part, of the evidence that the community had organized fundraisers out of sympathy for victims' families, and wanted justice, the court determined that a change of venue out of said community was necessary for the defendants to be afforded a fair trial. *Id.* at 379. The court stated, "We do not hold it to be an invariable rule that sympathy for a victim demonstrates antipathy to the alleged perpetrators of an offense. But such pervasive civic involvement in the fate of a victim, particularly when the events all transpire in a relatively small community, is a strong indication that the venue should be changed." *Id.*

The above factors deal with the criminal defendant's rights under the Sixth Amendment. Consider venue change requests from a prosecutorial standpoint, as was the case in *The Judge*. Although prosecutors are not personally afforded Sixth Amendment rights, courts have held that a criminal defendant's rights under the Sixth Amendment do not preclude a state from obtaining a change of venue. Courts have granted prosecutorial motions to change venue based on highly fact-specific situations. In *Hobbs v. Commonwealth*, for example, the Kentucky Court of Appeals upheld a state's change of venue over the defendant's appeal based on venue. 206 S.W.2d 48 (1947). The court found persuasive the affidavit of the Commonwealth's attorney, supporting the motion, and confirmed by two other citizens. In this case,

"the accused, Finley Hobbs, is a magistrate of Clay County and a man of wide influence; the defendants are related by blood or marriage to three of the most prominent and influential families in the county; and they themselves are well-known and have relatives scattered throughout the county. It is further stated that there had been many homicides and other crimes committed in the county in recent years, and because of the lawless conditions it had been difficult and almost impossible to secure arrests and convictions; that upon recent trials of criminal cases the many persons who were under charge and their friends had gathered at the courthouse and brought their combined influence and acquaintance to bear in the selection of juries for the trial of others. As a result of these conditions, it was alleged, the Commonwealth could not have a fair trial."

Id. Although Mr. Hobbs' conviction was reversed on other grounds, the court found no problem with the change of venue under these circumstances in 1947 Kentucky. *Id.* at 49.

Compare the state's change of venue request in *The Judge* with that of the defense attorney's request in *A Time to Kill*, which was denied. There was no unfair prejudice to the prosecution in *The Judge*, but what factors in *A Time to Kill* might should have led to a venue change?

LEGAL BRIEFS & MOVIE EXTRAS

*Robert Duvall's movie debut was in another law-related movie. He played Boo Radley in *To Kill a Mockingbird* (1962).

*When Hank Palmer was getting ready for a bike ride, he changes into an old Metallica t-shirt from the "Damaged Justice" tour, circa 1988-1989. On the back is the album cover art featuring an oversized judge's gavel. So cool. I am sure I had this shirt back in the day but will need a replacement now.

"Did you know 90% of the country believes in ghosts? Less than a third in evolution? 35% can correctly identify Homer Simpson's fictional town in which he resides, less than 1%

knows the name Thurgood Marshall. But ... when you put 12 Americans together in a jury and you ask for justice? Something just South of brilliance happens. Often as not, they get it right."

-Hank Palmer (Robert Downey, Jr.)

SELMA
(Paramount Pictures 2014)

Starring: David Oyelowo; Tom Wilkinson; Carmen Ejogo

Lesson: Constitutional Law

Plot: *Selma* depicts the peaceful protests for civil voting rights, from Selma, Alabama to Montgomery, Alabama, on March 7, 1965. The march was led by the late greats Martin Luther King, Jr. and John Lewis, among others. The marchers were met by Alabama state troopers, and were attacked with nightsticks, tear gas and whips, after refusing to turn back. The violent incident was caught on news cameras and the day became known forever as "Bloody Sunday."

Fifteenth Amendment: Voting Rights

Ratified by the states in 1870, the Fifteenth Amendment to the Constitution prohibits states from denying a male citizen the right to vote based on "race, color or previous condition of servitude." Unfortunately, however, many Southern states instituted obstacles, such as poll taxes and literacy tests, to deliberately reduce voting among African American men. Plus they faced resistance from the KKK and others who would beat them if they appeared at the polls. So black men were not encouraged or motivated to exercise their new right to vote. In short, the ratification of the Fifteenth Amendment did not end racial discrimination in voting.

The Selma March was the impetus for the Voting Rights Act of 1965. The Voting Rights Act denied governments the right to continue racial discrimination in voting by regulating against the use of such barriers to exercising the rights granted to black men under the Fifteenth Amendment. The Act authorized the federal government to oversee voting laws in southern states with a history of racial discrimination and interference with the rights of voters. A "coverage formula" was used to identify certain states subject to this federal oversight, which included federal "preclearance," in order for a state to pass any new election processes or voting laws.

In the wake of the Voting Rights Act, black voter registration drastically increased. Tangible evidence proved the federal legislation worked to more evenly protect Fifteenth Amendment rights. In 2013, however, the Supreme Court rolled back certain provisions of the Voting Act.

In *Shelby County v. Holder*, the Supreme Court declared the preclearance coverage formula unconstitutional. 570 U.S. 529 (2013). In doing so, the Court stated, that a statute's "current burdens" must be justified by "current needs," and any "disparate geographic coverage" must be "sufficiently related to the problem that it targets." *Id.* The coverage formula met that test in 1965, but no longer does so. ... Racial disparity ... was compelling evidence justifying the preclearance remedy and the coverage formula. There is no longer such a disparity." *Id.* at 530.

In other words, the Voting Rights Act worked, so it is no longer needed. This was a 5-4 opinion. Justice Ginsberg's dissent finds fault with the majority's logic. She stated: "Throwing out preclearance when it has worked and is continuing to work to stop discriminatory changes is like throwing away your umbrella in a rainstorm because you are not getting wet. ... The Court errs egregiously by overriding Congress' decision."

LEGAL BRIEFS & MOVIE EXTRAS

Selma is not 100% historically accurate, in terms of the sequence of events and other "liberties" that were taken for dramatic effect. It does, however, correctly portray the larger picture of what was happening in the south during those tumultuous times. We also see a different side of Dr. King. Yes, we see his heroism, but we also see his flaws and imperfections. His humanism.

*As I was working on this draft, John Lewis sadly passed away. He was the first black lawmaker to be honored to lie in state. We have come a long way. Of course, our current President failed to even acknowledge Mr. Lewis's life of "Good Trouble," so maybe we have not come as far as we can.

* Ava Marie DuVernay, the director of *Selma*, also directed the documentary *13th*, discussed in this book and other of my e-books. The relatively recent influx of minorities into filmmaking leadership roles has broadened the black history genre, breaking away from some of the earlier "white hero" focused films, such as *To Kill a Mockingbird, Mississippi Burning, A Time to Kill,* etc.

"Our lives are not fully lived if we're not willing to die for those we love, for what we believe."

- Dr. Martin Luther King, Jr.

TED 2
(Universal Pictures 2015)

Starring: Seth MacFarlane (voice of Ted); Mark Wahlberg; Amanda Seyfried

Lessons: Constitutional Law

Plot: *Ted 2* is of course the continuing story of the life of Ted, the talking stuffed teddy bear that grew up in Boston alongside his best friend John (Mark Wahlberg). Ted gets into trouble when he and his wife Tami Lynn try to adopt a baby. He becomes under the radar of the government, and his citizenship – and all of the unalienable rights associated with that status – is challenged. He hires an attorney, Samantha (Sam) L. Jackson (Amanda Seyfried) and sues for citizenship.

This movie is a sequel. By that definition alone, one can assume the movie is inferior to the original *Ted*. The original *Ted* was not too great of a movie; its sequel is downright ridiculous, disgusting, contains drug use, violence, language, filth, racism, sexism, antisemitism, and essentially is one of the most offensive movies I have ever seen. But that is only if the movie is taken seriously, which obviously no viewer would do.

The court scenes and posture of the legal action at play are so far-fetched they offer almost no value from a legal analysis standpoint, and as a legal professional, it is cringeworthy and almost embarrassing to watch. So why did I include it? It provides a backdrop for a discussion of the constitutional issues raised: the concept of "legal standing," as a procedural matter, and the more important issue, "citizenship" under the Fourteenth Amendment.

Article III: Legal Standing

Most of the discussions in this book surrounding Constitutional Law are regarding the Bill of Rights (the first ten amendments to the Constitution), due process, and equal protection. As a preliminary matter, the action against Ted warrants a discussion of Article III of the Constitution. Article III, generally, sets forth the framework for the judicial system in the United States.

The "standing to sue doctrine," as it is commonly called, is derived from Article III's limitation of the judicial power of federal courts to "actual cases or controversies." *Spokeo v. Robins*, 136 S. Ct. 1540 (2016). "The doctrine limits the category of litigants empowered to maintain a lawsuit in federal court to seek redress for a legal wrong." *Id.* at 1544. "[T]he 'irreducible constitutional minimum' of standing consists of three elements. The plaintiff must have (1) suffered an injury in fact, (2) that is fairly traceable to the challenged conduct of the defendant, and (3) that is likely to be redressed by a favorable judicial decision." *Id.* at 1547. That means that a party bringing or contesting a lawsuit must be able to show a sufficient connection to the legal issue and actual harm suffered as a result of the alleged legal wrong.

In *Ted 2*, the party that opposes Ted's personhood is a toy company. What possible legitimate interest to support standing could this company have in whether or not Ted is a citizen? None. This really ruins the credibility of the film for me. The Commonwealth of Massachusetts may have had standing from a public interest standpoint. That is the only possible party that could pass the standing test for opposing Ted's citizenship. If you think of another, however, please email me.

Also, because the court was dealing more with issues of law as opposed to fact, there would likely not have been a jury trial. They would have stipulated to some number of facts, such as, yes, Ted can think, like, love, hate, and talk, and smoke incredible amounts of weed. The case would be decided on legal briefs and oral arguments and the loser would have appealed to the First Circuit and ultimately to the Supreme Court.

Fourteenth Amendment: Citizenship Clause

Of course, the substantive law underlying Ted's case is citizenship under the Fourteenth Amendment: "all persons born or naturalized in the United States, and subject to the jurisdiction thereof, are citizens of the United States and of the State wherein they reside." The Citizenship Clause grants the right to enjoy rights, but only if you are a citizen.

As Ted's young lawyer notes in her opening statement:

A hundred and fifty years ago a slave by the name Dred Scott sued to prove that he was a person and not a piece of property. He lost. And as history has shown us, that wasn't justice. In every civil rights conflict we are only able to recognize the just point of view years after the facts. And when the next conflict comes along, we're once again blind to it as it's happening. Well, this is different you say, but it isn't. It is the same beast just wearing a different face, and it's happening again today. So I urge you, ladies and gentlemen of the jury, not to be a footnote on the wrong side of history. Don't wait too long to be right. Thank You.

She later echoes the sentimental when the trio was en route to New York to meet with a high-powered civil rights lawyer (Morgan Freeman). She says: "Look, I don't know what kind of mojo was in that wish you made when you were a child, but this bear is alive. And it seems to me that once the law devalues one kind of life, how soon before it devalues another? Who gets subjugated after the bear?"

Ted's case was analogous to the Dred Scott Case. Dred Scott was enslaved in Missouri, but his enslaver, Dr. John Emerson, moved Mr. Scott from state to state, including free states/territories. When Emerson died, Dred Scott attempted to purchase his family's freedom from Emerson's widow, who refused to sell. He then sued for freedom, fighting a losing battle that lasted over a decade. Mr. Scott's argument was that his presence and residency in free territories required his emancipation. Scott's lawyers argued the same for Scott's wife and claimed that their daughter's birth on a steamboat between a free state and a free territory rendered her born free. *Dred Scott v. Sandford,* 60 U.S. 393 (1857).

In probably the worst decision ever written, the Supreme Court held that the United States Constitution was not meant to include American citizenship for black people, regardless of whether they were enslaved or free. The Court decided that blacks were "not included, and were not intended to be included, under the word 'citizens' in the Constitution, and can therefore claim none of the rights and privileges which that instrument provides for and secures to citizens of the United States."

This was a 7-2 decision. Only two of the nine white men dissented. But luckily the North won the war and the Thirteenth and Fourteenth Amendments nullified the Dred Scott decision.

LEGAL BRIEFS & MOVIE EXTRAS

* Seth MacFarlane said the plot for *Ted 2* was in part inspired by Dred Scott's story.

Ted 2 has more references to other movies than any other movie I have ever seen. Here is a link discussing some of those pop culture references.

https://www.bustle.com/articles/92616-18-pop-culture-references-in-ted-2-that-are-bound-to-make-entertainment-fans-howl-with (last visited October 27, 2020).

13TH

(Netflix 2016)

Director: Ava Marie DuVernay

Lesson: Constitutional Law

Plot: A Netflix documentary, *13th* highlights often overlooked language in the Thirteenth Amendment to the United States Constitution, still carried over from its original ratification in 1865. The language essentially kept slavery alive as a form of criminal punishment. The film focuses on the use of involuntary servitude as punishment for crimes, and the manner in which southern states used this loophole to continue to oppress black Americans following the early years after the abolishment of slavery. It looks at oppression generally, asking the question: all of these years after the Thirteenth Amendment, are black Americans really "free?" What did it mean to be "freed" in the years that followed the Thirteenth Amendment? Is there some level of "involuntary servitude" still at play?

The film also examines the history of black oppression, from the arresting of black men for very minor crimes, and then "leasing" them under a government sanctioned work programs that resulted in mass incarceration and continued enslavement of black Americans. From lynching, to Jim Crow, to Nancy Reagan's war on drugs, to fatal shootings of blacks by police, the movie explores the intersection of race and justice in the United States, highlighting the years of systemic racial discrimination in this country.

For purposes of the "legal lesson," I am focusing this chapter simply on the Thirteenth Amendment.

Thirteenth Amendment: Slavery and Involuntary Servitude

In *Bailey v. Alabama,* a black man, Lonzo Bailey, contracted to work on a farm for a year at $12 a month. 219 U.S. 219, 235 (1911). He quit after a month and did not return $15 advanced to him. *Id.* at 236. Under Alabama law, Bailey's act was criminal. The statute in question stated, "[a]ny person who, with intent to injure or defraud his employer, enters into a contract in writing for the performance of any act of service, and thereby obtains money or other personal property from such employer, and with like intent, and without just cause, and without refunding such money, or paying for such property, refuses or fails to perform such act or service, must on conviction be punished." *Id.* at 227-228 (quoting Gen. Acts. (Ala.) 1907, p. 636.).

Mr. Bailey was not allowed to testify about whether or not he had just cause or good reason for quitting. *Id.* at 228. The Alabama jury found him guilty. *Id.* at 231. In addition to having to return the $15, he was assessed a fine of $30, plus court costs. *Id.* When he could not pay, he was sentenced to "hard labor for twenty days in lieu of said fine, and one hundred and sixteen days on account of said costs." *Id.* He appealed.

The Supreme Court noted that the words involuntary servitude have a "larger meaning than slavery." *Id.* at 241. The Court declared that, "[w]hile the immediate concern was with African slavery, the Amendment was not limited to that. It was a charter of universal civil freedom for all persons, of whatever race, color, or estate, under the flag." *Id.* at 240-241. A state statute, "if its natural and inevitable purpose is to punish for crime for failing to perform contracts of labor, thus compelling such performance, it violates the Thirteenth Amendment, and is unconstitutional." *Id.* at 239.

In 1916, the case of *Butler v. Perry* produced a different result. The Court refused a challenge by a young man in Florida to a state law that required all able-bodied men from the ages of 21-45 to work up to 60 hours on maintaining public roads. 240 U.S. 328, 329 (2016). The plaintiff was convicted and jailed for non-compliance. *Id.* at 330. He claimed his time on road maintenance was "involuntary servitude" in violation of the Thirteenth Amendment. The Supreme Court disagreed: the "term involuntary servitude was intended to cover those forms of compulsory labor akin to African slavery which, in practical operation, would tend to produce like undesirable results ... and certainly was not intended to interdict enforcement of those duties which individuals owe to the state, such as services in the army, militia, on the jury, etc." *Id.* at 332-333. The Florida law therefore "did not amount to involuntary servitude because a compulsory labor requirement, just like jury duty or military service, was a well-established duty owed by individuals to the state." *Id.* at 333.

In 1992, students and parents from Pennsylvania brought action against their school district, challenging the constitutionality of the school's community service requirement, as a prerequisite for graduation. *Steirer v. Bethlehem Area School Dist.,* 987 F.2d 989, 991 (1993). They lost. The Third Circuit held that an "educational requirement does not become involuntary servitude merely because one of the stated objectives of the Program is that the students will work without receiving pay." *Id.* at 1000. Without much rationale, other than comparisons to other "forced labor" situations, the Third Circuit held "that the mandatory community service program instituted in the Bethlehem Area School District as a high school graduation requirement does not constitute involuntary servitude prohibited by the Thirteenth Amendment." *Id.* One comparison the court made in finding the program constitutional is the fact that it is not involuntary servitude when a state requires attorneys to provide a certain number of pro bono legal services as a condition of practicing law.

The parents and students appealed but the Supreme Court did not grant cert. If a circuit split occurs on this issue in the future, however, the Court could very well revisit this issue.

LEGAL BRIEFS & MOVIE EXTRAS

*The Thirteenth Amendment may come into play in contracts law, regarding damages for breach. A contract for personal services that is breached generally cannot be remedied with specific performance. The proper damage award is monetary. *See, e.g., Beverly Glen Music, Inc. v. Warner Communications, Inc.,* 178 Cal. App. 3d 1142, 1144 (1986) ("An unwilling employee cannot be compelled to continue to provide services to his employer either by ordering specific performance of his contract, or by injunction. To do so runs afoul of the Thirteenth Amendment's prohibition against involuntary servitude.").

"Neither slavery nor involuntary servitude, *except as a punishment for crime whereof the party shall have been duly convicted*, shall exist within the United States, or any place subject to their jurisdiction."

–Thirteenth Amendment of the United States Constitution

ON THE BASIS OF SEX
(Focus Features 2018)

Starring: Felicity Jones; Armie Hammer

Lessons: Constitutional Law

Plot: This movie is a must see for any young girl who is thinking of a career in law. Everybody else should see it as well because it is an excellent film. Felicity Jones does a brilliant job in her portrayal of RBG. Armie Hammer also does a great job in his supporting role as her husband, Martin. *On the Basis of Sex* follows the story of Supreme Court Justice Ruth Bader Ginsburg, as she led the path to change laws discriminating against women. The tool by which she launches her efforts is the Equal Protection Clause of the Fourteenth Amendment.

Fourteenth Amendment: Equal Protection Clause

The Equal Protection Clause of the Fourteenth Amendment was established to prevent discrimination and to ensure that all citizens were equally entitled to the protections of the law. *Barbier v. Connolly*, 113 U.S. 27, 31 (1884). The Equal Protection Clause often comes into conflict with a state's police power to regulate public health, morals, and general welfare.

The Supreme Court recognizes that "when social or economic legislation is at issue, the Equal Protection Clause allows the States wide latitude . . . even improvident decisions will eventually be rectified by the democratic process." *City of Cleburne v. Cleburne Living Center, Inc.*, 473 U.S. 432, 440 (1985). When no constitutional or fundamental right is involved, courts will not scrutinize police power legislation under the Equal Protection Clause unless the law in question classifies as to a suspect or quasi suspect class. *See id.* The general rule is that legislation is presumed to be valid and will be sustained if the classification drawn by the statute is rationally related to a legitimate State interest. *Id.* This makes it difficult for advocates to challenge legislation that differentiates on the basis of sex, as long as the state can articulate a legitimate public interest.

This general rule only gives way when (i) legislation classifies by race, alienage, and national origin (suspect classes), or (ii) when legislation classifies as to gender (a quasi-suspect class). *Id.* A legislative classification as to race, alienage, or national origin is subject to strict judicial scrutiny, and the classification must be suitably tailored to serve a compelling State interest. *Id.* A gender classification enjoys a lesser scrutiny. Gender distinctions need only be "substantially related to a sufficiently important governmental interest" in order to be sustained. *Id.* at 441.

The first gender discrimination case the young RBG argued in court was *Moritz v. Commissioner of Internal Revenue.* At issue was a $600 "caregiver' tax deduction. It involved a 63-year-old bachelor who sought to use the deduction, as he was caring for his elderly mother. The Tax Code, however, essentially assumed that caregivers were women. The deduction applied to all women, but it only applied to men whose wives were incapacitated, dead, or if they divorced them. That her male unmarried client could not take the deduction is discrimination on the basis of gender. How brilliant that her first plaintiff suing over gender discrimination was a man?

Her opponent, an eager young IRS attorney, argued that a ruling in RBG's client's favor would put hundreds of statutes on unsteady legal footing. He took the initiative to use a "super computer" to generate a list, enumerating the laws that contain classifications "on the basis of sex." He felt quite confident that the Judge would not consider disturbing such a long list of presumably well-thought-out legislation that his (mostly) white male colleagues in Congress worked so hard to pass. That plan backfired.

RBG uses this list of laws to her advantage, stating her gratitude for the young lawyer's work in identifying for her all of the various potentially discriminating legislation open to challenge. She called it a "hit list." God I love her.

LEGAL BRIEFS & MOVIE EXTRAS

*Kathy Bates had a fun supporting role in *On the Basis of Sex*. She played Dorothy Kenyon, a strong, powerful lawyer and civil rights advocate who served as a mentor to young RBG. Born in 1888 and living until 1972, Dorothy Kenyon was a woman ahead of her times.

"Real change, enduring change, happens one step at a time. Fight for the things that you care about, but do it in a way that will lead others to join you."

-Justice Ruth Bader Ginsburg

JUST MERCY
(Warner Bros. 2019)

Starring: Michael B. Jordan; Jamie Foxx; Rob Morgan

Lesson: Constitutional Law

Plot: *Just Mercy* tells the true story of death row inmates in the 1980s in Alabama, and the attorney that saved their lives, Bryan Stevenson. Attorney Stevenson, played by Michael B. Jordan, is a lawyer, civil rights activist, and law professor. In 1989, fresh from Harvard Law School, he travels to Alabama to help death row inmates. He meets one of his first clients, Walter "Johnny D." McMillian, a lumberjack wrongly convicted of murder three years prior. The movie begins with a scene showing Johnny D. working in the woods, leaving in his truck, and being pulled over by the local police. It sets the scene for the injustices that follow and the activism and persistence of Attorney Stevenson contrasted to the complete incompetence and/or bias of Johnny D.'s court-appointed attorneys.

Whenever capital punishment is involved, the Eighth Amendment is invoked, in that it prohibits cruel and unusual punishment. Other sections of the Constitution apply to the constitutional rights of a criminal defendant facing the death penalty, such as due process and equal protection. I am focusing this Chapter on the constitutional rights afforded under the Eighth Amendment and ways in which death row inmates are treated by the Court with respect to capital punishment.

Eighth Amendment: Cruel and Unusual Punishment

A landmark Supreme Court case involving the Eighth Amendment and capital punishment was *Furman v. Georgia,*

408 U.S. 238. The *Furman* case considered the death penalty sentences of three black men, one found guilty of murder, two for rape. *Id.* at 240. A split Court, in a long opinion consisting mainly of concurrences and dissents, concluded that the death penalty did not pass constitutional muster in these three cases, due to the manner in which Georgia was applying and implementing its death penalty laws. The Court acknowledged that the death penalty was applied unequally against black men. In concurrence, Justice Douglas stated the obvious: "the death penalty inflicted on one defendant is 'unusual' if it discriminates against him by reason of his race, religion, wealth, social position, or class, or if it is imposed under a procedure that gives room for the play of such prejudices." *Id.* at 242. Accordingly, reversing all three sentences, the Court found that carrying out these three capital punishments would be cruel and unusual punishment and violative of the Eighth Amendment (as well as the Fourteenth Amendment, as it applies to the states).

The *Furman* decision resulted in state legislatures revising their capital punishment statutes to give some assurance that the death penalty would not be carried out in a discriminatory or cruel or unusual manner.

In 1976, blessing Georgia's newly revised statute, the Supreme Court backpedalled. With only Justices Brennan and Marshall dissenting, the Court declared that "the punishment of death does not invariably violate the Constitution," so long as states set objective "standards to guide and regularize juries" and make rationally reviewable the process for imposing the sentence of death. *Gregg v. Georgia*, 428 U.S. 153, 196-97. The Court found the use of a bifurcated trial to be especially important in protecting against cruel discrimination, in which a separate jury or fact-finder decides sentencing only after a conviction. *See id.* at 195. As other states followed Georgia's lead in drafting new capital punishment statutes, the death penalty promptly resumed.

Since deciding the Georgia cases discussed above, however, the Supreme Court has narrowed the permissibility of the death penalty under the Eighth Amendment to protect certain categories of convicted criminals. *See e.g., Thompson v. Oklahoma*, 487 U. S. 815 (1988).

In 2002, the Supreme Court held that the execution of mentally retarded criminals, even convicted murderers, constitutes "cruel and unusual punishment" and therefore violates the Eighth Amendment. *Atkins v. Virginia*, 536 U.S. 304, 321 (2002). The Court's rationale for carving out this specific exception to the use of capital punishment was because "mentally retarded defendants in the aggregate face a special risk of both wrongful conviction and wrongful execution." *Id.* at 320.

As *Just Mercy* makes clear, black men too, particularly in the South in the 1970s and 1980s, had their own "special risks" for wrongful conviction and execution.

LEGAL BRIEFS & MOVIE EXTRAS

*In Scene 1, when Johnny D. is pulled over in his truck, he puts his hands up immediately, before the police officer reaches his car. He is shown nervous, with his slightly shaking, workman hands held above the steering wheel where the officer can clearly see them through the windshield. He knows he needs to show that he is unarmed to reduce his chances of being shot. I can't tell you how I know this, but being shot was never a consideration when a pretty little blonde girl from Maine was pulled over for speeding in her mother's Chrysler during this very same time period (mid-to-late 1980s). She was too busy rummaging through her purse and her glovebox, searching for her insurance card, license, and registration, not waiting for the officer to approach because she was already late for the mall. Her day wasn't ruined; she had a good story to tell her friends, about her very first "warning" for speeding. It made me realize the number of ways in which "givens" such as our appearance or our geography shape our experiences.

*Another movie regarding the death penalty is *The Life of David Gale* (2003). This movie changed people's minds about the appropriateness of capital punishment.

YOU CAN'T TAKE MY DAUGHTER
(Big Dreams Entertainment 2020)

Starring: Lyndsy Fonseca; Hunter Burke; Kirstie Alley

Lessons: Family Law

Plot: Based on a true story, this Lifetime original portrays the real-life story of a woman, known in the movie as "Amy Thompson" (Lyndsy Fonseca), and the traumatic event that made her a mom. Amy was a healthy, young law student with a promising future ahead of her. One night, after she rejected sexual advances from an acquaintance, "Demetri"(Hunter Burke), he forced himself into her apartment, over-powered her physically, and raped her. Fortunately, the movie does not show the full horror she must have faced.

When Amy found out she was pregnant from the rape, she decided to keep the baby. All the while, Amy pressed forward with the rape trial as well as fighting for protection from abuse orders. She leaves Charlotte, North Carolina for Atlanta, Georgia, to start over. But years later, Demetri found her. Amy endured years of torment and harassment from her rapist. The worst began when Demetri found her in Atlanta and attempted to assert parent rights to Amy's daughter. Amy battled against laws that favored paternal rights over a woman's rights to raise a child resulting from rape without the fear of the rapist attempting to assert rights regarding the child. Because of the heavy burden required to terminate parental rights, some rape victims who become pregnant may instead chose to live in hope (and fear) that the rapist will never assert the presumed rights, only to be devastated at some point in the future when the rapist re-enters her life. That is what happened to "Amy." Ultimately, she decided to use her own legal skills to change the law.

Terminating Parental Rights of Rapists

Many state courts have had to address the issue of parental rights with respect to rapists or their parents who petition for rights to the victim's child, without the help of clear statutory guidelines or precedent. The biological parent is presumed to have constitutional parenting rights with respect to his or her natural child; a rape victim must file a petition in court to rebut that presumption in order to terminate parental rights. Terminating parental rights, generally, requires a stringent burden of proof to overcome that presumption.

Some states have enacted statutes addressing parental rights when incidents of rape result in a child, under which the standard for terminating the rapist's parental rights are relaxed. The problem with some of the statutes, however, was that a conviction or guilty plea is explicitly required in order to terminate the rapist's parental rights. Prior to 2015, states that required convictions (or guilty pleas) for purposes of terminating rapists' parental rights included: Connecticut (Conn. Gen. Stat. § 45a-717 (1999); Illinois (750 Ill. Comp. Stat. Ann. 50/8 (West 1999)); Indiana (Ind. Code § 31-19-9-8 (1999); Maine (19-A M.R.S.A. § 1658 (1997)); (Missouri (Mo. Rev. Stat. § 211.447 (1999)). Other states had no statute addressing the issue at all. Amy's state of Georgia was one such state. Amy's lawyer admitted that many judges feel that "a rapist father is better than no father at all." It should be noted that the real battle played out in Florida. Florida ultimately changed the law, which now requires only "clear and convincing" evidence that the rape occurred, as opposed to the higher criminal standard (beyond a reasonable doubt) that would be needed for a conviction.

The requirement for a conviction in order for a victim to terminate a rapist's rights is problematic because a rape conviction is not always a slam dunk. The crime may not have been proven beyond a reasonable doubt, for conviction purposes, due to some technicality or other factor. Maybe by the time the victim strengthened enough to report the rape, time has spoiled or eliminated evidence, or there is a statute of limitations problem. Worse than the failure rate of rape convictions is the sad fact that some rapes are never reported, due to fear, embarrassment, and other factors. There have been occasions, for example, where rapists have threatened their victims who wish to give birth to their child that they will assert their parental rights unless the victim agrees not to report the rape, or not to testify against the rapist. *See e.g.,* Ruth Sheehan, Rapists Lose Facet of Power, *The Raleigh News & Observer*, Sept. 6, 2004, at B1. For these and other reasons, victims may have chosen to remain silent about the rape, hoping the rapist will never assert parental rights, only to be surprised and devastated by such claim years later like Amy was.

Even in the states in which a criminal conviction was not *expressly* required, the statutes left uncertainty as to how, if at all, rape victims can be protected against such claims of parental rights. The question becomes, what evidence would be required, short of a guilty plea or a conviction, to have the rapist's parental rights terminated. Some state statutes remain silent as to this question, leaving uncertainty to rape victims about whether they will be able to convince a trial judge that her child was the result of a rape – and uncertainty about what point in the future she may be faced with such a challenge.

In 2015, however, President Obama signed the Rape Survivor Child Custody Act. This Act provided incentive to states to follow suit with Florida and change the law by making "grants to states that have in place a law that allows the mother of any child that was conceived through rape to seek court-ordered termination of the parental rights of her rapist with regard to that child, which the court shall grant upon clear and convincing evidence of rape." In other words, the Act was an effort to get other states on board with adopting a lower standard of proving rape for purposes of terminating parental rights. The goal was for state statutes to allow for termination in rape situations without the need for a rape conviction. Analyzing evidence under the looser "clear and convincing evidence" standard to prove rape broadens the ability for a victim to obtain sufficient evidence. For example, credible victim or other witness testimony at a hearing before a trial judge, substantiated by medical evidence, police reports, etc., may support a finding of rape for purposes of terminating parental rights. Perhaps victims underwent counseling, specifically addressing the rape, years before the rapists seeks parental rights. Such evidence should be considered where a conviction is not procured for various reasons, and a clear and convincing evidence standard to prove the rape, solely for purposes of terminating parental rights, allows for this.

Following the act, many states took advantage of this grant by taking appropriate legislative action to address the problem Amy faced in you can't take my daughter. Still, as i write this in April of 2020, there are still several states that require a rape conviction in order to terminate a rapist's rights, and some states still have no laws protecting rape victims from custody battles with their rapist at all. For a complete breakdown by state, see https://www.ncsl.org/research/human-services/parental-rights-and-sexual-assault.aspx (last visited October 27, 2020).

Protection from Abuse Orders

Amy also sought protection from abuse against Demetri, which should have been fairly easy under the circumstances. A protection from abuse order is a civil court order (i.e., "just a piece of paper") under which a court tells the abuser that he or she cannot have any contact with the victim and/or the victim's child(ren). State laws set forth who qualifies for such an order, but, generally, victims of extreme domestic violence qualify quite easily.

For protection from abuse orders, generally, the person seeking the order must have had a relationship with the alleged abuser. It is unclear whether a one-night rape situation would qualify under such statutes as a "relationship." Fortunately, however, most states have a separate statute for protection orders (also called restraining orders) for people not experiencing what is often referred to as "domestic violence," but who obviously need some protection, such as from abuse, harassment, or contact generally.

Had Demetri been arrested and properly charged with rape, bail conditions would have required he have no contact with Amy whatsoever, at least pending trial.

LEGAL BRIEFS AND MOVIE EXTRAS

*Lyndsy Fonseca, who beautifully portrayed Amy, is famous for her role as Colleen Carlton on the daytime drama *Young and the Restless* and for her role as Dylan Mayfair on *Desperate Housewives.* I would not be surprised to see Lyndsy as the starring lady in more films, Lifetime or big screen.

*The real woman in this story is actually Analyn Megison who now advocates for rape victims and women pregnant from rape attacks. See @analynmegison (Twitter)

*Help is available. **https://www.thehotline.org/help/**

CONCLUSION

Now that you have some law school behind you, you may automatically watch trial movies with a legal eye. You may find yourself objecting before the actors do. You may annoy those around you, but it is another valuable use of your education. As a true legal scholar, you will be able to spot the mistakes of the law when you watch a courtroom drama. Just remember not to let a film's flaws ruin your enjoyment of the movie and appreciation for its comedic or dramatic value. Despite some inaccuracies due to Hollywood influence, legal drama provides thought-provoking material for law students and legal scholars. These movies have been a staple of American theater for nearly a century and they always will be. Who knows, maybe someday a movie will be made about one of your cases!

OTHER RESOURCES FOR LAW STUDENTS

Coffin, Frank M. *A Lexicon of Oral Advocacy* (St. Paul, National Institute for Trial Advocacy 1984)

Dershowitz, Alan M., *Letters to a Young Lawyer* (New York, Basic Books 2001)

Fischl, Richard Michael and Paul, Jeremy, *Getting To Maybe: How to Excel on Law School Exams* (Durham, Carolina Academic Press 1999)

Herrera, Jennifer. *Formula for Success: The Psychological and Informational Handbook for Passing the Bar Examination.* (West Hartford, Graduate Group 1999)

Miller, Robert H. *Law School Confidential (Revised Edition): A Complete Guide to the Law School Experience: By Students, for Students.* (New York, St. Martin's Press 2004)

www.ingramcontent.com/pod-product-compliance
Lightning Source LLC
Chambersburg PA
CBHW020854180526
45163CB00007B/2501